T0154009

"The goal of the school system in most countries has generally had nothing to do with producing happy, creative, self-confident, autonomous children who will grow up to become happy, creative, self-confident, autonomous adults. Since schooling became mandatory in industrialized societies like the UK and the US, schools have been an ideological battleground between those who want to produce obedient workers and soldiers and those, like Robb Johnson, who would prefer to see a liberated humanity consisting of whole people, who are treated as such from birth, by their parents, by the schools and by all other social, political and economic institutions. This book is a brilliant crash course in the roots of the problem, the devastation wreaked since the post-Thatcher/post-Reagan austerity budgets and a return to Victorian ("family") values and how we might address all of these complex challenges. And it is as captivating a read as any good memoir, because that's exactly what it is. Robb Johnson lived through—and taught through—the backlash, working as a teacher from 1980 until very recently."
—David Rovics, musician and author of *Sing for Your Supper: A DIY Guide to Playing Music, Writing Songs, and Booking Your Own Gigs* (PM Press 2008)

Praise for *A Reasonable History of Impossible Demands*, 5CD box set (PM Press 2016)

"This stonking five-disc retrospective charts the development of one of this country's most important songwriters (no argument!). . . . This is one really essential purchase."
—David Kidman, *fROOTS*

The People's Republic of Neverland
The Child versus the State

Robb Johnson

The People's Republic of Neverland: The Child versus the State
© Robb Johnson
This edition © 2020 PM Press

ISBN: 978–1–62963–795–2 (print)
ISBN: 978–1–62963–811–9 (ebook)
Library of Congress Control Number: 2019946094

Cover by John Yates / www.stealworks.com
Interior design by briandesign

10 9 8 7 6 5 4 3 2 1

PM Press
PO Box 23912
Oakland, CA 94623
www.pmpress.org

Printed in the USA

Contents

Author's Note

This book was written and rewritten and rewritten again and again between 2016 and 2019. Partly this was because my friends at PM Press, Ramsey and James, insisted that too much bile and contemporary polemic were bad for both readability and enduring relevance—and they were right. Since the exhausted politics behind "education reform" car crashed and fell apart in the UK, we have seen a bewilderingly rapid shuffling of strategies of misdirection by the ruling class. Gove—previously remarkable for being far and away the most reviled reformist education minister and the one responsible for attempting to impose the most ludicrous hobby horses onto state schools—popped up during the Brexit campaign as an advocate of "Leave", famously declaring that the British public had had enough of listening to experts, and, as if to demonstrate the importance of having people who don't know what they're talking about in charge, then resurfaced as minister responsible for coping with the chaos that would ensue if Britain exited the European Union without having negotiated an agreement. Which was, of course, made all the more likely when the British winner of the "Donald Trump Lookalike Competition" Boris Johnson became prime minister in 2019. However, amusing the antics of such barefaced buffoonery might be on one level, it is both difficult and pointless to try to keep up with the "spectacle of the shuffle", pointless because it is essentially and apparently nothing more than endless distraction. Therefore, in one respect, this book has finally been rewritten so it reads as a historical record of a particular timespan. In 2019, the Labour Party was promising to end high stakes summative testing in primary schools and initiate a review of education with the intention of establishing a National Education Service, as well as talking about the importance of children enjoying access to creativity and the arts. Would this book become even more historical than polemical? Sadly not it seems, as the great British Public decided to vote for Getting Brexit Done rather than anything that threatened the greedy elite with the promise of some increased attention to issues of social justice. However, children will still arrive on this beautiful little planet with high expectations, and they will continue to deserve a much better experience of education than they have been subjected to here over the last thirty years thanks to the politics of "reform", the neoliberal project that set out to assert complete and politicised state control over the state schools most of our children go to.

Neverland—an Introductory Definition of Terms and Conditions

For nearly 150 years, going to school has been the norm for children in Europe and on those parts of the planet historically determined by European imperialism. This book is primarily a reflection on schooling and education based on my experiences working as a teacher in state schools in England from 1980 to 2015. The significant characteristic of this historical period was the imposition of education "reform". In this context, "reform" means the state asserting centralised control over all aspects of state education provision, guided by a combination of right-wing nostalgia and neoliberal free-market politics. As a result, state provision has favoured schooling rather than education, and the experience of the individual child is not valued as in any way central to the process.

This book looks at the background to the right's assertion of these values, contrasting them with the practical insights and understanding gained from my own working experience. This is not meant to be an academic study; the title is clearly indicative of a playful intent, as well as of a certain politics. This book is not about the never-never lands of the stupefying spectacle or the playpens of privilege and celebrity. This Neverland belongs to the people. "Reform" always freighted political intent, and this book does too, so if you lack the capacity to be angered that over four million children in the fifth or sixth richest nation state on the planet officially live in poverty and are unable to accept that this is clearly the consequence of government of the privileged, by the privileged, for the privileged—then probably this book isn't for you.

But if you are interested in "education", rather than nonsense like "teeching reeding thru fonix" or the gibberish of scores and outcomes, then I hope you might find this book of interest. Using England as a case in point, it considers how schools and education relate to the wider society in which they are located and how they relate to the particular needs and abilities of the people who experience them. In this book, I hope to show that schools and education are contested spaces that need to be reclaimed from the state and turned into opportunities that meet everybody's developmental needs, spaces where people can grow, not up, not old, but as individuals.

Prologue

Here's one brief narrative of one particular moment in the process of education experienced by one individual, who we'll call Charlie, and his friends and classmates on one particular day in the People's Republic of Neverland, Hollingdean branch.

> Charlie's watering the mud. He's got this plastic
> watering can
> That's half as big as his friend Zac, so he has to hold it
> in both hands.
> Charlie's watering the mud. He says, "I'm going to
> grow a tree.
> It's going to reach up to the sky, it's going to be as big
> as me".
> Little people, big ideas.
>
> Then Charlie says to Zac, "Now we have to paint it
> blue",
> So Zac and Charlie paint the mud, and Kasze joins in too.
> Immo watches thoughtfully, because Kasze's paint is
> sort of red,
> And as the mud turns sort of purple, "It will be
> beautiful", she says.
> Little people, big ideas.
>
> Keep on watering that mud, Charlie. Okay, sometimes
> it ends in tears,

But, then again, you might end up, Charlie, on the
    Galápagos Islands. . .
Now Nathan's watering the mud and half the class are
    growing trees,
And half the class are building rivers that one day
    maybe make it to the sea.
Kerry wants to paint the walls red but finds an acorn,
    green as spring,
So we dig a hole in Charlie's mud and drop
    tomorrow's oak tree in.
Oh yeah, little people, big ideas.[1]

Now very possibly, highly paid inspectors from the
Department of Dog Training, Weights and Measures might
start carping and tutting about "what is actually being taught
and learned here", because, sadly, they are unwilling or
unable to understand that their idea of "teaching and learning" is not education but a simplistic reduction of the processes
and experience of education to a limited and limiting two-
dimensional sociopolitical function, a mechanism constructed
to manufacture measurable outcomes. In this current, much
reduced model of "education", the teacher states, the pupil
restates, in a hierarchical relationship, where the effectiveness
of both parties in this transaction can be measured by testing
how much of the teacher's statement has been retained in the
restatement by the pupil. Schools become function machines,
like factories. Children, raw materials, go in at one end. The
teacher's only function is to add value to the raw material, and
we evaluate what has been taught and what has been learned
by measuring what comes out the other end.

    This is a travesty of education. Education is absolutely
not simply what can be described in terms of "measurable
outcomes". Measurable outcomes amount to reducing a life
to a series of statistics and dates that fill in the time between
birth and death, whereas, of course, life is so much more
three-dimensional and unruly and magical and immeasurable

than that. But it is convenient for those in charge not to have to consider that their statistics have these complexities, and it is also convenient to keep these statistics from developing much of an awareness of the richness and complexity of their lives, in case they get ideas above their station and start asking awkward questions.

Charlie, meanwhile, is happily watering the mud. Charlie has the water and the watering can, but, more than that, Charlie has an idea, and having ideas is getting pretty close to asking questions. Charlie shares his idea, engaging in inclusive, cooperative play, engaging eventually pretty much all of the rest of the class. Charlie and the class recognise that ideas are not closed borders but open doors you can go through and pursue with your own energy and reconfigure with the characteristics of your own imagination. And, seriously, if Charlie had not initially watered the mud, we couldn't have planted Kerry's acorn, could we?

Ah, but where, whinge the cops from the Department of Dog Training, is the teacher in all of this? Well absolutely everywhere, obviously, not only joining in with the adventure and chucking in the odd well-timed open-ended question and not minding if people are too busy to want to respond immediately but also very much behind the scenes making sure the scenery is in place, setting up the initial empowering environment replete with abundant watering cans, water, readily available paint that Charlie and Kasze confidently access, and facilitating that intangible essential, the empowering ethos that supports Charlie in his play, which then spills over into the realities and imaginations of the rest of the class, to the nicely judged intervention that suggests what we might do with Kerry's acorn. Should we wait to see if an oak tree actually grows and measure that to decide on the validity of the educational experience? Can you measure a metaphor?

And, anyway, just because you think you can't measure it, that doesn't mean it doesn't exist.

And, of course, Charlie Darwin was probably once upon a time a grubby four-year-old grubbing about in the mud, and, hey, look what that got us. . .

PART ONE

A BRIEF HISTORY OF MASS EDUCATION

All You Need Is Love and Comprehensive Schools

Little Edie Annie Spinks likes the Beatles and the Kinks
Living in a council house quieter than a silent mouse
never passed eleven-plus, rides the number 13 bus
To the secondary moderns where she gets forgotten
Mum and dad work all the hours, Edie's good at growing
    flowers
Edie likes to sing along to her favourite Beatles song

All you need is love, love, love
And Comprehensive Schools

Esmeralda Fortesque spends her whole life feeling blue
A lovely room, lovely home, a lovely garden all her own
She goes to such a lovely school, to learn her Latin
    grammar rules
How can you be lonely when you've got a pony?
She practises her scales for hours, she's not allowed to
    pick the flowers
Mummy's never ever there, Daddy likes the new au pair

All you need is love, love, love
And Comprehensive Schools

Every child should have the chance to learn and grow and
    sing and dance
It doesn't matter where you're from, cos you can go
    wherever you want
Round the corner over the moon beyond the stars it's up
    to you
Whether you're Edie Annie Spinks or Esmeralda Fortesque

All you need is love, love, love
And Comprehensive Schools

Remote Control

Let's start with a brief history of the hundred years of education development that formed the background not only to my teaching experience but, more importantly, to the imposition of the right's Great Education Reform Bill in 1988.

The wealthy and powerful had, of course, been educating their (usually male) children for centuries before the British state passed its first education act. Kings School in Canterbury claims to be the oldest school, having started in 597 (girls were only admitted in the 1970s), and Eton dates back to 1440. The cost of attending these fee-paying "public" schools was—and still is—far beyond the economic means of the majority of the British public. Mass education only came to be seen as an essential element of a successful modern society and economy in the latter half of the nineteenth century. Directed by the state, this was primarily education characterised by quantity rather than quality.

Compulsory attendance at schools funded by the state became law in Britain in 1870. The British state, concerned with maintaining Britain's efficiency as an industrial power and also alarmed by the growth of autonomous working-class education projects, passed legislation—the Elementary Education Act (1870)—making it mandatory for children to attend state-run schools. Schools would teach children just enough to enable them to function as efficiently as possible as workers in British industry. As the technology became more sophisticated, British industry needed workers with greater literacy and numeracy skills, so they would be able to make as much money as possible for British industry's bosses. Successive legislation meant state education became a reality for more and more categories of working-class children by the start of the twentieth century, effectively closing down any attempt by those within the working-class movement to organise independent schools and autonomous educational initiatives.

Prime Minister Gladstone also thought that Prussia's educated population had played a significant part in Prussia's victory over Austria in 1866. Throughout Europe, state education was perceived as a politicised institution intended to serve the interests of the nation state: "Society wants servile automata for its barracks and factories, and the mission of schools is to provide them", declared Victor Serge in France in 1910, adding, "the child enters school with his intelligence growing, alert and wanting to blossom. He leaves it . . . stupefied".[1]

The Prussian model was also perceived as the template for the growth in mass education in the United States at the start of the twentieth century. Former New York City Teacher of the Year John Taylor Gatto writes, "compulsory schooling on this continent was intended to be just what it had been for Prussia in the 1820s: a fifth column into the burgeoning democratic movement that threatened to give the peasants and the proletarians a voice at the bargaining table. . . . Divide children by subject, by age-grading, by constant ranking on tests, and by many other more subtle means, and it was unlikely that the ignorant mass of mankind, separated in childhood, would ever reintegrate into a dangerous whole".[2] Gatto cites *Principles of Secondary Education,* written in 1918 by Alexander Inglis,[3] which breaks down the purpose—the actual purpose—of modern schooling into six basic functions:

1) The adjustive or adaptive function. Schools are to establish fixed habits of reaction to authority.

2) The integrating function. This might well be called the "conformity function," because its intention is to make children as alike as possible.

3) The diagnostic or directive function. School is meant to determine each student's proper social role.

4) The differentiating function. Once their social role has been "diagnosed", children are to be sorted by role and trained only so far as their destination in the social machine merits.

5) The selective function. This refers not to human choice at all but to Darwin's theory of natural selection as applied to what he called "the favoured races".

6) The propaedeutic function. The social system implied by these rules will require an elite group of caretakers. To that end, a small fraction of kids will quietly be taught how to manage this continuing project, how to watch over and control a population deliberately dumbed down and declawed, so that government might proceed unchallenged, and corporations might never want for obedient labour.

Gatto adds that the outcome of schooling is a deliberately infantilised population: "Theorists from Plato to Rousseau to our own Dr. Inglis knew that if children could be cloistered with other children, stripped of responsibility and independence, encouraged to develop only the revitalising emotions of greed, envy, jealousy, and fear, they would grow older but never truly grow up".[4]

By the middle of the twentieth century, the authority of the industrialised nation state had been seriously weakened by the eruption of two successive world wars. In 1914, conflicts within the ruling class, divided along the lines of European nation state interests, caused the slaughter attendant upon imperialism to spill back from overseas colonies onto the domestic territories and populations of Europe. The ruling class response was effectively to arm and organise the working class along nation state dividing lines. Although this diminished the working class's capacity to think and act as an international organisation, the working classes and their political organisations were able to make significant political advances in different ways in different parts of Europe, including in those areas of the world previously controlled by European imperialism, particularly after the end of World War II.

In post-war Eastern Europe, this took the form of actually existing socialism, but that's another story. In Britain, it led to the establishment of the welfare state and the concept of political consensus. One of the state's primary duties was now defined as providing and running services—health, education, housing, public utilities—to meet the needs of the people. This rather cosy accord, a very British version of Lenin's New Economic Policy (NEP), also allowed for the continuation of institutions of privilege, particularly private schooling and private health care—doctors initially threatened strike action to oppose the creation of the National Health Service (NHS), unhappy at the prospect of having to treat the great unwashed fairly. Although major industries were nationalised and run by bosses on behalf of the perceived shared interests of government and people, there was ample opportunity for private enterprise.

This new understanding of the state's responsibilities impacted upon the mass education it was providing. Beginning with the Education Act of 1944, there was a significant expansion of provision; the Education Act ensured free secondary schooling for all children and also raised the school leaving age to fifteen. The act called for an expansion to both nursery and higher education provision and provided schools meals and milk for all primary school children. To staff these new initiatives, a new generation of teachers needed to be trained. Many had served in the armed forces during the war, and many of them were also animated by a commitment to the aims of the welfare state, the creation of a more equal society rather than a return to the class-ridden social system that was seen as being responsible for two devastating world wars. An integral element of this new vision of mass education would be an attempt to develop a pedagogy that valued quality of education and the quality of each individual's experience of education over the simple quantities of mass.

Alternatives and Radicals

Throughout the twentieth century, the issues of education and child development attracted the attention of radical thinkers and radical thinking around the planet. The state view of mass education as a means to instil basic skills along with its values of patriarchy, patriotism and religion was opposed by alternative voices insisting on alternative values. American anarchist Emma Goldman proclaimed:

> The underlying principle of The Modern School is this: education is a process of drawing out, not of driving in. . . . The Modern School, then, must be libertarian. Each pupil must be left free to his true self. The main object of the school is the promotion of the harmonious development of all the faculties latent in the child".[5]

and:

> I fail to understand how parents hope that their children will ever grow up into independent, self-reliant spirits, when they strain every effort to abridge and curtail the various activities of their children, the plus in quality and character, which differentiates their offspring from themselves, and by the virtue of which they are eminently equipped carriers of new, invigorating ideas. A young delicate tree that is being clipped and cut by the gardener in order to give it an artificial form will never reach the majestic height and the beauty it would if allowed to grow in nature and freedom.[6]

The compulsory schooling imposed upon the vast majority of children was opposed not only by polemic but by the establishment of alternative models of education. In Barcelona, Francisco Ferrer had set up the Escuela Moderna in 1904. In its prospectus he declared, "I will teach [children] not what to think but how to think". The school was co-educational, welcomed children from all classes, refused to operate a system of rewards and punishments, and saw no need for examinations and grades. In 1911, a Ferrer school—later known as the Modern School—was opened in New York. These initiatives offered an alternative pedagogy to the mass conformity that characterised state schooling. Ferrer's commitment to equality not uniformity actively promoted ideas of social progress and the importance of individual development.[7]

Austrian philosopher Rudolf Steiner asserted that the focal point of the education process ought to be the teacher's holistic understanding of the individual child. "The true teachers and educators are not those who have learned pedagogy as the science of dealing with children, but those in whom pedagogy has awakened through understanding the human being".[8] The first Waldorf school opened in 1919 in Stuttgart, based upon Steiner's ideas. Waldorf schools emphasise the importance of a holistic approach to development: "A teacher concerned with developing humans affects the students quite differently from a teacher who never thinks about such things".[9]

Two years after the first Waldorf school opened, Scottish educator A.S. Neill started Summerhill School, in Suffolk, England. Neill's philosophy provides a perfect articulation of a militant child-centred pedagogy:

> The happiness and well-being of children depend upon the love and approval we give them. We must be on the child's side. Being on the side of the child is giving love to the child—not possessive love—not sentimental love—just behaving to the child in such a way that the child feels you love him and approve of him. . . . A child is innately wise and realistic. If left to himself without adult suggestion of any kind, he will develop

as far as he is capable of developing. . . . My own criterion of success is the ability to work joyfully and to live positively.[10]

Summerhill School, however, like Waldorf schools, existed outside of the state schooling received by the majority of children. But by the time Neill wrote the book *Summerhill*, in 1960,[11] the post-war welfare state's understanding of its responsibilities toward children appeared to be enacting Bakunin's definition of the child's developmental rights:

It is the right of every man and woman, from birth to adulthood, to complete upkeep, clothes, food, shelter, care, guidance, education (public schools, primary, secondary, higher education, artistic, industrial, and scientific), all at the expense of society.[12]

It is also interesting to note how, as successive legislation made state education a reality for more and more categories of working-class children by the start of the twentieth century, teaching increasingly attracted socially committed individuals who saw in compulsory state education opportunities for subverting the intentions of the state and promoting social progress. It was the clash between radical, progressive teachers Annie and Tom Higdon and representatives of the established order, the Reverend Eland and the school managers, at Burston village school in rural Suffolk, in 1913, that precipitated Britain's longest running strike. Sixty-six children walked out on April 1 on a strike that lasted twenty-five years. In 1917, the daughters of Derby working-class anti-war activist, suffragette, socialist and vegetarian Alice Wheeldon, Hettie and Winnie, both trained as teachers, were arrested in front of the classes they were teaching when the state fabricated a charge of attempting to murder the British prime minister against the Wheeldon family.

Indeed, education has also attracted, albeit sometimes only temporarily, many individuals famous for their radicalism in other fields. Louise Michel was equally at home chairing the Women's Vigilance Committee in Montmartre during the Paris Commune and working in a classroom of children. Her radical approach to pedagogy—"it was something of a free-for-all, with highly unusual teaching methods"—often alarmed both colleagues and authorities—"You must close your school. . . . The other day, you were heard talking about humanity, justice, freedom and other useless things".[13] Vincent Van Gogh worked as a teacher in Turnham Green, West London, and George Orwell taught in Hayes and Uxbridge (West London again!). In France, both Simone de Beauvoir and Jean Paul Sartre spent fourteen years as teachers in various lycées, while radical teacher and Delhi university professor Randhir Singh declared: "Everything around me including my politics in shambles, I sought a new foothold in life. I started teaching. . . . After 'revolution-making', teaching perhaps holds the maximum possibilities for a non-alienated life".[14] Songwriter Leon Rosselson worked briefly as a teacher, singer Roy Bailey, who worked with both Leon and Tony Benn, had a day job as professor of sociology (co-editing the best-selling sociology book "Radical Social Work"),[15] and the 1960s pop culture "Mersey poets" Roger McGough and Adrian Henri taught French and art respectively.

The tension between radicalism and state control would become openly confrontational again in the 1960s and 1970s. The conflict between radical teachers and conservative employers, the conflict that caused the Burston strike in 1914, would resurface in the state schools of post-war welfare state England, when teachers attempted to assert the priorities of the children they taught over the remote social control function of education prioritised by the state.

Workers' Control

The creation of the post-war welfare state and the consensus politics of the post-war decades enabled a degree of increased participation of workers' organisations, particularly the bureaucracies of the larger industrial unions, in the processes of government. This would later translate into a confident rank-and-file tendency attempting to assert worker authority in the workplace. This was also to be a significant feature of teacher self-organisation in the 1970s. This section will look at how the increased confidence of the teaching workforce encouraged many teachers to address not only issues of their own professional well-being—successful industrial action to end the requirement to supervise school lunchtimes and National Union of Teachers (NUT) 1969 strike action in pursuit of better pay—but also to advance progressive pedagogies and, thereby, actively progressive visions of society.

The post-war consensus was constructed on a shared lived experience of recent history, where the ideology of the right had manifestly failed to meet the needs of the British people in the 1920s and 1930s, as well as failing to avoid World War II, and where the collective democratic endeavour of the people was understood to have ensured the military survival of Britain in the first half of the 1940s. The most obvious evidence of the strength of this narrative was the landslide defeat of Churchill and the Tories in the 1945 general election; it wasn't really until his death in 1965 that the sentimentalised Churchill myth—cleverly edited and shorn of its more embarrassing realities—was able begin to develop as an active political rather than vaguely nostalgic social narrative. In 1945, however, the working class were in uniform, armed and running out of patience. There were increasingly mutinous and increasingly successful strikes within the armed forces. As the rest of Europe was having to come to terms with the successes of armed communism—whether represented by the Red Army or anti-fascist partisans—the British ruling class responded by minding its manners. Implementing the reforms of the 1943 Beveridge Report to tackle the "five giants" of squalor, ignorance, want, idleness and disease identified by the liberal William Beveridge as blighting the life chances of the majority of the British population, they appeared willing to engage in dialogue with the representatives of British organised labour and to accept that these representatives had a right to expect to be consulted in matters of politics and governance.

These expectations were also present in the education workplace. As we noted earlier, an important aspect of the welfare state was an increase in terms of provision and scope of state schooling, which in turn involved an increase in the number of teachers, many of whom shared the general democratic expectations encouraged by the experience of the war and the election of the Attlee government in 1945. The development of teacher training into a degree course facilitated an increased number of teachers conceiving of themselves as reflective and autonomous workers empowered to make reflective and autonomous decisions about issues of education philosophy, pedagogy and best practice within their own workplaces.

Government education policy was itself shaped by a series of independent reports that considered the social function of state education in the immediate post-war decades. This was a significant period when committees set up by the state and empowered to provide guidance to government legislation produced a series of progressive reports responsible for orientating the organisation of state education around principles of equality and social justice rather than meritocracy and social mobility and around principles of quality and utility. The reports were the work of the Central Advisory Council for Education, which was established as a result of the 1944 Education Act. Its first report was *School and Life*, published in 1947, its last, the highly influential Plowden Report published in 1967. Its committees contained a mix of individuals from the traditional governing classes with backgrounds in charity work, government and industry but also individuals with practical experience of education. The Crowther report of 1959 noted that only 10 per cent of children from the poorest families got to grammar schools, recognising that class rather than ability determined the age at which children chose to leave school, while the Newsome Report of 1963 noted that those children classified as average or below average by their schooling were possessed of talents and abilities not addressed by the system classifying them. The Robbins Report (also 1963) explicitly stated education ought to concern itself with developing the individual citizen's capacities to reflect and create, that society had a duty to require not just good producers but good men and women. The Plowden Report of 1967 espoused progressive classroom practice, moving primary schools away from traditional chalk and talk methods of rote learning and instruction toward group work and learning by interaction and discovery.

The inadequacy of the social context and fabric to meet the needs of a significant number of children was recognised and the concept of positive discrimination established, with the creation of Educational Priority Zones intended to direct resources to children experiencing social exclusion. In 1965, Labour's then education minister Tony Crosland initiated the clearest systematic shift toward an education system committed to social justice, when he instructed all local authorities to prepare plans to implement comprehensive education in their secondary schools. This involved ending the existing system of selection by testing at eleven, whereby children identified by their test scores as being academically more able went to grammar schools—roughly 20 per cent of children—and the majority then went to what was generally experienced as a second-class education at secondary modern schools. Comprehensive education meant all local authority schools were to educate and meet the learning needs of all children of all abilities. He famously backed this up by apparently declaring loudly, if privately, "If it's the last thing I do, I'm going to destroy every fucking grammar school in England. And Wales. And Northern Ireland".

Although many educationalists, teachers and teaching organisations (e.g., NUT) supported and indeed actively campaigned in favour of these initiatives, there was often a significant lag in full implementation, as central government refused to provide full funding for recommendations like raising the school leaving age and providing nursery education for the under-fives. There was also no evidence of any real political will to attempt to address the anomaly of the continued untouched existence of the UK's most blatant affront to equality in education, the epitome of purchased privilege, the "public" school fee-paying system. We shall consider the effectiveness of "public" school education in producing fit for purpose government at later points in the text.

However, the child-centred, democratic aspects of pedagogy that characterised the more progressive private schools— the Montessori schools, the Steiner schools, Summerhill—that developed after the World War I now started to percolate into the teaching profession's discussions about good classroom practice with regard to educating the children of the working class. In 1960, Michael Duane, a friend of A.S. Neill's, became head of Risinghill Comprehensive in Islington and attempted to introduce some of Summerhill's values into the school's practice. Risinghill was closed in 1965, and school inspectors— readers can almost hear how bewildered and appalled they were in the sentence's terse conclusion—commented with some alarm on "an atmosphere of indiscipline which is difficult to describe". Yet it is interesting to note how Risinghill's radical initiatives, for example, humanist assemblies and pupil participation in school councils, are now standard elements of school life.

The 1960s also saw the ascendancy of a philosophy of education that prioritised autonomy as a pedagogical aim. The work of liberal theorists like R.S. Peters implied an understanding that education was to be valued for its own sake, because it enriched individual lives, enabling those individuals to adopt a "code or way of life that is one's own as distinct from one dictated by others", with the capacity to apply Kantian principles—"Act only according to that maxim whereby you can, at the same time, will that it should become a universal law"—when considering rule systems. His influential *Ethics and Education* was published in 1966. Peters defines "liberal education" as "a protest against confining what has been taught to the service of some extrinsic end such as the production of material goods, obtaining a job, or making a profession".[1] These ideas provided the philosophical framework for many teacher training courses, and thereby animated the practice of many new teachers.

Stepney and Islington

Two significant narratives illustrate how the tension between progress and reaction that had been developing in state education through the 1950s and 1960s came into full-scale, head-on conflict in the 1970s. In May 1971, teacher Chris Searle was effectively sacked for publishing a book of poems written by the working-class children of the school where he worked in Stepney. The school was the very traditional Sir John Cass Church of England School. Several of the teachers were Church of England priests, Searle would later recall, "one of whom would, on a daily basis, patrol the corridors complete with dog collar, academic gown and brandished cane. . . . There were five streams before you reached the 'Remedial' stream, which wasn't a class with small groups and more teachers to give close attention to students' learning problems. It was simply another class of more than thirty students with a single teacher: the rock bottom stream". When Searle was dismissed for producing *Stepney Words*, the children promptly went on self-organised strike and self-organised a march to Trafalgar Square:

> On the second day a large group of the strikers marched along the Embankment to Trafalgar Square, carrying banners. The secondary boys of the school on Ben Jonson Road (another poet!) nearly opposite Sir John Cass, Stepney Green School, had climbed the tall iron gates of the school to join the strike on its first day after their head teacher had tried to lock them in, and as the news was carried around the borough, the girls of Tower Hamlets School along Commercial Road came out, as did the students of Robert Montefiore School in Whitechapel.[2]

Following his sacking, Searle spoke about his experience at NUT meetings across England. In his autobiography he recalls:

> The meetings gave me a keen sense of young teachers' thirst for progress, for the championing of comprehensive schools and mixed ability teaching and the end of streaming, and for huge teacher-led changes in the curriculum. . . . There were young people who had lived and campaigned through the radical years of British university life, had experienced 1968 and all it meant, and were entering schools with deep commitments to the South African and Irish peoples, an end to the war in Vietnam and support for the trade unions and their resistance right across Britain.[3]

It took two years, but the dismissal was eventually ruled invalid. The education minister at the time was Margaret Thatcher. When Searle learned of the ruling, he issued a statement—quoted in full in the right-wing *Daily Express*—that declared:

> the meanest, most retrogressive and class-biased education minister for generations has been pressurised to decide in my favour because of the support and solidarity shown to me by classroom teachers, local children and parents and the National Union of Teachers, who have fought for me.[4]

Searle returned to Sir John Cass School "determined . . . to continue to attempt to develop, through imaginative writing, the generous, empathetic and fraternal instincts of these children". He developed a scheme of work with three main emphases; the local neighbourhood, the global conditions of the working class and the world of work. Searle later published the outline of this syllabus and examples of the writing that his pupils produced following this scheme of work in a book entitled *Classrooms of Resistance*. In addition to allowing for discussion and debate about contemporary events to feature as part of classroom practice the book argues "it was important to look to tradition and history, to find precedents in the past where individuals and masses of East End working people have similarly resisted or organised, or achieved advances which now benefited the children and their families". In the introduction he states:

> Education is only valid if it plays its part in supporting the total liberation of mankind, and not the interests of the ruling few. . . . [T]he priority was that these working-class children should learn to read, write, spell, punctuate, to develop the word as a weapon and tool in the inevitable struggles for improvement and liberation for them, and the rest of their class all over the world.[5]

Searle eventually got a job at another East End school, Langdon Park, a very different institution to the one he'd been sacked from:

Our School was quickly gaining the reputation of being a left-wing institution. Some parents humorously referred to it as the Kremlin, but they were always very supportive and laughed off its reputation because the students were happy there and worked very hard and with a potent enthusiasm: they saw the school as their own.[6]

The press had been surprisingly sympathetic to the schoolchildren's strike in 1971. However, four years later, when *Classrooms of Resistance* was published, the press response was significantly more politicised and more hostile, with the *Sunday Telegraph* asserting, "the sooner he is sacked, *pour encourager les autres*—of whom there are far too many—the better".[7] By 1975, the right was flexing its muscle with a backlash organised around the second defining narrative of the 1970s, the events at William Tyndale Junior School in North London.

The Labour government's commitment to comprehensive education provided a specific opportunity for a reactionary challenge to the politics of the post-war consensus. Education became a rehearsal for the right's resurgence in the late 1970s and the 1980s. Education—effectively a discourse about the future—gave the right a space where they were first able to effectively sidestep the gentlemanly post-war acceptance of consensus. This space allowed the right to construct a functioning populist attack on the egalitarian ethos that permeated the politics of the welfare state and created the gateway for subsequent attempts to overturn entirely the progress made by the politics of social rights and state provision.

In 1969, the academic journal *Critical Quarterly* started publishing a series of Black Papers (to be understood as the antithesis of the government's official White Papers) on education. They contained articles vehemently opposed to most of the contemporary issues associated with progressive educational development—comprehensivisation, child-centred classroom practices, student protests. . . . Their arguments were spearheaded by the personality of head teacher (later Tory MP and minister in the Thatcher government) Dr Rhodes Boyson, an advocate of strict uniform policies, corporal punishment and an ardent homophobe. Contributors included literati Iris Murdoch and Kingsley Amis (both of whom had recanted their youthful membership of the Communist Party when they were students at Oxford in the 1930s), and the Black Papers provided a veneer of intellectual and literary respectability to right-wing reactionary abhorrence at the concepts of equality and social justice becoming a social reality.

In 1974, the William Tyndale Junior School's attempt to effect a revolution of everyday life for children who didn't attend a fee-paying school represented everything the Black Papers and conservatives of both the right and the left detested and feared. The reactionary response of a vocal minority of staff and middle-class parents to the progressive initiatives of the majority of the staff at William Tyndale Junior provided the opportunity for the right to mount an effective attack on progressive education.

Rhodes Boyson enthusiastically gave full support to the disgruntled minority and their leading agitator, a support teacher who was also a devoted advocate of the literary theory that Christopher Marlowe was really responsible for writing many of Shakespeare's poems and plays, and the propaganda of the Black Papers hovered as a background presence in the arguments that developed both in the Inner London Education Authority and the national media.

The conflict arose because staff at William Tyndale attempted to reorganise both classroom practice and whole school policy in accordance with radical ideas about democracy, children's rights, autonomy, inclusion and creativity, with the children and their needs and interests being the starting point for teaching and learning (newspaper reports were aghast at finding pop music being heard in the school). New head teacher Terry Ellis and his colleagues wanted to create a school which, in Ellis's words, "geared its main educational effort toward the disadvantaged", which utilised a child-centred, integrated day methodology, which involved dividing the school day into alternating open and closed hour-long periods, with pupils free to choose what they did in the open sessions. This reorganisation of practice also included reorganising not only time but space and hierarchy. The staff sought ways to overcome the limitations of space imposed by the physical reality of the school building that also supported an ethos that sought to dismantle some of the arbitrary barriers and divisions that traditionally exist in schools between children and between children and staff.

> Drawing on the experience of the previous year, and a staff stability which had never been achieved before, it was decided to develop the organisation into the following structure.
>
> The children transferred from the Infants' were to be in two separated groups. . . . The rest were to be in five "vertical" groups, each not encompassing more than a two-year age span. . . . During morning sessions each group was to work with its own teacher on basic skills. Each afternoon, a wide system of options was to be offered. Ellis (the head teacher) was timetabled to work in the options system. All classes were moved to the top floor; rooms on the middle floor were made specialist areas for art and music. The hall, now fitted with bookshelves and soft chairs, became a central reading area, and maintained its function as an area for social gatherings of staff and children.[8]

Ellis and the majority of the staff were motivated by a pedagogy that was often animated by an understanding of education from a radical leftist perspective. This provoked a hostile response from vocal middle-class parents, who were effectively encouraged and organised by a small minority of staff who were highly critical of Ellis's pedagogy.

When you try to reach any understanding of what happened at William Tyndale School in the mid-1970s, it is difficult to unravel the educational issues from the political agendas. Teachers opposed to progressive education encouraged parental opposition, and with school managers and Labour Party members joining in, the opposition moved from issues of pedagogy to the level of political witch-hunt, with progressive teachers being demonised in the media for both alleged professional failings and alleged political indoctrination of pupils.

The conflict dragged on for over a year. The Inner London Education Authority (ILEA), the NUT, the Labour Party, the Infants School and, of course, the national media all got involved, generally on the side of the complaining "traditionalists. The junior school staff stuck to their principles and attempted to cooperate with an unending onslaught of meetings, procedures and inspections, but they were always attempting to negotiate reasonably with unsympathetic individuals, systems and hierarchies that were either institutionally conservative or simply unreasonably downright ideologically hostile.

It is obvious that the interventions by members of the Labour Party and the NUT—both individually and organisationally—aimed at challenging the decisions democratically arrived at by the majority of teachers and the head teacher and the support offered to the oppositional traditionalist teachers and parents by Rhodes Boyson freighted political agendas, but it was, of course, never those politics that the media wanted to focus on.

Over forty years later, however, we should note that much of the "radical" daily practice initiated by the staff at William Tyndale Junior School is now common practice that is recognised as facilitating the education process in state schools.

William Tyndale was castigated for establishing a sanctuary with its own teacher for children with challenging issues and behaviours. This is now considered a necessary resource in many schools.

William Tyndale was castigated for focussing support on children with particular impediments to learning, particularly those disadvantaged by ethnicity and behavioural issues. Looking at the achievement of particular groups and developing strategies to address particular needs is now standard practice. Now it is called "closing the gap", and educationalists understand equality as meaning not that everybody gets the same, but that everybody gets what they need. Which is what the Tyndale staff were doing, with their focus on the achievement within the school of particular ethnic groups and dedicated Special Educational Needs and Disabilities (SEND) support for children with behavioural problems.

Breaking down the rigidity of year groups—the age grouping of children by September birth dates (remember Gatto's identification of this as part of mass education's "divide and rule" strategy)—supports both the confident and the less confident child. Confident children will have more opportunities to develop their learning with older children, and less confident children will have more time to develop their self-assurance. A wider age range in the peer group also supports the development of a wider range of social skills. Vertical grouping is not particularly fashionable nowadays (so we leave out of consideration those many smaller schools or schools with varying yearly intakes where it is a practical necessity), but having worked in vertically grouped settings and in schools where the benefits of a more "family" arrangement of children are appreciated and opportunities for year groups to interact are actively pursued, I am convinced of the great value of these arrangements in addressing a diverse range of educational challenges.

Another characteristic the school was heavily criticised for was the head teacher's policy of democratising decision-making. While recent "reforms" have tended to encourage head teachers in the belief of their own divinity, my experience has been that there are also, nonetheless, head teachers who recognise that encouraging a genuine sense of ownership in workers is a good way to organise a work situation. Because it is good practice, and also perhaps partly because of the enormity of the bureaucracy and paperwork facing senior management, staff are often expected to participate in arriving at policies and deciding priorities for the School Development Plan (SDP). Indeed, one head at the last school I worked at espoused a vision whereby all adults working in the school would belong to a team concerned to determine and effect a particular priority of the SDP. Pupil representation in this process was also to be developed.

Great Debates

The subsequent 1976 Auld Report into William Tyndale School did its best to blame everybody it could (apart from the vocal middle-class parents and their vocal friends on the staff, obviously) and attempted to focus on individuals and authorities rather than pedagogies. Labour prime minister James Callaghan also appeared to be cautious in his response to the affair when he grandly announced a "Great Debate" on state education in a speech at Ruskin College, in October 1976, referring to "the new informal methods of teaching, which seem to produce excellent results when they are in well-qualified hands but are much more dubious when they are not". Underlying the speech, however, was a clear and barely concealed subtext that espoused an unreconstructed utilitarian valuation of state education, whereby schools existed to serve the needs of the state by providing future citizens trained in the skills the state decided it wanted.

Setting the terms of the Great Debate, "Sunny Jim" Callaghan attempted to conflate the supposed interests of parents with the economic interests of the state: "Let me answer the question 'what do we want from the education of our children and young people?' with Tawney's words once more. He said: 'What a wise parent would wish for their children so the state must wish for all its children'". Wise parents are apparently expected to be worried that education is failing to provide the requisite human raw material demanded by British industry; Callaghan stated:

I am concerned on my journeys to find complaints
from industry that new recruits from the schools sometimes do not have the basic tools to do the job that is
required. . . . I have been concerned to find that many
of our best trained students who have completed the
higher levels of education at university or polytechnic
have no desire to join industry. . . . Why is it that 30,000
vacancies for students in science and engineering in
our universities were not taken up last year while the
humanities courses were full? . . . To the teacher, I
would say that you must satisfy the parents and industry that what you are doing meets their requirements
and the needs of our children.[1]

Callaghan's speech clearly favours mass diligent study
of science and engineering, rather than engagement with all
those humanities, arts and subversive social sciences courses,
clearly of dubious value to industry. The clear lack of full
Labour government support for these curriculum developments gave legitimacy to the idea that the post-Plowden
developments in pedagogy were to be publicly questioned not
simply by educationalists but by all manner of hobby horse–
riding politicians and media pundits. The events at Willian
Tyndale Junior School and the way the media presented these
as evidence of a failing school came to characterise all progressive education and, by extension, evidence of the failure
of progressive education as a pedagogy. A book by journalists
for the *Times Educational Supplement* John Gretton and Mark
Jackson that called for government intervention to decide,
define and enforce standards in education was tellingly entitled *William Tyndale: Collapse of a School—or a System?*[2]

The moral panic that William Tyndall School engendered
also revealed two of the significant fault lines running through
state education since its beginnings that continue to remain
manifest and unresolved. They are not entirely unrelated; one
(partly referenced by Callaghan's concern that not enough

students were willing to do their bit for British industry) is the issue of access to culture, and the other is the issue of parental rights.

Access to culture is a real signifier of how "education" is understood. Is access to culture for the many of mass education or the few of paid-for privilege? William Tyndale's disposition of resources ascribed importance to art and music. Forty years later, we have a barely concealed state agenda in education that aims to limit access to the arts in favour of channelling the mass of the population toward subjects likely to generate profits for the employing classes. The national curriculum, both through prescribed content and ascribed valuation in terms of assessments, sidelines and diminishes the importance of art and music in particular and creativity in general. Higher education has experienced a similar process, with arts and humanities programmes being subjected to constant devaluation.

Partly this can be seen as the historical reaction of the right to anything connected to the 1960s. The 1960s represented an explosion of popular culture that—temporarily—happened outside of and in contradiction to the cultural establishment. The working class suddenly became the engine room for all manner of creative endeavours. Whereas previously working-class creativity—the music hall, for example—was effectively constrained within the confines of the existing class system, controlled by a confident aristocracy and business class and paying due homage to King and Country (music hall star Vesta Tilley was nicknamed "Britain's best recruiting sergeant" during World War I), the lower-class likes of David Bailey and John Lennon found themselves freely running riot and roughshod through and over an exhausted post-war landscape, welcomed with open arms as a novel diversion from the overwhelming glumness of respectable middle-class suburban dreariness by the jaded aristocracy and bored youth of the working and middle classes alike.

But while some working-class kids were going to art school and on to express themselves to great pop culture acclaim, not every working-class kid was Keith Richards learning how to play guitar in the toilets with Wizz Jones. Peace and love had less significance for the working class than their concrete experience, which remained largely characterised as continuing relative deprivation. Their sense of identity was expressed through adhering to core traditional attitudes and values and defined by their continuing negative relationship to capitalism's political and economic realities.

The access to and ownership of culture by the working class, the lower middle class, the underclass—the majority of people—is a complex narrative. An objective view of cultural development over the last two hundred years would inevitably conclude that it is the mass of the people who have increasingly provided the creativity that has galvanised art and music, from the democratisation inherent in mass-produced forms like the novel and the cinema to the democratisation consequent upon the influence of underclass musical forms, from the expressions of the experiences of black Americans in blues and jazz, hip-hop and rap to its echo in the expressions of the experiences of disaffected white youth in rock 'n roll and punk. But it's not real work, is it, not like being a coal miner or an engineer or research chemist or refuse collector or. . . is it? Sometimes it is presented—along with the Royal Family and the Lake District—as being part of what makes Britain Great, a tourist attraction. Cool Britannia—a trip down Penny Lane with the Spice Girls. But that was an invention of the early Blair years, and we all know how inclusive of the working class New Labour wasn't.

So perhaps it should come as no surprise to find that Chris Searle was sacked for encouraging working-class children to express themselves through the traditional preserve of high literary culture, poetry, or that the teachers at William Tyndale were roundly castigated in the media for playing pop music in their classrooms.

Denying children access to and ownership of the arts serves the purposes of the ruling class in several ways. However far short of its revolution popular pop culture fell, it nonetheless managed to pose—or be perceived as posing—a real threat to capitalism and its ruling class. It was not just John Lennon who had security agencies monitoring his activities—Ewan MacColl, a driving force in the UK's post-war folk revival, was monitored by MI5, while his brother in-law-in the US, Pete Seeger, was blacklisted for his politics. If you deny children access to this sort of culture, you deny them access to the ideas it freights, and you exact your revenge upon it for having had the temerity to challenge your authority in the 1960s. If children are not asking awkward questions or thinking they can establish their own agendas, then they are more easily manipulated into fitting into your agenda—cannon fodder, factory fodder, consumer fodder, subclass fodder. . . and if you deny them access to culture, you subtly dehumanise them, so it is easier to ignore them when they die, either for you, or because they are surplus to your requirements.

At the start of the 1970s, the organised working class were convincingly demonstrating that probably all you needed to change the world was not love or any other of pop culture's expressions of individual liberation and self-assertion but a mass picket by most of Birmingham's workers at Saltley Gate. The twenty-first century has seen the popular feel-good film and stage musical *Billy Elliott* background its narrative with the violence of the miner's strike.[3] This provides a bit of added contrast and drama and acts as a metaphor for the defeat of the traditional working class, their jobs, communities and stereotypical values. The narrative here is "individual salvation is attained through art". But just as not all the working class were going to be able to earn a living playing guitar in the 1960s, they were unlikely to be any luckier at earning a living dancing in the 1980s.

Access to both traditional high culture and the forms of popular culture that twentieth century pop culture has evolved into has become increasingly economically restricted. In 2015, pop journalist Stuart Maconie quoted the "highly debatable" statistic "that as much as 60 percent of the pop charts of recent years has been occupied by privately educated musicians".[4] Specialist popular culture further education colleges now exist that claim to teach students how to be popular culture workers; both culture and learning have been instrumentalised and gentrified. What are we educating the working class for—a lifetime as spectators and the expectation that their place is to form audience rather than perform action?

This question of expectation is also central to the issue of parental attitudes to state education and the rights many parents want to exert over their children. Many working-class parents were as hostile to the progressive ideas put into practice at William Tyndale School, just as the middle-class parents were. Both the local education authority and Prime Minister "Sunny Jim" Callaghan were happy to suggest that the state shared their concerns.

Some might argue: well, of course the state has the right to expect to get what it wants from state education, because, after all, the state is paying for it. Well, no, not exactly. The figureheads of the state are not putting their hands into their variously very well-fattened wallets and coming up with a fistful of offshore untaxed readies. The state is paying for state education with the people's money. The state would define itself as the structure of governance to which the people abdicate responsibilities for—rather than the sum of the people described by—a particular geographical area. Nonetheless, most states tend to present themselves as in some way governing on behalf of the interests of "the people", like wise parent Callaghan. The state replicates itself and its priorities through the values it endorses and the model it provides of "wise parenting". These values background both working-class and Labour Party antipathy to the progressive education initiatives at William Tyndale and elsewhere. It is often both surprising and disappointing how conservative Labour Party radicals can be when it comes to education. They are progressive left leftists until it comes to matters like the school uniform, which they suddenly insist is absolutely essential for a good education. Indeed, I have also been amused to find anarchists complaining that they have trouble maintaining discipline with and authority over "their [*sic*] children". Archetypal anarcho-troublemaker Mikhail Bakunin wasn't impressed by the concept of the sanctity of parental rights:

> the child must be trained and guided, but . . . the direction of his first years must not be exclusively exercised by his parents, who are all too often incompetent and who generally abuse their authority. . . . The child belongs to no one, he belongs only to himself. . . . It is society that must protect him and guarantee his free development. It is society that must support him and supervise his education.[5]

Recently we have seen how the state chooses to alter its definition of wise parenting to suit its political objectives. For Callaghan, wise parents want to keep industry happy; for Thatcher, Major and Blair, wise parents want to exercise parental choice and send their children to schools that appear to good advantage in league tables and Office for Standards in Education (Ofsted) reports. Perhaps recalling how parents at William Tyndale School had put a stop to dangerously progressive ideas of education there—parents were encouraged by the state to take an active formal role in running state schools, with the creation of school governing bodies that included parent representatives. For Cameron's first term as prime minister, wise parents were those who favoured academisation and who set up free schools. Then, in his second term, it was announced that most parents have the wrong skill set, the wrong sort of wisdom to be governors—perhaps because many parents had by then wised up to the damage being done to our schools by a restrictive curriculum and diminishing funding, some even going so far as to take their children out on strike to protest against this in May 2016.

Parents, of course, are just as likely to be as wise or as foolish as they ever were, however the state chooses to present them. Parenting is not anything the vast majority of people have any training for. Parents, because they vote, are generally accorded a degree of respect and a set of rights by our representative democracy that children, who don't vote, are denied. Unless, of course, the parents are working-class. The introduction of compulsory schooling, like legislation setting restrictions on child labour, often caused considerable economic hardship in families that relied upon children's earning potential to make ends meet. "The family" is one of those social sacred cows, particularly favoured by those politicians who like to promote "family values"—a thin veneer for the more dubious values of patriarchy and paternalism, social respectability and conformity. Family values emphasise relationships sanctioned by religious or civil authority rather than the free associations of autonomous individuals and have a history that favours obedience rather than discussion or dissent. They are used by the right to posit the family as a microcosm of society, where people are expected to know their place and do as they are told by figures of institutional authority. In this understanding of family, parents are expected to become the state's surrogate police force, the first agents of socialisation and repression.

Authority is not my idea of parenthood, just as ignorance is not my idea of childhood. Nonetheless, parenthood does carry with it as many if not more responsibilities than rights. Parents have the responsibility to try to respect the integrity of the child. Children are neither fashion accessories or little footballers fathers can live out their own thwarted dreams through. Children benefit from both support and space. I have always thought that becoming a parent does not inevitably diminish one's capacity to think objectively about one's child, but it is a poor parent who doesn't instinctively think their child is just the best thing ever to happen to them and the universe—even if objectively they recognise this may well paradoxically hold true for the estimation in which every other parent holds their child. That is why—as Bakunin insisted—we need a society that safeguards and facilitates the development process of each individual child. We need schools and educationalists who are able to see all children for what they are, each one the best thing ever to happen to their universe, and each one belonging to themselves and their futures. And that is why we need schools and educationalists rather than central government deciding what happens in schools and in education. That is also why we need properly funded free state schools, a comprehensive system committed to meeting each individual's need, and why we don't need or want the nasty system of private "public" schools offering the best privileges your money can afford. Each and every child needs to receive an education characterised by quality and equality, because no child gets to choose where they are born. And each child is indeed the best thing ever to happen to the universe.

You can trace the skeleton of such thinking in the strategies that teachers at William Tyndale school evolved to meet the needs of their pupils, which can be seen as attempting to meet the needs of the whole child. Half a century after Emma Goldman wrote, "The modern school, then, must be libertarian. Each pupil must be left free to his true self",[6] modernity in education was still not necessarily what those in positions of authority and influence in society wanted to see happening in their schools for working-class children.

The William Tyndale witch-hunt was fuelled by parental assertion of the primacy of *their* parental rights over *their* children over the professionalism of the teachers. It represented the triumph of opinion over knowledge and provided a clear warning that teachers could no longer take it for granted that their professional status and knowledge could withstand populist politics and media prejudice. The moral panic also represented a backlash against all the libertarian developments in education that had noticeably been seeping into the state system over the previous decade and some of the questions those developments had thrown up. Do parents know what is best for their children? Does the state know what is best for its children? It wasn't just youth culture talking about "My Generation" or the Vietnam generation asking awkward questions of the Auschwitz generation any more. Practitioners in the social structures expected to process young people into society were also asking awkward but eminently sensible questions about that process, questioning both the social function of state education and the nature of the society it was operating in.

Complete Control

The very public controversy generated by the events at William Tyndale Junior School revealed the extent to which reactionary opinion could enlist support from both the media and the general public. William Tyndale School accelerated the right-wing backlash against the perceived radicalism of the 1960s. That great cultural signifier, the 1964 film "A Hard Day's Night", has a scene where the clearly lovable Beatles are confronted in a railway carriage by "a representative of conservative opinion". Beatle Paul wants the window open: "There's more of us than you, we're a community, like a majority vote. Up the workers and all that stuff".[1] The audience, and by extension the nation's sensibilities, are expected to side with the Beatles and their clearly lovable if generally sloppy notions of post-war social progress. Six years later, those sloppy notions of social progress having led Beatle John into bed-ins with non-white performance artist Yoko Ono, the nation's sensibilities were starting to incline more toward the side of "a representative of conservative opinion" and his outraged declaration, "I fought the war for your sort!" Speaking as the milk-snatching education secretary in Edward Heath's 1970 Tory government, Margaret Thatcher had scolded: "Go back, you flower people, back where you came from, wash your hair, get dressed properly, get to work on time and stop all this whingeing and moaning".[2]

Norman Tebbit, Thatcher's perfect hatchet man, was particularly apocalyptic about the consequences of the ideas of the 1960s percolating into the daily water supply of the

general population—note the prevalence of educational terms
(I have to say he seems to be fulminating about a very different
planet to the one I was living on):

> Bad art was as good as good art. Grammar and spelling
> were no longer important. To be clean was no better
> than to be filthy. Good manners were no better than
> bad. Family life was derided as an outdated bourgeois
> concept. Criminals deserved as much sympathy as their
> victims. Many homes and classrooms became disor-
> derly—if there was neither right nor wrong there could
> be no bases for punishment or reward.[3]

Just over ten years after Callaghan initiated the Great
Debate, Thatcher's Tory government, having deliberately
taken on and largely beaten the miners and their communities by provoking the miners' strike of 1984, felt able to turn
its attention toward "reforming" social democracy—the social
characteristics, values, practices and structures that had
evolved with the welfare state. Thatcher declared this to be
her aim within a year of becoming prime minister: "We are
trying to roll back the tide of Socialism. We must get 'stuck
in' and sort out our problems in our traditional British way
instead of asking the Government to intervene every time".[4]
Ironically, for the nation's schools, this involved greater state
intervention to sort out what the right defined as problems.

Teachers' traditional mechanisms for negotiating with
their employers, the local authorities, through the longstand-
ing Burnham committee, were first to go, done away with in
favour of more direct central government control over teaching conditions and salaries. Then, significantly, school praxis—
what teachers did in the classroom, what and how they taught
and what and how children learned—was brought under
central government control by the imposition of prescriptive
government legislation.

With the 1987 Great Education Reform Bill (at the time
known by its acronym: GERBill), the state began the process

of asserting complete centralised government authority and control over the education offered to its children. Initiatives like the national curriculum, SATs testing, publication of SATs results and ranking schools by results in league tables replaced professionally evolved pedagogy with a state-run highly politicised instrumentalisation of schooling. The class nature of the "reform" legislation was clear from the outset: fee-paying "public" schools were not to be subject to these initiatives. State classrooms, however, were to be turned back into the kind of Victorian learning factories thoroughly satirised by Charles Dickens in 1854 in the novel *Hard Times*, the classrooms of Coketown, with children "little vessels then and there arranged in order, ready to have imperial gallons of facts poured into them until they were full to the brim".[5] And then some.

PART TWO

THE STATE OF STATE EDUCATION

Oliver Twist

Oliver Twist, who doesn't exist apparently now,
Sits at the back picking his scabs in my literacy hour,
But he's dreaming such dreams, dreaming such dreams.

The minister says: "These are the ways we raise standards".
But which box do you tick when Oliver Twist's thinking in
    rainbows?
And dreaming such dreams, dreaming such dreams.

His grandad Tim Winters, two teeth left like splinters, says,
    "Well I was the same",
So it's nobody's fault, you're on income support, you've got
    yourself to blame.
For dreaming such dreams, dreaming such dreams.

In the canteen, there's cabbage and beans and the odd
    dead samosa,
But you have to choose between a pudding and a juice if
    you're on free school dinners.
That would be dreaming such dreams, dreaming such
    dreams.

Oliver Twist, now you just look at the state you're in.
There's a box you can tick for a new nuclear submarine,
There's a box you can tick for a millennium dome,
But pudding and juice, that would be dreaming. . .
That would be dreaming such dreams, dreaming such
    dreams.

Oliver Twist, now you just look at the state we're in.

Zealots and Their Hobby Horses

In 1987, state education became the recuperated property of the ruling class. That this was a political rather than an educational intent is apparent from the lack of educational knowledge and experience of the prime movers of the "reform" agenda. Apart from the alarming Rhodes-Boyson, whose headships of various secondary modern and comprehensive schools were characterised by strict discipline policies enforced by caning, none of the noted advocates of education "reform" had any relevant background in or experience of education theory or, indeed, state education itself. All the key ministers in charge of education in the Thatcher government and intent on "reforming" it shared similarly privileged backgrounds—Kenneth Baker (Baron Baker of Dorking now) with degrees in history and international law, worked for Royal Dutch Shell before becoming an MP. In the case of Sir Keith Joseph, it was fee-paying "prep" school, then on to Harrow "Public" School, then off to Oxford for a degree in jurisprudence. Indeed, even the "minister for flogging", as Rhodes Boyson was known when he became a member of Thatcher's government in the 1980s, had enjoyed the opportunity offered by selective education to go on from Haslingden Grammar School to attend University College Cardiff, the University of Manchester, the London School of Economics, and Corpus Christi College, Cambridge. These men enjoyed affluent, privileged backgrounds that facilitated their progress to elite universities, which in turn facilitated their career progress into government. Their "thinking" about education was primarily determined by the ideological perspective of their class rather than by any objective interest in the principles and practice of state education as it has developed in Britain. They viewed education with the experiences and the values of their class, which are the experiences and values of wealth and privilege, arrived at through business and commodity. They therefore applied the values of business and commodity to public services: "best practice" must be determined by successfully measured outcomes directed at meeting the needs of British business. State education should once again be aligned with the political and economic interests of their class, the ruling class, not the reality of the needs of children whose life experiences are far removed from their own privileged upbringings.

The reforming urge became legislation with Tory education minister Kenneth Baker's announcement in 1987 of a forthcoming Great Education Reform Bill—commonly known at the time by its rodent-recalling acronym GERBill. The following year the GERBill became law with the Education Reform Act that gave us a national curriculum determined by central government and its ideological hobby horses, and which promptly took away five days of my teacher's holiday for GERBill training purposes—how to ride hobby horses—and never gave them back. These central government diktats would usually be represented by an avalanche of acronyms; you'd have the SEF, the SDP, the ECM, there would be FSM, G and T, EAL, SEND. There would soon regularly be the latest guide to the latest goalpost moving Office for Standards in Education (Ofsted) guidance, an unhealthy and abundant spew of data analysis, with meaningless gibberish about targets, levels and even sublevels, none of which ever bore any real corresponding relationship to any child you were actually supposed to be educating.

At first Baker wasn't able to bring in a payment by results system (the "reformers" had to wait nearly thirty years before "performance management" made "performance-related pay" a reality again). But 1988 saw the introduction of a national curriculum, knowledge of which could be and would be tested regularly. There were Standardised Assessment Tasks—SATs—tests at seven, eleven and fourteen, later reduced to tests at seven and eleven years of age (but as we will discover there would later be added phonics testing for six-year-olds and an unhealthy obsession with getting some sort of baseline test as soon as the hapless four-year-old set foot in a reception class). SATs results were published with schools being ranked like football teams in league tables, ostensibly facilitating parental choice, but in practice often simply ensuring working-class schools got less money. Parents with domestic circumstances more likely to be able to support children considered "able" in test situations would therefore be likely to choose to send their children—and therefore the funding that goes with them—to successful schools, a covert but very effective reversal of the welfare state's practice of targeting resources to support children in situations of deprivation.

The "reform" agenda was resisted to some extent by teachers and the teaching unions, but that resistance was weakened, first by the general sense of demoralisation experienced by unions and the organisations on the left in the wake of the miners' strike, and then by a misplaced faith in the possibilities offered by the Labour Party electoral landslide of 1997, fronted by the plausible Tony Blair, who declared his three priorities to be "education, education, education".

However, as in so many other respects, it was hard to tell New Labour education priorities apart from Tory education policies. (Let's not forget that Thatcher liked to boast that the creation of New Labour was her finest achievement.) A government report in April 2009, the first chapter titled "The Evolution of the National Curriculum: From Butler to Balls," asserted:

> In more recent decades there has also been a significant level of consensus across the political parties as regards the need for a national curriculum, what its purposes

might be and how it should be structured and supported. . . . The 1944 Education Act, introduced under the Conservative President of the Board of Education, R.A. Butler, put in place publicly provided primary and secondary education for all. . . . The strength of the teaching profession and its representative bodies at this time inhibited attempts to introduce greater central direction of the curriculum.[1]

New Labour was fully in favour of "greater central direction of the curriculum" and the continued effective exclusion of the teaching profession and its representative bodies from the processes of decision-making, a significant exception being the positive influence educationalists were able to exert on the creation of the Early Years Foundation Stage (EYFS) curriculum introduced in 2006.[2]

As the years passed, the curriculum was refined to increasingly focus on measurable outcomes. Thanks to a 2006 report by Sir Jim Rose (who last taught in a secondary school in the 1970s), primary children were to be taught English—possibly one of the least phonetically regular languages due to the diverse constituents of its etymology—through a phonics-based approach to language. This devalues and excludes both the child's own developed language skills and also the idea that language is primarily about communicating meaning, expressing ideas and imagination. But it is measurable. Six years later, in 2012, five- and six-year-olds were being subjected to a "phonics screening" test, having to bark their way correctly through forty words, half of them real words and half of them gibberish. Children's Laureate Michael Rosen is a determined opponent of reducing language learning to the measurement of systematic phonics teaching. In "Phonics: A Summary of My Views", he writes:

> Billions of pounds are being spent implementing programmes of study for 4, 5 and 6 year olds that have

no evidence to support their implementation when we widen the testing to include irregular texts, real texts and comprehension.[3]

This is not just an issue faced by six-year-olds in English state schools. The real beneficiaries of these programmes of study are the commercial interests marketing them. By the second decade of the twenty-first century, schools in England were facing issues of marketisation of teaching and learning remarkably similar to those faced by schools around the world, as the Global Education Reform Movement reconfigured publicly owned assets like state schools purely as opportunities for profit. Teachers in Australia would find themselves faced with the same mechanical phonics-based approach to the teaching of reading and writing as teachers in England.

Grandiose initiatives in the USA with snappy titles like No Child Left Behind or Race to the Top and the implementation of the Common Core Standards (CCS) education "reform" system tied school funding directly to both outcomes and classroom practice, which profited private edubusiness companies—if you don't do the tests, you don't get state funding. Edubusiness generates between $20 and $30 billion a year, and the UK company Pearson, the planet's largest education company, makes more than $9 billion a year. Bill Gates, whose support and money have ensured the implementation of the CCS programme, announced a vision of education 2009 that effectively completely marketized learning:

> When the tests are aligned to the common standards, the curriculum will line up as well—that will unleash powerful market forces in the service of better teaching. For the first time there will be a large base of customers eager to buy products that can help every kid learn and every teacher get better.[4]

In England the connection between testing and funding has been slightly more fig-leafed, with funding tied to outcomes by the publication of SATs results league tables. Although presenting as a less direct mechanism, this nonetheless impacts on classroom practice by effectively coercing schools to "teach to the tests"—if you don't do well in the tests, you won't get the funding. Poorly funded schools are likely to attract fewer pupils and therefore receive less money—as Billie Holiday observed in her sardonic nifty little critique of capitalism "God Bless the Child": "Them that's got shall get/Them that's not shall lose".[5]

The state's "greater central direction" and increased Kafkaesque bureaucracy and workload within schools, combined with punitive inspections and performance management systems, now coerce schools into purchasing schemes of work that offer the promise of guaranteed curriculum coverage as a matter of course across all age ranges. Even four- and five-year-olds in the EYFS have been marketized through testing. The EYFS, introduced during the Blair years in 2008, is a rarity in that you can clearly detect the presence of educationalists and early years practitioners behind its drafting. It is surely one of the very few positive significant outcomes of Blair's noisy commitment to "education x 3". Perhaps its existence is due to that inch of difference Richard Neville, editor of the 1960s underground magazine *Oz*, identified as the difference between Labour and Conservative government by which the magazine he edited was able to operate or not. Perhaps it is an indication of how unimportant the hobby horse–riding politicians and pundits consider the under-fives to be. Generally, their idea of education cannot comprehend anything you can't mark as correct or incorrect on an answer paper, and four-and five-year olds clearly don't do their learning on paper. Nonetheless, in 2015, when the government first attempted to introduce a system of formal "baseline" assessments for four- and five-year-olds entering schooling, EYFS settings trialling this testing had to choose one from six very different commercially available schemes designed to label the children with scores that would be carried forward throughout their primary school career. The government's main intention was that the score would be used when the child was eleven to judge the effectiveness of the school. The trial was an expensive shambles. Most settings opted for the scheme that was the most child-friendly and observation-based, which was neither that well thought-out nor what the government wanted anyway. It was rumoured that this earned the company that produced the scheme a nice little £10,000,000. Undeterred by either the widespread opposition to baseline tests or the fiasco that was their first attempt at imposing standardised tests on four-year-olds, in 2017, the government simply invited firms to bid for a baseline assessment contract worth £9.8 million.

And, of course, although the older children are the easier it is get them to answer questions in writing, on paper, the veritable herd of elephants in the room is that we all know—really, incontrovertibly—that all this tests is whether children can answer a particular question at a particular point in time. It doesn't tell anybody what they actually know.

Goon Squads and Thought Policing

A traditional and simplistic way of motivating progress has been the use of the carrot and the stick. "Reform" has simplified this process further by using a stick and another stick.

In this section we will look at the preferred sticks used in this "reform".

The rigorous system of nationally standardised testing and publication of results is designed to ensure compliance from schools as institutions, with schools passing this pressure downward to ensure compliance from children and teachers. Pressure on schools has been further increased by the central government's "reform" of how state schools access funding. The state initially began by cutting the funding to local education authorities; outsourcing services to private contractors further diminished the authority of local government. Then the function of local authorities was reduced to little more than diffusing central funds to individual schools, which suddenly had full control of a limited budget and equally suddenly needed to fund a new level of bursar bureaucracy, with none of the "economies of scale" that allowed local authorities to effectively manage a number of settings and to direct funds strategically to meet local need. Central government then embarked on a year-on-year underfunding of all individual school budgets.

The more the state washes its hands of responsibility, the more those responsibilities turn into opportunities for private profit. Turning our public services into privatised commodities has been a slow but steady process. Outsourcing school clean-ing services or school meal services on a "best value" basis was a particularly effective easy win strategy that went hand in hand with degrading local authorities and local democracy through underfunding. The process is brutally simple: under-funded services are soon seen as underperforming. They are then sold off to "the market", because the fiction is that "the market" will run them more efficiently.

The same mechanism that was used for piecemeal privati-sation of services has now been applied to schools. "Failing" or "underperforming" schools are to be rescued by the deregula-tory "academy" initiative, which allows schools to be run more in line with business practices associated with "the market". Academy status was originally a short-term attempt by Tony Blair's New Labour government to direct money to failing schools not performing well in the league tables without government having to do too much intervention. (This was a favourite tactic of the Blair government; as little central gov-ernment direction and as much free-market funding as pos-sible—unless of course it wanted to bomb somewhere). This mechanism was then seized upon by the Tories as a ready-made blunt instrument with which to effect widespread priva-tisation of state education. Academisation removes the school and all its assets from local authority oversight and the commu-nities they serve, and there is no mechanism for getting these assets back. Sixty-one per cent of UK secondary schools and 21 per cent of UK primary schools had been "converted" to acad-emies by 2017. Academies are operated by private companies yet funded by central government (public money). Academies enjoy a greater degree of freedom to employ who they like and pay who they like however much they like. The one common factor seems to be that head teachers and senior management manage to pay themselves a great deal more money than they would earn in state schools controlled by local authorities. Children attending academies don't appear to achieve better results than children attending local authority schools, but head teachers attending academies can achieve salaries of over £200,000 a year. Another worrying feature academies seem to share is a fondness for excluding pupils. In April 2017, the *Guardian* newspaper found there were forty-five schools that had given at least 20 per cent of their pupils one or more fixed-period exclusions in 2016–2017. Five were run by local authorities, six were free schools, and the rest were academies, with one of them, the Outwood Academy Ormesby, in Middlesbrough, excluding 41 per cent of its pupils.

Academies have also directed funding away from local authorities and contributed to the impoverishment of local authority provision. There is now no effective layer of local authority support for schools—or for children. Underfunded local authorities feel they have no choice but to cut school support services—specialist curriculum advisers, specialist learning support teams for children with particular additional needs—that could mediate the impact of legislation on individual children and schools. Any support services for vulnerable children that continue to exist depend on schools "buying" their provision, and as school funding decreases, so does the ability and will to spend money on supporting children with particular learning needs. Children with particular behavioural needs are excluded from mainstream schooling and attend units run by private providers.

A further deregulation of schooling was effected by the Tory government's 2010 "free" schools initiative, a policy that hoped to see parents setting up their very own teaching establishments. These were expected to be middle-class hobby horse outfits, with no requirements to abide by nanny state niceties like employing qualified teachers or paying them properly or even sticking to the national curriculum, but they would, nonetheless, be lavishly supported by central government funding. The policy has been a dismal failure, despite ministerial willingness to chuck hundreds of millions of pounds worth of public funds at these private enterprises. Often free schools have been set up as effectively non-inclusive faith schools, and many free schools have, like the government's policy, turned out to be dismal failures. National Union of Teachers (NUT) research discovered that by April 2017 £138.5 million of tax-payers' money had been spent on sixty-two free school projects that either closed, partially closed or failed to open at all. The total sum of money spent on free schools up to April 2017 was over £3.6 billion—roughly £8.6 million per "free" school. Meanwhile, state schools were seeing a year-on-year decrease in their funding. In January 2019, the campaign group School Cuts Coalition estimated:

> 91 per cent of schools will experience real-terms cuts between 2015 and 2020. Some of those cuts have already happened, some are yet to come. All of them are damaging to children's education.[1]

The "reform's" ultimate stick of choice, however, has surely been the studded and lead-weighted cosh known as the Office for Standards in Education (Ofsted), a national, centralised inspectorate, or government punishment tool, as it is more commonly understood by those who experience it.

Before the creation of the Ofsted in 1992, the quality of provision in state schools had been largely the responsibility of local authority advisers, whose interventions were supportive rather than punitive. The Ofsted, centrally organised with no local knowledge or connection, conducts an inspection process that visits schools at random, solely to evaluate the school's performance against Ofsted's current guidance for inspection. Over the years, Ofsted criteria have focused increasingly on evidence and outcome and changed in particulars and details whenever it appeared schools had worked out how to meet the current Ofsted inspection criteria. There has been a tendency to reduce the amount of time inspectors spend poking about and being a nuisance in your classroom, which for most teachers obviously might seem a good thing (although you would think if anyone were interested in inspecting what actually happens in schools, they might want to look at what actually happens in classrooms), instead having schools self-evaluate using an Ofsted online form. So for much of the year school management expends its energy hunched over a computer filling out the self-evaluation form and harassing teachers for endless amounts of evidence and data with which to fabricate an online school profile upon which the Ofsted inspectors then base their judgements.

As the inspection process implies, the school's measurements of outcomes are now more important than the actual children in the school. The imposition of summative SATs testing at seven, eleven and fourteen meant schools once again became places where children were labelled as failures. The imposition of Ofsted standards meant that schools could now be labelled as failures too—and schools labelled as failures in Ofsted judgements would then get turned into academies run by private companies.

Most school inspections are carried out by Additional Inspectors (AIs) employed by private companies known as Regional Inspection Service Providers (RISPs). The inspectorate has been continually dogged by questions about the qualifications of its inspectors, many of whom have no teaching experience or background in education. Forty per cent of AIs were not rehired by the Ofsted after a contract change in 2015. It epitomises the cavalier approach by privatised services to issues of their own quality and impartiality of provision. The head of Ofsted in 2016, Sir Michael Wilshaw (salary close on £200,000 per annum), previously worked as director of education for the thirty-four-school ARK Academies chain. His successor Amanda Spielman—initially rejected for the role because she had no teaching experience, a decision unilaterally overridden by the then education secretary Nicky Morgan in a July 7, 2016, letter[2]—also enjoyed a management position at ARK.

Ofsted is a fine and shining example of how no opportunity is missed to exploit public services for private profit. Both structurally and functionally, it is an instrument of privatisation. Ofsted's inspections are summative judgements, with no effective mechanism to support schools graded as in need of improvement or failing. That is supposed to be the responsibility of the local authority, although government cuts to local authority funding means local authority education departments are skeleton affairs, with support either cut or inadequately funded and inadequately staffed. Failed schools are, therefore, highly liable to be taken over by academy trusts, effectively a back-door privatisation by state intervention. Schools graded as failing or placed in "special measures" by the Ofsted will undergo repeat Ofsted inspections—but if a failing school converts to an academy, the visits simply stop. Attempting to get an Ofsted judgement overturned is extremely unlikely to succeed and is professional suicide. Ofsted inspections and judgements have even been responsible for the literal suicides of several teachers and head teachers.

As levels of workplace stress and workload pressure increase to unmanageable levels, and teachers are driven to increasingly rely on off-the-peg commercial schemes of work from edubusiness profiteers like Pearson, which are guaranteed to provide easy solutions to issues both of curriculum coverage and workload, the individual skills and the individual needs of individual children diminish in importance.

Denying teachers control of content, combined with the centralised determination of which particular set of facts are to be poured into the little pitchers, has been a continual and central feature of the "reform" project. This is a slightly subtler stick with which to beat children to ensure that as citizens they respond as the state would wish them to. If you control both what and how children learn, you can go a long way toward controlling what and how they think and, by extension, what they do and think when they are adult citizens.

The initial national history curriculum was a breathtakingly blatant triumph of Tory thought policing. It offered units of unconnected nostalgia—Victorian England hopped over World War I completely and skipped blithely forward to the

Blitz, thus denying children the opportunity to understand events as a continuity, with cause, effect and consequence. This also absents from learned history significant if troubling events like World War I and the Bolshevik Revolution.

A later national curriculum review in 2014 relaxed the amount of central direction and control over the content of the primary curriculum in England, but by then the majority of teachers have neither the experience nor the training necessary to view the opportunity to exercise control over curriculum content as anything other than yet another imposition of increased workload. Nonetheless, there is continual clear evidence of the same instrumentalist control of knowledge exercised by the central government, with infant children pointlessly talking about their language in terms of diagraphs and split diagraphs. It is like watching dogs being trained to walk on their hind legs. Their rare poetry lessons will be structured to tick off learning about "connectives" or "suffixes" rather than being experienced as an opportunity to play with language, explore meaning and develop an expressive voice. I don't imagine Billy Shakespeare saw his sonnets primarily as a chance to tick a box or two. Me, personally, as a creative writer, teacher and general human being with an MA in English literature, well, to paraphrase the great Joe Strummer, I don't know what a split diagraph is, and I don't like it. In the case of the play *King Lear* . . . the novel *Wuthering Heights* . . . the song *London Calling* . . . knowing what a split diagraph is is about as useful and significant as a very small fart in a very large thunderstorm. Young children are far better off going on a bear hunt with Michael Rosen. Writing in the *Guardian* in 2008, Rosen summed this reductive process up perfectly: "Literature is being shrunk into literacy". He adds:

> I don't think that it's possible to help all children become fluent readers and writers ("lever up standards" if you will), unless they discover the value of what humanity has produced in the printed word. One of the

most potent forms that the printed word offers to us all is literature.[3]

In the speech he made the previous year accepting the Children's Laureate award, Rosen detailed how schools erase the "value" of literature, the dimensions of meaning and communication—and enjoyment—from the experience of "reading" they offer children:

> reading . . . starts off by being something that has to be done quite explicitly without the use of books, followed by being something that is done when you read a reading book not a book, followed by being that thing you do when a teacher has some questions to ask you about what you have just read.[4]

By hollowing meaning and communication out of language, by denying children ownership of their own language, by reducing language in schools to an academic task rather than a vital, active pleasure, reconfiguring it as the measurables of nonsense like spelling, punctuation and grammar (SPAG), you strike a population dumb when they could be learning how to make their words sing. You control the language they use to think with. Young children are now again being taught joined up writing—another distraction from the idea that you write in order to express your ideas. By facing children from six years old with a curriculum content that must be consumed, you confine the focus of that thinking to consumption, and you limit questioning, because you have a curriculum designed to arrive at particular answers. By facing children from six years old with a narrowing of learning experiences that prioritise particular answers that become measurable outcomes and a curriculum divided into compartmentalised subjects, you disable creativity and imagination and discourage children from making connections in their learning.

Joined up writing—yes. Joined up thinking—no.

Paulo Freire is also very clear on the value the ruling class places on ignorance: "From the point of view of the dominators of any epoch, correct thinking presupposes the nonthinking of the people".[5]

Tony Benn, arguing in favour of comprehensive education, makes the same point when he talks about why the ruling class might be so opposed to it:

> And now the comprehensive ideas come in, there's a recognition that everybody is entitled to have access to knowledge. And I don't think the people at the top are very keen about that. There's a great suspicion of public education because educated people are much harder to control and uneducated people are told what to do.[6]

That this programme of thought policing has proved politically successful is surely demonstrated by the ease with which vast sections of England were persuaded to vote against their economic self-interest during the 2016 Brexit referendum by a Brexit campaign that substituted a media-led mendacious populist narrative for reasoned objective analysis. We have already noted former education minister Gove, a fervent advocate of "free schools" run by enthusiasts and untrained amateurs, popping up on behalf of the right-wing "Leave" campaign to assure us that we don't want to listen to people who actually know what they're talking about. But after nearly thirty years of the national curriculum, not to mention over thirty years of tabloid-scale media mediation, why would you necessarily expect people to engage with concepts of objectivity and meaning in their public discourse?

"Reform" has ensured that the greatest impediment to good practice in state education is now the state itself. From steady traditional classroom practitioners to visionaries with brilliant aspirations, all teachers have been hammered by successive tidal waves of legislation. Teaching and learning have been reconfigured as something you can test, and the unquestioned dogma is that by testing you can "raise standards" and make sure children and teachers are doing what they are supposed to do and what they are being told to do.

Teachers have been deliberately deskilled and devalued. By imposing a curriculum and then a set of teaching standards that prescribe school and classroom priorities and practice, government denies teachers the opportunity to exercise any real professional authority. By therefore deskilling teachers as a profession, that legislation has to all intents and purposes killed both the good practice that took place in "chalk and talk" classrooms and the good practice developing post-Plowden initiatives. "Reform" has effectively redefined good practice as simply the best way to do bad things.

And this has become systematic practice. Academy chains collapse, children with particular needs who might lower a school's outcome statistics either get abandoned because schools operate a triage system based on percentages of children achieving predicted grades or simply disappear through the cracks in the system, heads of academies are found to be guilty of everything from falsifying exam results to serious financial mismanagement that makes what may or may not have happened at William Tyndale Junior School look like a lark in the park. "Reform" may look increasingly like the emperor's new clothes, but it nonetheless still has a couple of spectacular distractions up its non-existent sleeve. Rule number one of any ruling class: if in doubt, wave your national flag about a bit.

British Values

A conservative government is organised hypocrisy.
—Benjamin Disraeli

In 2011, the British state decided what its schools needed to promote were red-white-and-true-blue "British Values". This section will look briefly at the context that backgrounds this and how these values were reflected by the government that devised them.

Britain, of course, is generally a little coy about admitting it is a state. Usually it prefers to cloak itself modestly in the quasi-mystical notions of "Britishness", the land of hope and glory, the mother of the free, a monarchy, a realm, the mother of all parliamentary democracy. British people are encouraged to identify with a succession of mildly eccentric monarchs— Henry VIII and his six wives, dumpy little Victoria and her beloved Christmas tree of a German husband. Us peasants are clearly expected to bow the knee, tug the forelock and charge the guns at Sebastopol, because we are encouraged to think of ourselves as loyal servants of the holy mystery that is royalty. Your king and country want *you*. There is this mystification of subservience, that somehow we are serving someone, some "thing", infinitely more special than we are—Charles I was very keen on the idea that he had been directly ordained by God to tell the rest of us what to do. This was why the forces of parliament and fledgling democracy, such as they were, decided to cut his head off in 1649. Unfortunately, it only slowed the royal family con down by a generation.

In 1984, my friend Robert, communist shop steward in Ghent, travelled to Kent to show solidarity with the striking miners. He says he was very much surprised to find that in almost every home he went to, there was a picture of head of state Her Majesty Queen Elizabeth II on display. Nonetheless, it was very much the full might of "the state", a disposition of state force deliberately politically organised by the government in advance, that the miners and their communities were up against.

In 1984, ironically, it became manifest that "the state" is not just something that happens abroad or in George Orwell's novels. "The state" is the result of a historical accumulation of political and social power. In Britain, this has resulted in a systematic disposition of economic and political power, the British system of class, within which society—the way we live our lives—has been organised. The state organises economic resources and the distribution of wealth generated by the people who live within its often arbitrary borders. The state is ultimately never value-neutral; it has a historically proven tendency to prioritise the interests of those powerful groupings that have gained access to the mechanisms of economic, political and social control. The mining communities provided the most effective and most effectively autonomous organisation of the working class in Britain; in the 1970s, they successfully challenged the authority of the government, went on strike and in so doing provoked the 1974 general election called by the Conservative Heath government, which said government promptly lost. Thatcher was determined to use the full resources of the state—the legislature, the media, the police, the army—to break the miners, and by breaking the miners and their communities with a state-provoked strike to break the organised working-class movement as a whole. To their shame, the leadership of the Labour Party and the Trades

Union Congress (TUC) chose to side with the state rather than the organised working class.

Nonetheless, the fiction continues, and there is the tendency to understand the state in terms of a benign monarchy operating in balance with the Mother of Parliaments™. Yet the development of the British state, like any other state, is a history of the organisation and disposition of power within particular geographical limits, the state's borders. In the case of the UK, we can identify the Norman invasion of 1066 as responsible for formalising a distribution of power, the consequences of which we live with today. This state was characterised by conquest and a subsequent division of territory among loyal soldiery.

Within five hundred years, however, the basis for power was shifting away from territory to a class of citizens who generated wealth and hence accumulated power through means other than land ownership. Two hundred years later, the wealth and power of the merchant slave-dealing class was being eclipsed by the rising economic muscle of the machine owners and industrialists. Throughout this process, successive waves of economic interests had demanded a greater say in the affairs of the state, arguing that—from the barons facing down King John at Runnymede with their Magna Carta through the parliamentarians executing a politically anachronistic monarch to the Great Reform Act of 1832, whereby the cities of the Industrial Revolution gained electoral representation—the state ought to represent the interests of the people who created its commonwealth. By the end of the nineteenth century, this demand for representation and the continuing process of democratisation had spread to the working class, whose representatives argued that as all wealth is not created by ownership but by labour, the state should represent the interests of the majority of its population, the working class. The concept of rights, the right of every person to participate equally, was also finding expression in an increasingly militant women's movement.

Logically, the history of increasing democracy is a convincing argument in favour of the understanding that, in reality, the state is nothing more than a formal organisation of resources whose function is to meet the needs of the people within its geopolitical borders.

The narrative runs like this. Once upon a time, the state was dressed up in the feudal paraphernalia of landowning aristocracy and the regalia of royal families. Then the state became a matter of economic privilege, apparently more accessible to more and more people (wealthy men), as it dressed itself respectfully in the promises of parliamentary democracy. And sometimes it seemed as if all the wealth generated by the people, all the immeasurable wealth of their individual hopes and dreams and hidden lives, would become the guiding principle upon which the fabrication of the state would be predicated. And that's when Mrs Thatcher started talking about rolling back the frontiers of socialism.

As a result, we now have the apparent paradox of non-existent state responsibility—the triumph of privatisation, no state ownership of anything much any more, with even policing prisons being in the profiteering hands of private companies—yet state authority increased in potency to an almost totalitarian capacity. That authority now manages its geographical territory as a client state serving the interests of the neoliberal empire.

The globalisation of ownership—for example, French state-owned companies already own various lucrative parts of the National Health Service (NHS) and tender for public utilities services, and much of Britain's shambolic privatised rail system is owned by state-owned European railways—and global trade agreements currently up for ratification, designed to enable multinationals access to ownership of utilities and services on a worldwide basis, and the increasing unaccountable power of transnational corporations surely make the "nation state" largely irrelevant, reducing it to the level of sentimental nostalgia, like that for a particular type of folk dance.

Nonetheless, ironically, it is by appealing to those nation-state narratives that the right has managed to seize control of "the state" and legitimise its "rethinking" of the unthinkable, washing its hands of state responsibility and turning those responsibilities into opportunities for private profit, up to and including the nationally beloved NHS. The state, cheered on by the media, continues to trumpet traditional "British Values" when it comes to what ought to be taught in state schools.

The Cameron government had used nationalism from the outset as both ideology and a weapon of mass distraction. In 2011, in a speech about the causes of terrorism at conference in Munich, Cameron declared that multiculturalism had failed, arguing that what Britain needed was a "stronger national identity". For schools, education around issues of inclusion and diversity were replaced by "British Values".

Britishness was used in pursuit of state aims as both distraction and coercion. When I was a teenager, going to the cinema always involved, at the end of the evening, a cheerful stampede to get out of the auditorium before the National Anthem was played. Now the singing or not of this clunking song in favour of a family of German aristocrats is employed by the state and its media as a political point to be scored against a leader of the Labour Party, who apparently didn't sing along at his first ceremonial event as leader, and who might not be as compliantly New Labour as they'd like. Now schools have been directed by the state to ensure teaching promotes "British Values". These values include absolute respect for the law—so no teaching about the likes of Robin Hood, Captain Swing, the Tolpuddle Martyrs, the suffragettes, Mahatma Gandhi or Nelson Mandela—and such fresh-air concepts and generally incontrovertible generalities as democracy, individual liberty, respect and tolerance. Presumably because schools weren't promoting them anywhere near actively enough, the promotion of "British Values" became a legal requirement in 2013.

These "British Values" are little short of toxic. Some practitioners attempt to assert that these values are not so much

British as values shared by all humanity. A closer examination, however, might suggest that indeed these values, because their immediate reference points will be the context of British history, are, indeed, particularly and unfortunately "British".

Uncritical respect for the law is, of course, only one sentence away from the "only obeying orders" defence that the Nuremburg courts rejected in 1945. Respect for "democracy" in the context of the UK's ideas of democracy is also problematic: while trade unions now have to have more than 50 per cent of eligible members voting for a ballot to be valid, there is no similar threshold for parliamentary elections—instead, there's the UK's interesting "first past the post" idea of democracy, which, in 2015, meant 24 per cent of the electorate voting Conservative combined with 5.2 per cent of the electorate voting LibDem lumbered the UK with the austerity-wielding Cameron-Clegg government.

Respect for individual liberty sounds a good starting point in theory, but in the context of the ethos of the historical British state, this translates in practice as liberty without social responsibility, the liberty to make money at the expense of others, the liberty of "hate speech" pretending it's "free speech"—"I'm not racist, but. . ." Then there's the "value" of "tolerance", a particularly pernicious and quintessentially British characteristic; Tom Paine eloquently anatomizes this in *The Rights of Man* when he declares:

> Toleration is not the *opposite* of intoleration, but it is the *counterfeit* of it. Both are despotisms. The one assumes to itself the right of withholding liberty of conscience, and the other of granting it.[1]

The reality of "British" respect for individual liberty and the dubious value of "British" tolerance are much in evidence in the ongoing state sponsored scapegoating of Muslims, with Office for Standards in Education (Ofsted) threatening to mark down any school where pupils or staff wear a niqab and instructing inspectors to interrogate primary children who wear a hijab about why they wear it. I wonder at the contrast that represents with the way—in spite of widespread populist opposition—the UK state in the 1970s recognised it was important for Sikhs to wear a turban. Perhaps that is a whole different dialectic, but I am still amazed at how the right to wear what you choose to wear has suddenly become so irrelevant when it comes to Muslim women. If I am honest, I was a bit sad when my female Muslim colleagues started covering their heads in the early 1990s when I bumbled into the staff room but, on the other hand, being aware of the problems of patriarchy and masculinity and having been accustomed to being categorically excluded from "women only" spaces in the past, it wasn't like it was a problem. Some of my friends choose to wear a hijab. I choose to wear a "Straight to Hell" Clash T-shirt. By 199whatever, no one was likely to spit at me on the street for so doing. Nowadays, sadly, wearing a hijab in the UK requires a lot more commitment than wearing a punk rock T-shirt.

Is the British state really threatened by women who present themselves in ways that are in accordance with their particular faith? When, in 2006, senior Labour politician Jack Straw wrote that he felt "uncomfortable" talking to Muslim women who cover their face, adding this was "a visible statement of separation and difference", Tory politician Greg Hands escalated the argument by insisting people felt "intimidated" by women who covered their faces. More recently, in 2018, privileged ex-Eton, ex-Oxford University white male Boris Johnson decided to exercise his privileged white male individual liberty and champion a woman's right not to be told what to look like by male authority figures, by declaring that women wearing burkas looked like pillar boxes. The stereotyping of Muslims is cheap populism, and the blatant similarity to the stereotyping of Jews that led Europe to the Holocaust is an act of cynicism that is beyond irony.

In terms of the dominant (white) cultural norm of masculinity, these are clearly women *not* doing what women are supposed to do to keep blokes happy, the standard model being girls uncovering themselves as public entertainment on page 3 of a bloke's favourite daily tabloid.

Schools have traditionally been to varying degrees "soft", unconscious, institutional transmitters of "Britishness" and of nationalist culture and values. The introduction of the formal requirement to transmit "British Values" made this transmission of nationalism a statutory duty. Two years later, the Prevent Duty became law. All schools and registered early years providers were subject to a legal duty to monitor children and report them if they suspected they might be being radicalised. This, unsurprisingly, led to a comedy of errors that sometimes errs toward tragedy and sometimes farce. In the summer of 2018, Little Ducklings Nursery in Brighton was failed by Ofsted inspectors for its inadequate understanding of the Prevent strategy. The right-wing media were obviously in something of a dilemma as to how to respond to this newsworthy item of a nursery not doing enough to prevent radicalisation of its toddlers. Usually only too happy to support anything that contributes to the Islamic terrorism moral panic, most newspapers decided in this instance to bash that old shibboleth from the glory days of Thatcher, the "nanny state".

If you question its motivation, you might well be told the Prevent Duty is concerned with all radicalisation, all "extremist" politics opposed to parliamentary democracy's methodology of representation arrived at by voting. Theoretically this includes preventing the activities of far-right white racists, although the state seems to show a marked reluctance to apply their definition of terrorism—violence used in pursuit of political aims—when responding to white racist attacks. Recent statistics suggest that nearly a third of Prevent referrals now relate to radicalisation by far-right extremism. However, in reality and in practice the Prevent strategy is legislation that operates in accordance with populist Islamophobia. It was and remains focused on the Muslim community, and its likely outcome is an increased sense of alienation and oppression within the Muslim community, leading to an increase in individual radicalisation.

Perhaps the targeting of Muslim women, like the dehumanising of people labelled migrants, is also an indication of insecurity on the part of the state, an awareness of its precarious hold on governance and authority. The more bankrupt the regime, the greater the need for scapegoats. The state has nothing like a genuine democratic mandate; in the 2015 election, with just over 66 per cent of the people entitled to vote bothering to do so, the government received a mere 36.9 per cent of the votes cast. The government consistently fails to meet its own targets in its self-declared austerity programme and governs—or not—a population that can apparently suddenly erupt into widespread riot, as it did when police shot dead an unarmed man, Mark Duggan, in Tottenham, in 2011. It is a state whose government can consist of a small elite friendship group from "public" school and Oxford University, with a barely concealed or even denied history of obnoxious and sleazy public and private expressions of "individual liberty", a group whose members will happily stab each other in the back whenever the opportunity arises. In 2015, the disgruntled Tory Lord Ashcroft, miffed that Cameron hadn't given him a promised role in government in 2010, asserted that the future prime minister had inserted his penis into the mouth of a dead pig as part of an Oxford initiation ritual. Should we be surprised that his response to this revelation was neither a denial nor his resignation?

By 2016, it was objectively manifest that it was the Cameron government that was terminally inept and was failing. It spectacularly misjudged the extent and the downright nastiness of the nationalism it had habitually stoked and invoked and so mishandled its own "Remain" campaign that it lost its own referendum. Meanwhile, in education, the flagship policy of "reform", the covert privatisation of the academy programme, was likewise by that point manifestly unsuccessful and clearly failing. Evidence both that academies didn't generate better results than local authority schools and that academy status facilitated outrageous acts of corruption by head teachers given too much power and money became too widespread to ignore. Anti-academy campaigners began achieving the unthinkable—stopping their schools from being turned into the personal fiefdoms of ambitious heads.

Faced with the wheels seriously falling off its academisation project, in March 2016, the Tories abandoned any pretence of concern for educational standards or parental choice, and even any old tosh about democratic process, when chancellor George (christened Gideon) Osborne (qualifications: private schooling, Oxford history graduate and Bullingdon Club member, *Daily Telegraph* journalist with a personal fortune of £4,000,000) announced that *all* schools would have to become academies within six years. This is what British democracy looks like in practice; money on its hind legs in every respect, with education policy being dictated not by a minister of education but by the Chancellor of the Exchequer. However, this announcement was not at all well-received by a broad spectrum of society. Bosses of existing academy chains voiced their concerns about the viability of this enforced policy, and, on May 3, parents took their children out of school, in an unprecedented nationwide schools strike, to demonstrate their discontent at what the state was doing to its schools and their children. The policy of enforced academisation was then cancelled within a week by Justine Greening, the secretary of state for education generally referred to in the bet-hedging Tory media as having "possibly" been educated at a comprehensive school (tricky one that: if comprehensives are so awful, do they by rights have any business producing future Tory MPs and ministers of state?)

Which of course brings us neatly to the other great distraction the right employs when it comes to education, that it is a useful and desirable selection process and an excellent and effective promoter of meritocracy and social mobility.

Social Mobility and Post-Society

> They are casting their problems at society. And, you
> know, there's no such thing as society. There are indi-
> vidual men and women and there are families. And no
> government can do anything except through people,
> and people must look after themselves first.
> —Margaret Thatcher, 1987

Just because the state currently likes to think it can avoid any meaningful social responsibility doesn't mean that society doesn't exist. The human animal is sociable and friendly by nature—again, young children instinctively delight in each other's company—and society, collective organisation, is essential to the survival and well-being of the individual human animal. We are pretty feeble organisms, without fur or particular physical prowess. Cooperation and society have always been necessary conditions for us. Our leaders have always accumulated power either by being the biggest psychopathic bastard in the tribe or the richest psychopathic bastard in the country, but their leadership has always meant nothing without the rest of us. However much our current leaders wish to abolish society, it is nonetheless the wealth created by human society, people working together, that furnishes them with their privileged lifestyles.

School and schooling constitute the process by which young people progress from familial to social structures. Whether you do this by forking out over £30,000 a year to Eton or buying your child a bus pass to the nearest comprehensive, the general consensus is that the young need to go through this process, these microsocieties of education, where children discover, develop, rehearse and refine the skills they will be utilising for the rest of their lives as social beings. Except, of course, as far as the state is concerned, and as far as those parents who identify their values with the values of the state are concerned, that isn't what schools are for at all. Schools are there to identify and certify the worthy. In Britain, we like to shy away from the obvious conclusion that, as far as the state is concerned, schools are primarily institutions of social control, Illich's "powerful churches"[1]—control the children and you control the future. Like the hierarchy of the family, something else we prefer not to mention, the hierarchical configuration of education serves the function of repressive conditioning identified by radicals like Victor Serge and Emma Goldman at the start of the twentieth century: "The ideal of the average pedagogist is not a complete, well-rounded, original human being; rather does he seek that the result of his art or pedagogy shall be automatons of flesh and blood, to best fit the treadmill of society and the emptiness and dullness of our lives".[2]

Over the last thirty years, there have been two fictions promulgated by the right about the function of schools. On the one hand, they ascribe the ills of society to bad schooling rather than bad government or bad economics, while, on the other hand, they present good schooling as airlifting deserving cases out of the abyss, so they can access their proper, more elevated station in society. The first uses a simplification of the idea that state education is somehow primarily responsible for the state of the nation. Successive bad governments have laid the blame for failures of the nation state at the door of a school system they scapegoat as being infected with the progressive ideas of the 1960s, the application of the practices of democracy and equality that they present as inhibiting the right's mantra that individual enterprise is the engine of a healthy society. The scapegoating of what they identify as faults in schooling as somehow responsible for what they perceive and present as faults in society has provided significant background noise for the populist "reform" discourse. Politicians love their populist snappy little slogans, like lazy old comedy acts relying on their catch phrases for easy laughs. Conservative party campaigns have been particularly adept at oversimplifying political discourse into emotive one-liners. Thatcher had such great success when unemployment was nearing the million mark with the slogan "Labour isn't working" that she was able to triple that figure within three years, and Cameron's use of the idea of a "broken Britain" enabled him to preside over an austerity government that a 2017 issue of the medical journal *BMJ Open* identified as being responsible for the "economic murder" of 120 thousand people a year.[3]

The "reform" agenda that concentrates attention on failing schools and failures in schooling serves as an effective distraction. This, says the government, is where the fault lies. The "reform" agenda implies schools have failed to teach children effectively, and, thereby, schools (rather than successive governments) have failed to meet the needs of Britain. The "reform" distraction implies that by returning to traditionalist practices—testing, rote learning—we will "raise standards", and by achieving ever better test results, schools will somehow be mending broken Britain for us all.

The second fiction presents education as being directly related to increased economic prosperity for individuals. Education is no longer the liberal education of intrinsic value but the neoliberal certifier of better employment prospects in the free marketplace, leading to increased individual economic prosperity. Always a little less reticent about these issues, the USA's Common Core State Standards (CCSS) website features a quotation from the CEO of State Farm Insurance Companies, enthusing: "State-by-state adoption of these standards is an important step toward maintaining our country's competitive edge. With a skilled and prepared workforce the business community will be better prepared to face the challenges of the international marketplace"[4]—so not much of a Great Debate about the purposes of education going on there, then. Better employment prospects have come to be configured as the main desirable outcome of education. In reality, of course, successive governments have actively pursued anti-working-class policies that have significantly reduced employment opportunities. All the mantras of "reformers" about raising standards and the necessity of everybody and everything being above average are revealed as meaningless gibberish if there are not actually enough jobs for everybody or not enough "good" jobs to go round. Nonetheless, the fiction that schools can and should lift deserving individuals out of obscurity or deprivation into suitably salaried social leadership roles commensurate with their innate intelligence and/or ability (the two generally considered interchangeable terms) remains potent.

This second fiction is so successful—or perhaps so deeply ingrained in the collective understanding of society—that it is now often uncritically parroted by elements of the Labour Party. It brings with it, however, the reintroduction of the idea of school as a selection process, a return to its pre-comprehensive function without actually using the words "grammar school". When people talk about schools identifying merit, they use the traditional criteria of academic success as an index of value, whereby schooling equates social value with its measurements of particular manifestations of intelligence. Backgrounding this is the comforting intellectual respectability of Plato's ideal of a society organised as a meritocracy. Social mobility is offered as a practical mechanism that works toward realising Plato's utopian theory. Social mobility is also, of course, a polite way of saying "embourgeoisification", which is, of course, merely a polite way of saying, "I get more money than you lot do".

The self-interest of the state and the self-interest of some parents coincide around this mutually acceptable and mutually self-serving fictional configuring of schools as institutions operating on behalf of a meritocracy. Schools are supposed to identify and promote those individuals of merit from among the general herd, demonstrating what, in a quote earlier in this book, Alexander Inglis described as "the diagnostic function" (deciding whereabouts in the social hierarchy each child belongs) and "the differentiating function" (sorting children for their future role in the social machine and training them accordingly) of schooling.[5]

The consequence is the accompanying fiction that having been selected by the school system, having been to the "best" schools and universities, those who run society are those best suited for the job.

Schools have traditionally labelled individuals such that society—often represented in this context as "employers" or "British industry"—knows what they'll be good for as adults and where they will fit into the industrial machinery. This sorting process has traditionally been an important feature of the schooling system. Schools prepared children for adult hierarchies by ranking them in their classrooms too. Children were "streamed" within schools or "set" within classes according to ability, then, as a consequence of the result of a test taken when they were eleven, were selected for a first-class or a second-class secondary school. Children were again summatively tested to ensure they left school with a set of certificates summing up their abilities and, therefore, their future usefulness and worth to employers, British industry and the state. In times of full employment, schools are policed by the idea that if you "work hard", you will "get a better job". In times of widespread unemployment, schools are policed by the idea that if you "work hard", you will stand a "better chance of getting a job". But it is always hard work leading to academic achievement that will be the signifier of merit and, thereby, facilitate access to the higher levels of the schooling hierarchy that, in turn, are supposed to provide access to future roles of greater social responsibility and greater economic income.

"People from my sort of background needed grammar schools to compete with children from privileged homes like

Shirley Williams and Anthony Wedgwood Benn", whinged Thatcher in 1977.[6] "Social mobility" essentially endorses a view of society that is competitive rather than cooperative, and, therefore, harmonises with recently ascendant right-wing thinking. In the absence of a national selection process like grammar schools, the mindset of meritocracy has considered alternative strategies to support social mobility and provide assistance to the aspirational likes of the young Margaret Thatcher (not that the young Thatcher was ever in reality particularly poorly educated or economically underprivileged). In 2011, the Education Endowment Foundation was set up by the Sutton Trust with a Department for Education grant of £135,000,000. Ostensibly aimed at improving the attainment of the poorest children in the worst performing schools, its reports into what it sees as "best value" in terms of test results are impacting on ideas of "best practice" in schools. "Best value" is, of course, determined by measurable outcomes like league tables and the nonsense of year-on-year percentage increases in summative testing scores. The Sutton Trust was set up by Sir Peter Lampl OBE, "to improve educational opportunities for young people from non-privileged backgrounds and increase social mobility".[7] Having taken the grammar school route to Oxford, he was disappointed on his return to England twenty years later, after making lots of money in America, to find there were hardly any people like him going to Oxford any more. Sir Peter's aim is "democratising selection" rather than equality of education. This is merely addressing symptoms instead of causes. Properly addressing equality in education means addressing the causes of inequality in social background.

When Justine Greening was appointed education secretary in 2016, much was made of the fact that she had very likely indeed attended a state comprehensive school in Rotherham. This, she says, convinced her of the importance of the link between education and social mobility, her own trajectory being from schoolgirl in Rotherham to MP for lovely middle-class Putney. The *Daily Telegraph*, concerned that the social group least likely to go to university is white working-class boys, enthusiastically agreed: "Justine Greening's appointment as education secretary gives real hope for social mobility—and the white working class" it enthused.[8] So soon it won't only be plucky little Putney voting for white working-class MPs, there will be busloads of socially mobile candidates who have learned to scrub up nicely at universities to choose from, and if they've learned their Latin properly like Michael Gove wants them to, why, you'd hardly be able to tell them apart from the former members of the Eton Rifles, who up until Justine Greening's appointment as education secretary, provided the general bulk of your average Tory government.

Unfortunately, "real hope for social mobility" Greening only spent two years as Ed Sec, obviously to the bitter disappointment of all loyal and aspirational white working-class boys who read the *Daily Telegraph*.

"Social mobility" is now often mispresented as a priority of the function of state education since 1945. This is an interesting and significant revision of the aims of post-war state education. Indeed, the 1960s saw a great deal of social mobility, as being working-class became both fashionable and in some areas of popular culture an asset that resulted in social success and economic wealth for particular individuals. But the prime aim of post-war education had less to do with ideas of social mobility—hence the dismantling of that great system of second-class privilege, the grammar school, always touted as the fast track for bright working-class kiddies to middle-class respectability—and much more to do with ideas of social justice. All children deserved and had the right to an education that empowered all children not just those with an aptitude for passing particular selection tests on a particular day and included as a right access to further state funded education. That this is no longer a priority of state education means that expectations that schools will somehow address issues of inequality by rigorously teaching whatever the government tells them to teach is simply setting schools up to be seen to be failing. Loading such responsibility onto schools also means they conveniently take the blame for the government's own failures. Austerity is an important sounding word intended to distract attention away from the fact that government intends to run society with no concern for social justice or compassion and has no intention of providing a positive future for all its future citizens. Instead—let us cherry pick and advance the poor we deem deserving; everybody else has to know their place in the undeserving and unwanted lower orders—and like it or lump it. When a system selects and earmarks winners, that system also selects and labels losers. Will that great meritocratic system also address the issue of those chaps who, no matter how high the school fees that daddy pays, are just no good whatsoever at Latin—gels whose only talent appears to be wearing hats to watch a horse race—or the dim-witted results of the sort of aristocratic inbreeding so beloved of royal families, perhaps? Will they be turfed off their privileged monied perches to swap places with the brightest of the white working class?

Prince Chinless, this is Rotherham, and this is your new bedsit accommodation.

Somehow, I think not.

PART THREE

TEECHAS AND TEECHIN

Teacher. The one who makes the tea.
—Roger McGough, *First Day at School*

In Buttercup Class We Smile

Ben's dad's out of prison, Ben can't sleep at night,
Ben gets so excited he wets the bed with fright,
He'll come to love his daddy in a little while,
It's the ropes and the rules of big boy school
But in Buttercup Class we smile.

Wayne's dad went to the Post Office to get some cash for
          beer,
He took his shotgun with him, now he's looking at ten years.
Mum sees Wayne just like him in a little while,
It's the ropes and the rules of big boy school
But in Buttercup Class we smile.

Kylie's mum says Daljit's mum is a junkie and a whore,
Now there's blokes going round with baseball bats and
          petrol poured through doors,
And someone's in for serious grief in a little while,
It's the ropes and the rules of big boy school
But in Buttercup Class we smile.

April saw them come in and what they did to mummy,
Rajan saw the bad man stick his knife in uncle's tummy,
He knows his uncle won't be back in a little while,
It's the ropes and the rules of big boy school
But in Buttercup Class we smile.

These green and pleasant gardens I played in as a child.
The winter came and turned them all to stone.

Jobs turned into benefits, booze turned into dope,
Homes turned into bedsits, and the shops ran out of hope,
You do your best, nonetheless, for a little while.
Despite the ropes and the rules of big boy school
But in Buttercup Class we smile.

So, will they learn the hard way, like their dad's and mums
How much Father Christmas never really comes?
I hope they may remember for a little while
Despite the ropes and the rules of big boy school
In Buttercup Class we smiled.

A Conflicted Situation

If you keep two angels in a cage
They will eat each other to death.
—Adrian Mitchell, "A Warning"

I started writing this section on the day after there was a shoot-
ing at a school in Santa Fe. On May 18, 2018, ten people were
killed. Ironically the first victims to be named were two people
who were to some extent unlikely to have been there. Cynthia
Tisdale was a supply teacher. Her son told the *Washington
Post*, "She started substitute teaching because she loved to
help children. She didn't have to do it. She did it because she
loved it". Seventeen-year-old Sabika Sheikh was there as part
of a Youth Exchange Study programme. Her father told AFP
in Pakistan, "We are still in a state of denial. It is like a nightmare. . . . There is a general impression that the life is safe
and secure in America. But this is not the case". I also note
that in the book I am currently reading, *American Heiress*, the
author Jeffrey Toobin also refers to violence in schools: "a
grand jury report in July 1973 showed that there had been
forty-two assaults and one murder on school property in the
past year, as well as almost $1 million in property damage".[1]

Happy days/angels in cages. . .

When I started teaching, no school had a coded push
button key fob intercom entry system. Now, every school I go
to has one. In the US there is a serious discussion about arming
teachers. So I am conscious that this book is about making

Neverland a reality, while the everyday reality is that schools are located in societies that, like their governments, are increasingly failing to meet the needs of their people. Schools, once transmitters of society's values, are now instrumentalised by the state as enforcers of state policy, and schools and children have become prime targets for lethal acts of aggression by alienated individuals unable to form social attachments.

Humans depend upon attachments. The human animal as a species has historically survived by forming attachments. However, by sending its young to institutions outside the family unit, European society developed a tradition of education that is characterised by separation. By the nineteenth century, the British ruling classes promoted an ethos of distance between parents and children, with nannies responsible for running the domestic nursery, children being seen not heard, then being packed off to boarding schools, a distance that was echoed to varying degrees throughout the industrialised Western world. Schooling for the masses replicated to a lesser extent this ethos of separation and distance on a schoolday rather than school term basis.

Teachers in Britain have often had their role understood as being defined by the Latin phrase "in loco parentis"—in the place of the parents—with regard to the children in their class, the children that they teach. Parents may feel the values they want transmitted to *their* children by school are the values they feel they are entitled to transmit—the values of *their* family. Teachers in state education, however, are now primarily required to transmit the state's values to children. To ensure this, in addition to its centrally directed curriculum, the state has imposed the Teaching Standards document on teachers, which inevitably conditions what happens during teacher training courses. Theoretical frameworks, concepts like "child development", have been replaced by training organised around this shopping list of basic skills and work practices. The Teaching Standards are like the instructions you get with flat pack furniture. At no point do they ask you (as we were asked in our philosophy of education course) if you think the classroom is a conflict situation. (I decided I did. I wasn't sure at the time what to do with this answer, but that was probably a significant choice signposting the way toward Neverland.) The most overt expression of any intellectual framework is the duty to adhere to the state's definition of "British Values", which is a significant part of the document's description of a teacher's duties.

When I started writing this book, I had a look on the "so you want to become a teacher" government website. Funnily enough it still laid great emphasis on the idea that people want to become teachers because they want to do some social good. The website calls it "making a difference"; there are photographs of neatly uniformed nicely multi-ethnic young persons having lightbulb moments around a beaming, caring *teacher*. And then there is this hilarious box trumpeting "earn up to 67k". In your dreams. In reality, your starting salary will be about £24.00 a year, and there is a good chance you'll give up teaching within five years. In 2016, nearly a third of all teachers were quitting within the first five years, while, in 2017, the figure was 50 per cent within the first four years . . . and these alarming statistics are more or less replicated in the US and Australia.

The state has now also introduced initiatives that aim to circumvent traditional pathways involving graduate level study that might include areas of learning deemed unnecessary by and in conflict with the state model of teaching and learning. The state wants docile and compliant pupils and teachers turning up at the exam factories every day and doing as little thinking about and questioning of what they are doing and why they are doing it as possible. From time to time, there are announcements that ex-forces personnel are to be fast tracked to the classroom, promoted as being exactly the kind of role models children need nowadays (keen on discipline, good at following orders), not to mention being a way to address the issue of shortfall in teacher recruitment.

This bright idea, despite being generally very media-friendly, seems to have no significant impact whatsoever.

You don't have to join the army to bypass teacher training at the further education degree level. The School Direct scheme promises "on the job training while you earn a salary",[2] thereby minimising the likelihood of you being distracted by any pesky pedagogical thinking, while the Teach First initiative for 2020 offers you five weeks of introductory training in June before starting working in a classroom in September.[3]

But I have to say, all of the student teachers who have turned up in the schools I have been working in were clearly not animated by the prospect of making 67k a year or by ending up in a leadership role in their own social enterprise but by the aspiration to "do some good" and make a difference. But this aspiration is largely unexamined and unsupported by their training process. Student teachers were always absolutely amazed when I said that when I started teaching, we decided for ourselves what we taught and how we taught it. Teachers and head teachers, increasing numbers of whom have only ever experienced the national curriculum model of schooling, both as children and as adult workers, who have nonetheless chosen to commit to education and to making a difference, may well find in practice that their values are in conflict with the authoritarian values of the state. Instead of transforming lives, they find themselves transforming life into data, instruments in a mechanistic bureaucracy whose aim is to maintain the appropriate production levels in the exam factory, like assembling the appropriate number of flat pack utility furniture units. Lacking the perspective you get from a training programme that encourages professional reflection rather than bureaucratic compliance, and with the majority of working teachers never having experienced conditions of professional autonomy, they find it difficult to maintain and pursue their aspirations to make a real difference when the state, the curriculum, the Office for Standards in Education (Ofsted) and the school's senior management pressure them to prioritise simple curriculum coverage and measurable outcomes, a quantitative rather than qualitative approach to learning.

Teachers deliver the curriculum, train the dogs and test how long they can walk on two legs. Learning, which has become the dominant cliché catchphrase to describe what children are doing in schools, is becoming reduced to the ability to stand on your hind legs and regurgitate correct answers in test situations. The perversion of language is almost Orwellian. When I was studying for a Postgraduate Certificate in Education (PGCE), the Philosophy of Education course tutor Sylvia Denning rather surprised us by asking us what we thought the work of a teacher involved. We all thought this was a bit obvious, so we gave blindingly obvious answers that essentially came down to an instructional model of teaching, with possibly the suggestion that good teaching might contain elements of the inspirational modestly offered for consideration too. Sylvia smiled and asked us to note that the word "education" had its roots in a Latin verb meaning to lead out of. The work of a teacher, she suggested, ought to consider the implications of the idea that a teacher is primarily an educator. The purpose of education is to develop, to help draw out the potential that is already present in every child.

The state clearly does not want to accept that all children have potential and isn't interested in whether they have diverse skills and abilities or not. The state wants them trained according to the interests of the state. The state wants them scored and selected according to their usefulness to the ideology of the state. The state wants them to be little pitchers filled up with state sanctioned skills and knowledge by a compliant workforce of M'choakumchilds. The utilitarian philanthropist "wise parent" Gradgrind (who turns out to be anything but) defines the scope of his concept of teaching: "Now, what I want is Facts. Teach these boys and girls nothing but Facts. Facts alone are wanted in life. Plant nothing else, and root out everything else. You can only form the minds of reasoning animals upon Facts; nothing else will ever be of any service to them". The Facts are administered by the teacher, M'choakumchild, and children are "little vessels then and there arranged in order, ready to have imperial gallons of facts poured into them until they were full to the brim".[4]

This antiquated instructional model (a poor excuse for a pedagogy) is now the default setting in the majority of class-rooms, as teachers struggle to cram into children the body of knowledge prescribed by a curriculum over which they have no professional and—apparently—very little personal control. Instead of the pre-Plowden stereotype of "chalk and talk", children now gaze at "interactive" whiteboards and endure what is—however patronisingly animated and brightly col-oured—instruction by PowerPoint. Planning is what you did this time last year to show that you are covering the curricu-lum. "Teaching" is reduced to racking up the day's screens. "Learning" is reduced to memorising their instructions. The only significant refinement added to the Gradgrind model of schooling by the "reformers" is their insistence on weighing the pitcher before, during and after the pouring in of the cur-riculum, predicting how heavy the pitcher will be next time they test it and comparing that against national standards of average pitcher weight development, to prove value has indeed been added. It is hard to see this as a difference worth making. Teachers will need to develop the ability to create and maintain a safe space, a distance that is both protective and subversive, between the demands of the state and the needs of the children. It is only in such liberated zones that genuine education can take place and a real difference can be made.

Problems with Authority

A dog's obeyed in office.
—Billy Shakespeare, *King Lear*

Teachers, whether they recognise it or not, have real issues with authority. There is the obvious issue of the way society line-manages its schools, which the agenda of "reform" has obviously prioritised and weaponised. But there is also the perennial problematic of how teachers respond to the "authority" the traditional model of schooling has invested them with.

The recent history of education reform is also the recent history of the centralisation of state power. Another bleak irony: the Conservatives like to present themselves as the party upholding the general libertarian values of freedom and democracy; in practice they have actively disempowered local democracy because of the potential challenge posed by councils to their political authority. For most of the twentieth century, state education was the responsibility of its local education authority (LEA) and was to some degree responsive to local democratic elections. With the Teachers Pay and Conditions Act of 1987, which abolished the Burnham Committee, the mechanism for pay negotiations between representatives of the teaching unions and their LEA employers, central government started the process that steadily eroded this layer of local democratic control. The introduction of the national curriculum the following year effectively did away with any real influence LEAs had over their schools. Local authorities are still nominally responsible for the state schools in their area but with hardly any legal power or economic resources to do anything significant.

Effective education does not depend upon but is made much easier to effect if there are buildings and an infrastructure that support it. That means effective education is encouraged by schools that are built with an architecture that fully supports our post-war educationalists understanding of what constitutes good practice and are supported by an elected and accountable local democracy that ensures schools meet the needs of the people rather than the ambitions and egos of their head teachers. The disempowering of LEAs and the restrictions on funding available to local authorities have impacted considerably on state schools and their capacity to enact effective education. The cutting of local authority funding affects the physical provision of school buildings, forces local authorities to sell off assets—playing fields for children, buildings used as teachers centres, which had provided space to support professional development initiatives and union activities—and strips away the education advisors, teachers, teams, and support services that provided oversight and quality assurance and ongoing guidance and support to schools at a local level rather than the punitive one-off inspections of Office for Standards in Education (Ofsted).

This is the point where we are supposed to say: ahh, but governing bodies now have the authority to fulfil those functions of oversight and guidance. Well, having been a governor a couple of times and having known many governors, both fine and foolish, I think the best and politest answer is: that is not always the case. Too often head teachers can too easily work governing bodies to their will. Governors are the embodiment of the intensely forgettable Conservative Prime Minister John Major's woeful attempts to elevate armchair experts and general busybodies into positions of actual responsibility, for which nothing other than their sense of their own importance and the importance of their own opinions qualified them.

These now compose the individual school governing bodies that replace the functions once carried out at local authority level by professional paid workers under the oversight of democratically elected local councillors. The state has managed the trick of ruthlessly centralising real power, while devolving much time-consuming responsibility to governing bodies, who then have to split the business of management into various committees responsible for overseeing the business of translating central government legislation into daily practice in schools. School governor is a voluntary unpaid position filled by local authority nominees, various co-opted individuals, and elected representatives from the parent and staff body. Here's the paradox—although the post requires no formal or particular experience or qualification, there are nonetheless training courses you are advised to attend. This would seem to suggest that it is not necessarily a position of responsibility anybody could fill, providing they possessed the sturdy "mum's army" common sense exemplified by anybody who reads the *Daily Mail*.

However, as noted earlier, it seems far too many parents who don't read the *Daily Mail* are becoming governors. Indeed, by 2016, there were clearly far too many non–*Daily Mail*–reading governors cropping up all over the place on governing bodies and very vocally and very effectively opposing proposals to turn their schools into academies. When Chancellor Osborne announced the policy of total enforced academisation by 2022, then education secretary Nicky Morgan piped up that there should be new skill set criteria for the unpaid job description of governor, presumably to democratically weed out the undesirables. Governors needed to have business skills, Nicky Morgan proclaimed, because nowadays schools needed to be able to stand on their own two feet.

Banks we happily prop up, bale out, subsidise. . . Schools, on the other hand, have to learn to stand on their own two feet. Of course, a simpler solution to the question of how to ensure our schools are effectively managed might be to revert to the previous and effective practice of managing schools with professional objectivity and oversight through local democracy and local authorities, where our taxes pay people qualified to do the job to do it properly at a local authority level. Instead, *austerity*, that most wicked expression of Newspeak, whereby the global economic problems caused by the catastrophic mismanagement of money by a few greedy bankers is used as an excuse to hammer flat any likelihood of opposition to central government policy. Austerity has been used to justify the implementation of a year-on-year programme of decreasing central government funding for local authorities. There is now no effective line management for schools, other than a remote and unresponsive central government. Left to stand on their own two feet, schools are told to network, to engage with the concept of "schools supporting schools", which too often simply means the head teacher with the shoutiest ego in the cluster group gets to tell everybody else which hobby horse to ride and how to ride it.

Someone asked, when I told them I was writing a book, what the message of the book was. I thought too briefly and replied too quickly that the message is: never trust anybody in authority. Although it sounds so obviously glib as to almost be a cliché, it is nonetheless one of the conclusions I think my experience has led me to. Neverland—like anywhere else, really—indeed works best as a People's Republic, a cooperative where each contributes according to their ability to make sure that each receives according to their needs. Hierarchy invariably puts particular individuals in particular positions of authority, where their perspective suffers accordingly, and they find themselves considering the requirements of the hierarchy or the needs of the institution, which, however unreal, often accumulate a self-perpetuating virtual reality of their own, rather than the needs of the people, which are the reason the People's Republic exists in the first place. All of us have experience with how positions of authority change those invested with that authority. We wonder, as those in positions of hierarchical power enact some bizarre piece of nonsense or tyranny, if power has corrupted them, or if all along they had really been secretly hiding the corruption within them.

Positions of authority are associated with notions of personal ambition and personal reputation, and, obviously, there will be a temptation to allow reputation and ambition to affect the "leadership" decisions you make, particularly when most leaders will have actively pursued a "leadership" position in the first place. *Leadership* is in and of itself a politically loaded concept, and the idea of the importance of "leaders" and "leadership" has been fed into the language of education increasingly during the period of reform. At Hertford Infant and Nursery School, we tried to insist that we had curriculum coordinators not subject leaders. Leaders, however, was what we were told we ought to be calling ourselves if we had any position of particular responsibility. Maybe there are some people who get excited by the idea that they might be thought of as "leaders", and some so sadly damaged that they hunger after "leadership" positions, so they can domineer, harass, boss and bully people to their heart's content. But, more often, particularly as a consequence of the government's interference in education, people in authority in schools cease to be able to recognise as important what happens to teachers and children, because the demands of their position and the perceived demands of the school as an institution are now so overwhelming that they skew all other sense of value and purpose.

Pressures of increased bureaucracy and administration that would once have been undertaken by paid and trained bureaucrats and administrators at the local authority level have led to the rewriting the head teacher job description, replacing the teaching component with senior management functions. As distance between management and practitioners increases, it becomes obvious to teachers that yet again their boss's agenda isn't their agenda.

Any position within a hierarchy brings with it a hierarchical perspective. The challenge is to maintain your autonomy within the hierarchy, to be able to evaluate the hierarchy's values against your own, and when the two conflict to attempt to act according to your values not the hierarchy's. Not an easy matter; hierarchies and institutions tend to want to own you body and soul, and, for teachers, the steady attrition of the state's attempts to exercise complete control over the teaching profession, from the notion of "accountability" to the very definite prescriptions set out in the government's Teaching Standards document, has significantly eroded the concept of professional integrity.

I like to think that I only ever became an early years coordinator to prevent the priorities of the school hierarchy from interfering with our good practice and as a strategy to avoid being told what to do by people who didn't actually do the work. I did quite like being able to make people's performance management targets and reviews as painless as possible. But you would have to ask the people I worked with whether these good intentions were translated into workplace praxis. The road to promotion is littered with good intentions. The important question is how those in authority who started out with good intentions manage—or not—to maintain the integrity of the distance between their good intentions and the demands of the hierarchy's agenda.

Schools are cursed with the historical legacy of being institutions established at a time when hierarchy, patriarchal hierarchy at that, was the dominant form of social organisation. Of course, it is not just schools that are afflicted with the mindsets of Victorian autocracy. Many of us still—as Johnny Rotten once so perfectly sneered—love our Queen, and we also now love our celebrities (among whom we find ourselves numbering, at a minor level, the aforementioned increasingly disappointing John Lydon), with the same forelock tugging reverence that we were once supposed to show our aristocrats, ministers, elders and betters.

Schools and teachers are expected to exercise authority on behalf of the state and socialise children, imbuing them with state-sanctioned values. Respect for hierarchy is a subtext that runs throughout the life of the school. Assemblies, for example, are expected to happen daily and be predominantly Christian in character, with one of the attributes that makes everybody gathering in the school hall "an assembly" being that gathering showing "reverence for a higher being" (not just the head teacher, whose being in this instance is not quite higher enough). Forms of address—"sir, miss"—and regimented standing up and sitting down reinforce the understanding of respect not as something mutual but as something hierarchical. Royal weddings often involve an unexpected day's school closure, and no one ever suggests this demonstration of subject loyalty might be detrimental to a child's education. I found Carlisle train station, an otherwise suitably business-like dour northern hub of rail transportation, festooned with red-white-and-blue Royal Family artwork displays from local loyal primary schools when it was Mrs Windsor's ninetieth birthday. Latterly, schools have been encouraged to have two minutes silence at 11:00 a.m. on November 11, not so much to think about the generation slaughtered by and for the royal families of Europe between 1914 and 1918 but increasingly as an expression of support for "our boys keeping us free" in places like Afghanistan, an expression of respect for that most hierarchical and ranked of organisations, the military. Teachers and head teachers as individuals who have chosen to commit to education and to making a difference may well find their values in conflict with these reflections of the authoritarian values of the state.

It is easy—or at least easier—for teachers to collude with the state's authoritarianism, to become uncritical in their acceptance of their institutional capacity to exercise power and impose the values of the institution onto the people whose needs it is supposedly serving. It is also easy—or at least easier—for teachers to slip themselves into that hierarchical mindset and uncritically assert themselves as simple authority figures in order to impose their will in the classroom.

Once again, as a supply teacher, having deliberately deskilled myself in this respect, I marvel at the uncritical ease with which teachers impose their will and their order on children. I am not sure they even consider that the classroom might be a conflictual setting—thirty people with individual needs and agendas arbitrarily expected to conform to a situation in which they have no agency receive only intangible recompense at best (a star, a sticker, a tick, a smiley face, golden time, extra playtime, whatever) that is run according to the dictates of a salaried official—let alone reflect on whether that is the best way to make a difference. It has always angered me the way some teachers use their authority to determine, often through manipulation of language, the values governing what takes place in a classroom, imposing a set of values that enforces their agenda over the interests and aspirations of the children. The term "learning" is now ubiquitous in schools to describe what children are doing and is somewhat cynically used by many teachers instead of the old term "working", as if calling it so makes it so. When we play, learning is a consequence, but particularly for young children, play, not learning, is the intention, the "for its own sake" that animates their activities. This is now erased from the school process. Now when children make constructions with reclaimed or recycled materials—even the very terminology removes the playfulness of the old descriptive noun "junk"—they are understood as "learning how to join two surfaces together" or something similarly incidental to the child's intention, which is to make, by combining their imagination with their motor skills in an enjoyable process of personal praxis, something that wasn't there before—a robot, a house, a mess, whatever.

Just because our teacher says that "we are having fun learning our phonics" doesn't mean this is objectively true. What is objectively true is that all power does indeed offer opportunities for corruption, and absolute power offers very dangerous opportunities for absolute corruption, which is one of the reasons we should be opposed to academisation of schools. Headship of an academy carries with it an increase in powers that effectively make the school the head's private business empire, with the headship role becoming much more that of a CEO role, accompanied by a £100,000-plus salary a year to match, and the senior management, like a board of directors, paying themselves the inflated salaries of their choice.

Thirty years ago, the idea that you could run the great welfare state public services of health and education along the lines of business was considered manifestly absurd. Both worked to meet the needs of people; it was not as if raw materials were being transformed into products that had a value in the marketplace. But, step by step, the reformers have reconfigured the public understanding of these services, representing them primarily as structures and institutions rather than functions and processes. Instead of thinking of state schools as the process whereby children are educated, state education has come to be understood as a set of physical assets, as an expenditure, where there are measurable outcomes that can be used to ensure we are getting our money's worth. And now you hear such nonsense everywhere. Out of nowhere at a recent social gathering, I found myself pinned to the conversational wall by a bloke who had worked for the BBC, who was insisting on telling me that you couldn't just accept a teacher saying they'd done a good job; you had to be able to measure the goodness or not of the job done. He'd been a parent governor, he said, implying he clearly knew what he was talking about. I did afterwards wonder if you were allowed to accept somebody who worked for the BBC saying they'd done a good job or clearly knew what they were talking about on the strength of attending three governing body meetings a year.

Schools are now face to face with the only authority capitalism really recognises, the authority of money, and the only value capitalism really recognises, the value of profit, where value for money means really just getting as much as you can by commodifying as much as you can and giving as little back as possible whenever you can. Only you're doing this where children's lives are the basic currency.

As the mindset of privatisation has worked its way through public services, starting with utilities like the railways that can be run—badly—for profit or housing, which can be easily relocated into an existing market, the valuation of the accountant has come to replace the accepted valuation of education. Structures and institutions are more easily representable in terms of value for money, their interactions reduced to transactions, and their efficiency ranked by measurable outcomes (however partial or meaningless). A standardised curriculum is imposed, a system of testing is imposed, the results are published and schools ranked by their performances, thereby proving whether or not they've done a good job. Complex processes are reduced to simple numerical scores. What cannot be so simplistically measured is, of course, ignored and, together with the overt messages of value contained in the content selected by the government for its curriculum, this has the effect of sidelining those skills and attributes of children and areas of education that aren't easily measured. It is easier to appreciate attributes like creativity, imagination, curiosity, empathy and cooperation than it is to measure them, but I suspect these are not attributes the reformers wish our children to take with them into the job marketplace in any case. Performance management now links productivity outcomes to workers' pay. Targets are set at the beginning of the performance management period. (The central government intention is for the school to try to get teachers to accept being tied to some specific figure—X number of units will make Y amount of progress by the end Z amount of time.) If this target or any of the others the school has decided upon for the teacher isn't met, the teacher can then be denied a pay increment.

The language of measurement and value becomes the inappropriate descriptor of a teacher's function and a child's development. Schools have generated a linguistic bureaucracy that makes teachers focus on administration rather than children. Language is used not to understand or represent reality but to fabricate convincing virtual realities. It is misused with breathtaking disregard for meaning. Now we do have raw materials—they used to be called children—and we do have finished products—they used to be called children too—the quality of which, and, therefore, the apparent marketplace value, is identified by the measurement under test conditions of how much of the teaching it was supposed to be taught has been sufficiently learned to pass those test conditions. Children who pass more exams are worth more to the school than those who don't.

The internal values of the school have been reconfigured with terms like "value-added" . . . "impact" . . . "achievement". The school my sons went to rejoiced in the slogan "Putting Achievement First". When the head proposed turning the school into an academy, he was keen to assure the student body, in case any of the children feared otherwise, that an academised school would still be putting achievement first. Most parents we spoke with in the campaign to prevent the school becoming an academy rather preferred the idea of putting the children first. Funnily enough, in Brooklyn, in 2016, there was exactly the same slogan "Putting Achievement First" on a bus stop advertisement for a charter school. It is now rare to find a state school in England not engaged in a slightly politer version of the same sort of sloganeering and self-promotion. School railings are invariably decorated with banners carrying the school's snappy one-liner slogan and the latest Ofsted report carefully edited to provide the most favourable quotation about the school's performance. Private nurseries advertise themselves similarly on billboards and in local newspapers. Everyone wants to tell potential punters— sorry, prospective parents—how good they are at achieving.

If education simply becomes "achievement", then it becomes an outcome of linear progress and a hierarchy of knowledge and skills. Competition and a hierarchy of winners and losers not cooperation is the model used to incentivise the performance of pupils, teachers and schools. This also impacts upon the nature of the relationships within the classroom. Teachers are pressurised by the need to achieve outcomes and to drive children toward these outcomes. Such a situation encourages teachers to resort to positioning themselves as authoritarian arbiters of what does and does not take place in the classroom. This is not professional authority, however; this is simply the exercise of authority within a hierarchical structure. It is not a situation conducive to the reciprocal dialogue identified by Freire as good educational practice or supportive of the democratisation that some progressive teachers were working toward in the 1970s. Although Searle was criticised for substituting his values in his scheme of work for the state's traditional values of patriotism and Christianity, those values included a commitment to discussion and debate and attempted to dismantle the hierarchical distance between teacher and taught:

> [W]e both undertook to revolt against the divisions that I, as teacher, paid functionary of the State, and they, as pupils, expected pawns of the employers, worked to transcend . . . by a comradeship of the classroom which would undermine the very roles and conflicts the society was making for and between us.[1]

While professional authority, along with democratically elected local authority, has now been replaced by centralised political authority and the authority of the marketplace, schools still retain a traditional model of patriarchal authority in their internal organisation. Staffing structures are vertically organised ladders of pay and authority, with the promise of increased power and salary accumulating at the top levels of the ladder. Again, money is identified with authority. Gender is also identified with authority; recent figures for England revealed that in primary schools 15 per cent of the staff are male, but 27 per cent of heads are male, while in secondary schools, 38 per cent of the staff are male, but 62 per cent of heads are male. The bigger the school, of course, the bigger the budget—and the bigger the head's salary. Salaries for state secondary school patriarchs are often quoted as being in the region of £150,000 a year, while academy CEO-style heads are happily writing themselves salaries in the region of £500,000 of taxpayers money a year.

At the moment, state funded schools in the United Kingdom are supposed to be not-for-profit organisations. Advocates of continuing "reform", unsurprisingly, look favourably upon the idea that the businessification of schools might logically lead to schools being run for profit. Are we surprised to learn that the former Ofsted lead inspector Christopher Woodhead is also an enthusiastic proponent of such a development?

Oh, the excellent authority of money!

PART FOUR

THE CHILD

Shall I tell you who is strong?
Child, you are strong,
You have nothing and your hands are small
But the world spins like clay on a potter's wheel
And you will shape it with your hands.
—Edward Bond, "Old Woman's Song"

The Orange Class News

You get Kelly's knee, Craig's thumb, Rosie's rabbits and
    Gohar's mum
Turtle James, Mona's twins, the computer games where
    Omar wins

Who's lost their teeth and got new shoes? This is the
    9 o'clock Orange Class News.

You get Hari's dad and MacHaroon, Ruchi-Cuchi and Mr
    Moon
Nasher's motor, Harminder's James Bond, Taffy's daffy and
    now where's James gone?

You get Rylan's smile and Gagan's grin, and David's
    uniform's absolutely ruined again, Mr Johnson. What
    do you do with them all day long? In my day we did
    spellings, in my day we did tables, all you seem to do is
    save the bloody rainforest.

Adam's judo and Emily's cough, and Matthew's stories go
    on and on and—
There's Meera's cousins and Partha's pigeon and Barney
    the dog done poo in the kitchen
Of Long John Lawrence and wake up Lauren and well,
    whose turn is it to weigh the classroom hamster?

So it's every morning, on the mat, who did this and—who
    did that?
It would be nice if every kid only ever made the news like
    Orange Class did.

Forget the stupid things that grown-ups who never did do
This is the 9 o'clock Orange Class News.

The Essential Anarchist

Each child born is born an anarchist.
—Robb Johnson, "At the Siege of Madrid"

The child, compared with the shifting slippery shape of the state, remains pretty much a constant. You get complaints about children not being children any more, you get totalitarian regimes claiming they are creating a "new type of man" and you get local conditions of culture and history and societal values seeping in from the word go, but, basically, the human animal doesn't evolve or alter anywhere nearly as much as the society it finds itself in. The human animal does, however, have to express itself through the social languages it finds around it. As we have noted, the British state has attempted to control those languages through its assertion of control over schooling and, we might add, through its assertion of control over social relations and organisation (turning the working class into the unemployed class) and assertion of control over culture (through commodification and the mediation of the media)—all these strategies have attempted to exert almost medieval standards of complete control over the language of social discourse. This control shows particular intent and attention to the way that control of that language exercises ideological control over political debate. Between them, schools and media impose models of thinking and not thinking, of value and non-value, that are intended to be understood as more real than individual experience, action and reflection. So maybe children appear differently than they did in your experience of the past, partially because they have to work in a different language than the one you grew up with—toddlers, presented with a real old retro paper book, will be observed attempting to swipe pages rather than turn them, and five-year-olds will, as noted, talk about diagraphs as if that was somehow important learning for a five-year-old. But that's just the language not the thing itself. The thing itself is still what it always was, an improbable and random flame of unique consciousness, wide-eyed, happy to be here, and curious to find out more.

People, eh?

You've got to love them, haven't you? Here we are, billions of us, doing our best in metaphysically impossible conditions, happy pigs, unhappy Socrateses. We are, all of us, simultaneously nothing special and the centre of the universe. Most of us, the vast majority us, are generally okay. Clearly, there are some individuals for whom something somewhere has gone wrong, so they become oppressors and exploiters, police and thieves, fascists, celebrities, bosses, mass murderers, politicians (sometimes, far too often, both at one and the same time). Beckett's humorous final insult in *Waiting for Godot* is "critic", mine might possibly be "Ofsted inspector".

But children . . . they love the world. Che Guevara said, "true revolutionaries must perceive the revolution, because of its creative and liberating nature, as an act of love. . . . Let me say, with the risk of appearing ridiculous, that the true revolutionary is guided by strong feelings of love".[1] Children are very much guided by strong feelings of love. Each child carries the revolution wittingly or unwittingly under their breath and under their coat, like Brecht's Galileo carries the truth under his breath and under his coat, loving the world as they do. *Love* has become a rather overworked and frequently devalued word, both as a noun and a verb, but it is nonetheless a pretty good description of a significant human characteristic and motivating factor. One of the positives about having worked as a teacher and having spent twenty-three years of my working life in the early years is that you get to see human beings as they are, at their best, usually—although increasingly not always—before things go wrong. Before capitalism sinks its teeth into them. Before the state makes sure their great expectations—which are really only that the world will respond in kind to their innate love of being alive—get well and truly disappointed. Children are humanity in its essence, and they—we—are hardwired to want to love the world.

Perhaps it is this active, conscious commitment and capacity that makes our brains that little bit different from—say—the brain of my great friend Ginger the cat, whose level unperturbed gaze greets me from the screensaver every time I turn this iPad on. Paulo Freire, author of the aforementioned *Pedagogy of the Oppressed*, notes that "animals do not consider the world; they are immersed in it. In contrast human beings emerge from the world, objectify it, and in so doing understand it and transform it with their labour".[2] However, sometimes—all too often, in fact—children find that the world is organised to deny them their transformative energy. I would also add that humans are particularly characterised by their capacity for attachments that involve complex, sometimes irrational, counter-intuitive choices and behaviours. Attachment for humans is not just a biological necessity; attachment is also a psychological necessity, and what is often remarkable about our monsters is their history of failed significant attachments coupled with their persistent irrational substitute attachments—Hitler's famous fondness for dogs, for example. One child I taught who had experienced a very loveless start to his life, contemplating a mill pond on school journey, was adamant he would rescue an animal in danger of drowning there but not a person. Indeed, the remarkable quality of indifference that is otherwise only found among humans, and generally in fictional forms like Alain Delon's performance in *Le Samourai* (does that man ever take a shit, I find myself wondering?) may well be existentially satisfying but remains essentially fragile and fictional—and even Delon's character turns out to have a fatal weakness for canaries. . .[3] With humans there is this inescapable capacity for attachment to have an irrational and an aesthetic quality to it, and this is what transforms attachment into love.

Of course, Ginger feels no need to develop or own an iPad, with or without my frequently troubled gaze greeting him every time he switches it on. Attachment is a much more straightforward matter for Ginger, and, if I am honest, probably doesn't ever entirely escape the rationality of transaction (although I do feel that our relationship has developed with at least a modicum of affection for me on Ginger's part, but that could be just because I know where the cat treats are kept and can be persuaded more frequently than anyone else to dish them out). Whereas, surely, as humans, most of us have at some point been aware of and troubled by the irrationality of our attractions and the impossibility of certain of our transactions.

Love is both rational and irrational. Children are also both rational and irrational. Far too many adults underestimate a child's ability to engage with reason, perhaps because they only notice the child's delight and engagement in the irrational, the imagination, and the playfulness that they have had squeezed out of them in their experience of "growing up". Children have a great capacity to commit to delight for its own sake, with none of the ulterior motives of outcome that govern learned adult behaviour.

An anecdote: it is school journey, and we are on the beach at Swanage at sunset. H (a very thoughtful and reflective eleven-year-old) takes out her instamatic camera and points it at the beautiful horizon. P (a thoughtful but more practically inclined eleven-year-old) sensibly counsels her friend, "It won't come out". "It doesn't matter", says H, as she clicks the camera.

Another characteristic of childhood is that it is a period when the individual's growth and change is at its most manifest. The young human is notorious for being subject to phases of biological development. Yet each of these developments, which in many ways help construct the social identity of the individual, takes place individually, at differing rates and to differing degrees. There is the legendary "terrible twos", there is the young child's deep necessity for movement, which makes the traditional characteristics of formal schooling—sit down, be quiet, do your (written) work—categorically inappropriate for young children, particularly for boys; their bodies release luteinising hormone at around four years of age, affecting them the way testosterone levels affect adults. Gender is, of course, not a divide but a spectrum, but there are generally different rates at which different motor skills develop in boys and girls, and those of us at the boy end of the spectrum will have been likely to have found our brain development in the frontal cortex, caudate and temporal lobes (the thoughtful and analytical parts of the brain) lagging behind those of us on the girl end of the spectrum by as much as twenty months for much of our childhood. And then there's adolescence. . . These are the species-specific biological realities of "growing up", and to these must be added the challenges of a reflective consciousness that has to engage with "decentring", balancing your own needs and aspirations with everybody else's and coping with the awareness of self.

Decentring is a grandiloquent term for what is often more prosaically termed "caring and sharing". Rather like love, these are two words that have somewhat lost their potency through overuse, although the meaning and social behaviour that they freight remain as socially potent as ever. Children have a pretty good instinctive capacity for empathy. They are also pretty good at cooperating rather than competing. My experience of working with children convinces me that children are infinitely happier and, therefore, in utilitarian terms, more effective as learners when they are functioning in a cooperative and empathetic caring and sharing environment. That is surely stating the obvious; when we are happy, we are better able to function and contribute. Nonetheless, since the Romantics started getting all introspective and maudlin as the Industrial

Revolution kicked in, we find ourselves in the paradox of a cultural tradition where suffering and unhappiness have been seen as requisite elements to the creative process. In *The Third Man*, Graham Greene's serpentine superman Harry Lime, who, like Milton's Satan in *Paradise Lost*, gets all the best lines, is able to plausibly assert that three centuries of Swiss brotherly love produced the cuckoo clock, whereas thirty years of the Borgias produced the Renaissance. This belief that tyranny and suffering are the most efficacious conditions conducive to production has translated easily into the ethos underlying the treatment of children in many if not most classrooms up until the latter half of the last century.

As adults we are often faced with evidence that seems to support the idea that happiness is not conducive to "progress". Paradoxically, unhappiness is seen as a great generator of creativity. The "world wars" of the twentieth century saw the development of sciences that have since come to determine the subsequent development of much of the way human society is organised, from jet engines to computers, as well as expensive and costly initiatives like space programmes. Hey, thanks for the Velcro! Much easier for a four-year-old than laces. And thanks for nuclear energy and all the ingenious cruelty of modern weaponry. Discontent—certainly with the discovery of the teenager in the 1950s—has become synonymous with adolescence (rather than class?), and with the explosion of pop culture in the 1960s, adolescence became synonymous with creativity, making a direct link between behaviour and biology, as well as between culture and biology. The effect of biological change—menstruation and menopause—is seen as a significant factor for women. Men on the other hand are . . . what? Set in stone after their last shift of adolescent testosterone? Incapable of growth? Forever little boys lost in big boys' clothes? I think I read somewhere all our body cells are replaced every seven years. How much of a constant am I anyway, even ignoring Sartre's categorically conclusive proposition that existence precedes essence?

Goalkeepers

When I was growing up my team was Tottenham.
Number eight was always Jimmy Greaves.
Jimmy Greaves was always inside right,
Referee your offside rules do not apply to me.

Then there was the goalkeeper, Pat Jennings,
The safest pair of hands at White Hart Lane,
The safest pair of hands in Northern Ireland,
Where British rule would soon be sending British troops
    again.

And the ball is always heading for the corner of the net,
You're reaching out for something that you're never going
    to get.
Sometimes you will, sometimes you won't.
Sometimes you do make the save, sometimes you don't.

So who would want to be the team's goalkeeper,
The last man standing on the line,
The safest pair of hands you can depend on
When the game runs out of extra time?

Both my dad and Albert Camus were goalkeepers.
Albert learned to fight the plague between the posts.
He held the line although the line was history,
He held the line although the line was lost.

And the ball is always heading for the corner of the net,
You're reaching out for something that you're never going
    to get.
Sometimes you will, sometimes you won't.
Sometimes you do make the save, sometimes you don't.

There's this photo of eleven schoolboys grinning,

Arms round shoulders, kit don't match, but do they care?
Cos their captain's sitting centre with their trophy
And behind him, keeper's cap on, that's my dad standing
 there.

Later there's the man, defying gravity,
High-jumping in mid-air, but best of all
Is the photograph where he's forever flying,
All his being stretched to make the save and catch the ball.

And the ball is always heading for the corner of the net,
You're reaching out for something that you're never going
 to get.
Sometimes you will, sometimes you won't.
Sometimes you do make the save, sometimes you don't.

Later when I'm going through Ron's papers
There's this statement dated summer 39,
For fellowship and freedom, and there's my father
In those sentences at seventeen my father underlined.

Socialisation and the Essential Anarchist

In every cry of every Man,
In every Infants cry of fear,
In every voice: in every ban,
The mind-forg'd manacles I hear.
—Billy Blake, "London"

No wonder then we have evolved schooling, a process of dedicated developmental institutions that, if they won't help people with their menopause or their existential problematics, will at least help our children negotiate puberty and arrive at the far shore of adolescence. A few life skills wouldn't do any harm either, and for most of us they'd certainly be of a lot more practical use than a maths GCSE. Certainly, the Maths O Level that I somehow managed to acquire, which was a pre-requisite qualification to be accepted on a teacher training course, has proved of no use whatsoever in my subsequent life or career. In the mid-1980s, a friend who was a deputy head of one of Hounslow's secondary schools surveyed what mathematics their pupils actually used in practical situations once they left school. He found the majority of pupils went on to work in retail situations, using mathematics they had learned by the time they were eleven. He was contemplating how these pupils could spend their time between eleven and sixteen being taught something other than complicated mathematics they would never need and didn't like, but then the national curriculum came along and put an end to all that child-centred speculation. Later, in 2010, plans to extend the values and broad thematic organisation of the successful Early Years Foundation Stage (EYFS) curriculum upward into the wastelands of the national curriculum vanished, like equalities, off the Department of Education's agenda the moment the Cameron government got elected.

By 2015, half of Cameron's cabinet were privately educated, whereas only 7 per cent of the population as a whole is privately educated. Commenting on this discrepancy at the time, our friends from the Sutton Trust concluded:

> It is good to see more comprehensive educated cabinet ministers, reflecting the schools attended by 90 per cent of children. But with half of the Cabinet still independently educated and half having been to Oxbridge, today's figures remind us how important it is that we do more to increase levels of social mobility and make sure that bright young people from low and middle-income backgrounds have access to the best schools and the best universities.[1]

Perhaps a more objective response might be that it is surely unacceptable that positions of authority are so disproportionately accessed by the privilege of having attended particular gateway institutions.

Access to education is subject to the interests and decisions of the ruling class, and, as with state schooling, access to further "higher" education has been recuperated by the state. It is not just the abolition of the grants funding system for students, replacing this entitlement with the disincentives of loan and debt. Teachers and lecturers working in further education have seen their pay, conditions and pensions savaged by central government. Access to education and the quality of the experience of that education have been revealed as variable according to the priorities of the state, itself a variable subject to the ruling class's control of the historical process.

It is also clear that the very concept of childhood, and so the situation of the child, has been similarly variable. One could make the case that childhood in Britain only became a universally accepted condition in the nineteenth century. Nineteenth-century reformers put children at the centre of novels and passed legislation to prevent their employment (frequently such employment providing essential family income). A century later, it would be the economic prosperity of post-war USA that initiated the identification of a further related childhood condition, the teenager. Capitalism has not been slow to identify the potential market childhood offers. Disney has expanded from cartoons to a major cultural arbiter, with its Disneylands and Disney channels and Disney stores, the world's second largest media conglomerate in terms of revenue. Some older teachers I have known grumble that "children have changed". I am not sure I agree: I think children just wear very different clothes now to the rags and hand-me-downs from the adult world that we used to dress them in. Nonetheless, a childhood where you are deliberately and ruthlessly targeted as an economic opportunity, considered primarily by large powerful economic interests as a potential consumer, is bound to provide a challenging experience that takes some making sense of. The child, however, enters the world with the same qualities of enquiry and eagerness that children always have. It is the languages it learns and the clothes we make it wear that make it malleable, a creation of history, of a particular social organisation.

Sometimes this process of socialisation turns children into monstrous adults. We know that societies can condition people to perform terrible actions, whether it be climbing out of trenches and marching in parade ground formation toward murderous machine-gun fire on the Somme or carpet-bombing Cambodia. None of that, the stupidity and cruelty of adults, is necessarily the fault of the child, but it does lead one to question how the child ends up in such situations. What did we teach, and what did the child learn?

Currently in England, the purpose of education is—if it is offered for any consideration at all—limited to a conservative set of utilitarian outcomes—good scores lead to good jobs for good dogs. One constant outcome, which, of course, runs back through Callaghan's Great Debate all the way to the initial Elementary Education Act of 1870, is that education is intended to make Britain better at being "great". But if we consider the context in which monstrous adults are cultivated out of ordinary children, don't we often find that their education had been geared toward meeting the priorities of the state? What social attachments are schools encouraging when they teach "British Values" or make children salute a flag every day? These are practices that endorse attachment to the state and, therefore, to the state's priorities. Are these priorities we should be concerned with in education?

Certain characteristics of the state may vary, and with the political shift in the balance of power between the people and the state in the immediate post-war decades, as we noted in the section "Workers' Control", it did indeed appear that with the welfare state, the character of the British state had significantly changed. The model of state education that we think of in Britain is very much influenced by the ideas and opportunities of the post-war consensus of the 1950s and was later further influenced by the libertarian blossoming of the 1960s. There was the growing sense that education should be organised to meet the needs of, to support the development of, to enhance the well-being, the life chances, the confidence and competence of the individual child. The emergence of an educational praxis organised around the paramount importance of recognising and meeting individual ability and need might suggest an overlap with the values of the "reformers", who come from a political tradition that is fond of trumpeting the values of individualism. Whereas their idea of the individual is always qualified by the determinations of class, wealth and privilege and favours competition as the generator of individual success, my understanding of the individual is very different and is not framed by the vertical indexes of differential but by the horizontal perspective of commonality. Roger McGough expresses it rather neatly in his poem "Streemin"; "look at the cemtery/no streemin there". Sadly, of course, the streemin that is a consequence of our class-based system of social organisation does very real damage to the life chances and the life expectancy of the many to enhance the well-being of the few.

We already hear far too much about people who do us no real tangible good whatsoever and far too little about those people who keep the wheels of our lives turning. As I always used to say to my sons when I was pushing their buggies to playgroup or to the library for a story session or off for an adventure involving chocolate cake or whatever, and a large wagon was trundling slowly down the road collecting the rubbish or the recycling: "When was the last time the Queen emptied the bins for us, eh?" This text has so far been overrun by the names of the "reformers", people who have neither experience nor a clue as to what constitutes good practice in education, whose access to power, and, thereby, the authority to enact their prejudices and hobby horses on the rest of us has been won not by appropriate knowledge or aptitude but through their access to the privilege afforded by the accumulation of surplus wealth. Surely no one, in their right mind or not, would allow Michael Gove to perform major surgery on their child, just because he went to Oxford and his wife writes for the *Daily Mail*—but we allow him to insist that what our children need is "more rigour and basic skills" (not to mention Greek and Latin) in our schools. In the US, just because he is ridiculously, obscenely wealthy, Bill Gates is a major promoter of charter schools, the US equivalent of academies, which is linked—*quelle surprise!*—to moves toward "increased e-learning", a future that envisions no teachers, just technicians to help children log on.

That may be good news for Bill Gates, but is it good news for teachers and children to be heading toward a culture of learning that effectively dispenses with the possibilities of non-programmable human interaction? The sense of touch reduced to a touch screen. The possibilities of imagination and reflection reduced to algorithm. Of course, when it does away with the mystery and alchemy of human relationships, this is a future that also does away with those awkward and expensive unpredictable variables, teachers. Computers are like the boss's idea of the ideal worker and the Victorian idea of the ideal child. They do what they are told, they are seen but not heard, and they don't join unions.

Here's another anecdote.

I was handing leaflets out about the dismalness that was the state's plan for baseline testing of four-year-olds one Sunday afternoon as part of the Brighton and Hove National Union of Teachers (NUT) anti-baseline picnic. Two people who were clearly all the world to each other, a dad and his three-year-old daughter, passed by and took a leaflet. I can't remember her name, so I'll call her Emily, which is a name I have always rather liked. Emily was a small person with Downs Syndrome. I believe that Emily is every bit the equal of Bill Gates. We each have different skills and proclivities and attributes. When I need my drains unblocked I will call in Dynorod, and they will send the Dynorod operative skilled in the use of a long stick. When I need my spirits lifted I will listen to Bruce Springsteen singing "Born to Run". Sadly, Bruce's attributes mean he has earned considerably more through singing than the person who works for Dynorod has earned from unblocking drains. However, when my drains back up and excrement bubbles up through the manhole outside my back door, putting "Born to Run" on the turntable is not going to be my first response. Bill Gates is not much use either, and I am sure at some point someone may want to write a computer programme that unblocks drains, but its efficacy will depend on affordability, with cheaper, popular affordable versions not working particularly well. No doubt there will be an endless choice of hardware, like there is an endless choice of televisions, laptops, washing machines etc., none of which work particularly well, and the operating system will be run by Virgin media and only accessed through a labyrinthine call centre in Mumbai, and it will be utter bollocks nine times out of ten. Society functions, both if at all and at its best, through cooperation and skill sharing. Someone unblocks your drains when you need them too, and someone sings "Born to Run" when you need them to, and Emily and her dad give each other a unique companionship that is beyond words and, indeed, beyond price, because it is at the level of the deepest of attachments, and it is the mystery and alchemy of individual lives, individual stories coinciding perfectly in a shared string of moments, an afternoon together in the park.

Whatever our abilities, every child matters. Indeed, this is the title of government legislation—reduced to the acronym ECM—that was a response to the failure of the state to protect the life of eight-year-old Victoria Climbie.

The Every Child Matters initiative of 2004 was intended to ensure every child, whatever their background or circumstances, has the support they need to:

- stay safe;
- be healthy;
- enjoy and achieve;
- make a positive contribution;
- achieve economic well-being.

An initiative of the Blair Government, it is one of those instances where, following an event that so appals society's mediated discourse, the state has to decide upon an appropriate response. Occasionally, terrible events occur that the media cannot manage to ignore or mediate. The drowning of Alan Kurdi in 2015 and the Grenfell Tower fire in 2017 were similar examples of the media and the state being backfooted by catastrophes they could not immediately manage. The abuse and killing of Victoria was an event that demanded a state response. Every Child Matters was the government's attempt to establish measures to safeguard vulnerable children by formalising the rights of children within British society.

Vulnerable socially disadvantaged children have been attending state schools ever since legislation established state education. In 1913, teacher Kitty Higdon was reprimanded by school managers for lighting a fire without their permission, which she had done to dry the clothes of children who had walked three miles to school in the rain—this was the incident that precipitated the longest strike in Britain (1914–1939), leading to the establishment of the Burston Strike School. Nearly half a century later poet and primary school teacher Charles Causley was angered when people thought he had invented Timothy Winters.

> Timothy Winters comes to school
> With eyes as wide as a football pool,
> Ears like bombs and teeth like splinters:
> A blitz of a boy is Timothy Winters.
>
> His belly is white, his neck is dark,
> And his hair is an exclamation mark.
> His clothes are enough to scare a crow
> And through his britches the blue winds blow.
>
> When teacher talks he won't hear a word
> And he shoots down dead the arithmetic-bird,
> He licks the patterns off his plate
> And he's not even heard of the Welfare State.
>
> Timothy Winters has bloody feet
> And he lives in a house on Suez Street,
> He sleeps in a sack on the kitchen floor
> And they say there aren't boys like him any more.
>
> Old man Winters likes his beer
> And his missus ran off with a bombardier.

Grandma sits in the grate with a gin
And Timothy's dosed with an aspirin.

The Welfare Worker lies awake
But the law's as tricky as a ten-foot snake,
So Timothy Winters drinks his cup
And slowly goes on growing up.

At Morning Prayers the Master helves
For children less fortunate than ourselves,
And the loudest response in the room is when
Timothy Winters roars "Amen!"

So come one angel, come on ten:
Timothy Winters says "Amen
Amen amen amen amen".
Timothy Winters, Lord.

Amen!

Governments expect initiatives like ECM to be widely welcomed as they are presented as attempts to address the issues of social exclusion and educational disadvantage through legislation. Schools are now overtly configured as outposts of state intervention, preventing and identifying causes for concern. This is a role developed even further with the government's Prevent strategy, which insists that schools police children and their communities to prevent radicalisation. But consider the ambition of these new duties: Are schools really to be held responsible for ensuring children "achieve economic well-being"? There has been a steady expansion of attention to safeguarding and child protection issues in schools. Responsibilities have become duties. The social work aspect of teaching—Annie Higdon lighting a fire to dry a soaked child—has experienced something of a mission creep. Teachers are now expected to be proactive monitors of children's behaviours in order to be able to trigger police raids on families whose child draws or says something that sounds like it might possibly be evidence of something a bit militant.

There is an increasingly blatant disjoint between stated aims of state legislation and the reality of how these aims translate into real consequences, real "outcomes". In practical terms, for example, however rigorous a diet of phonics blending and segmenting a Timothy Winters might now enjoy, it is ludicrous to expect that this would enable him access to a future where he will stay safe, be healthy, enjoy and achieve, make a positive contribution and achieve economic well-being on Suez Street.

Little Vinnie Jones

Little Vinnie Jones wants to be an artist
But he lives up in the flats
In one of them big blocks up the hill
Where they don't have any trees and they don't have any
    gardens
They got wheelie bins and black sacks
A bus stop and that's it.
Don't ask me why

When we do PE he always does it barefoot
His dad delivers pizzas
Mum looks 17
But he's really good with words and he's really good with
    numbers
He's really good at making things
He's everybody's friend
Don't ask me why

Government says: we don't have any money
They're cutting this, they're cutting that
Work more, pay more, get less

Paying for the people in the nice big houses
With their gardens behind high walls
Where they never feel a thing
Don't ask me why
I don't like the rich

Little Vinnie Jones wants to be an artist
How many pizzas does it take
To get to Monet's garden?
How many kids you think ever wanted to be artists
But got stuck inside a flat
With some pound shop felt tip pens?
Don't ask me why
I don't like the rich. . .

Wrong Questions and Wrong Answers

"Bitzer", said Thomas Gradgrind. "Your definition of a horse".

"Quadruped. Graminivorous. Forty teeth, namely twenty-four grinders, four eye-teeth, and twelve incisive. Sheds coat in the spring; in marshy countries, sheds hoofs, too. Hoofs hard, but requiring to be shod with iron. Age known by marks in mouth". Thus (and much more) Bitzer.

"Now girl number twenty", said Mr. Gradgrind. "You know what a horse is".

—Charlie Dickens, *Hard Times*

Every Child Matters (ECM) addresses none of the structural reasons why children like Timothy Winters continue to find themselves living in places like Suez Street, in a Britain where we see a year-on-year increase in statistics relating to child poverty—in 2018, the figure was 4.5 million children living in poverty,[1] despite Britain being then ranked generally as about the fifth richest country in the world. Clearly, however well intentioned, this is merely another failure of the state, imagining disadvantage and deprivation can be simply magicked away by a few fine words that teachers then have to translate into effective affective practice. The other option of course is simply to redefine poverty. In 2015, as official figures for child poverty rose from 2.3 to 2.5 million, the Cameron government's response was to describe the measurements used as "deeply flawed" and initiate a "new series of indicators including exam results"—which suggests teachers are to be held responsible for child poverty now rather than government economic policies.

For a number of reasons, schools have been expected to bear increased responsibility for society's problematics. This is partly because in some areas the school is the most effective and functional institution for miles around. Parents, however depressed their life experiences are, generally care deeply about their children. Monsters and those crushed beyond endurance by their own dismal life experiences are rarer than their representation in the media would have us believe. Based on their historic role as care providers and their capacity to focus on the well-being of children, schools provide opportunities for families and individuals to develop positive self-images and to rediscover their self-confidence and their life skills in the shared safe spaces that schools can offer to communities.

In the days when local authorities had budgets they could spend meeting local needs, I worked for a couple of years as a community teacher in a large infant and junior school, located on the socially deprived and depressed northwest frontier of the London Borough of Hounslow. The school served a couple of small council estates, one low-rise one from the 1950s that was predominantly but not exclusively inhabited by white British families and a larger more modern high-rise estate that was predominantly but not exclusively inhabited by British Asian families. The reason the school had a community teacher was partly to ensure the school met the needs of its community but also partly because the school was the only effective council institution in the area, making it the most effective conduit to support the local people.

Both communities experienced social exclusion. A shared experience of exclusion was simple geography, the location of the estates as far away as you could get from any social amenities. Both communities also experienced the institutional exclusion that often goes with schooling. Teachers are likely to present as part of a culture that is predominantly reflective of the values of the white middle class. In primary schools, this dominant culture is often further refined as being reflective of the values that are white, middle-class and female.

White working-class boys, for example—or the stereotype this term represents—as already mentioned, a cause for concern for that great and fearless champion of equality the *Daily Telegraph*, would have a much better experience of education if they weren't faced with institutions primarily organised to confer success upon those children best able to conform to the stereotypical values of middle-class females. The younger the child, traditionally the more "feminine" the institution in terms of staff and curriculum. Boys find themselves in their first classrooms in situations run by women, where the intention is clearly to get them to be quiet, do good listening, sit still and engage in activities requiring fine motor skills that—unlike girls of a similar age—they are as yet unlikely to have developed. This is not how the stereotypical boy and indeed the stereotypical working-class individual best likes to learn. They work best when they can use their energy in an environment that values autonomous, active, explorative, investigative patterns of learning. This catastrophic mismatch has only been utterly worsened by the sort of "back to basics" curriculum emphasis imposed by those governments the dreadful *Daily Torygraph* has so enthusiastically supported. From the beginning, those who are the least able to conform to the values of school are being set up to fail the most, always struggling with "learning delays", as the linear demands of the rigid national curriculum rush headlong forward without them, a train of learning that must accelerate with pace, rigour or whatever is the latest state-sponsored slogan favoured by the latest team of dog-training inspectors, running to the government imposed immutable timetable. These governments have also not helped the self-image of the white working class by destroying their employment prospects and communities and then castigating them as benefits scroungers far more to blame, along with public services, than greedy bankers for the financial meltdown of 2008.

Nonetheless, every child does matter. Every child is objectively as unique and meaningful as your child, just as every individual is a consciousness that is the apparent centre of the universe, just like you.

It is easy to get sentimental about children. The younger they are, the cuter they are generally perceived to be. By the time they reach eighty, they are definitely no longer cute and are liable to be warehoused, and sometimes abused, in run-for-profit care homes. Current government initiatives are preparing young children for this by encouraging their incarceration in run-for-profit nurseries from as early an age as possible, so their feckless working-class parents will have no excuses for not getting a job.

I remember, when I was working with private nurseries as part of a local authority project in support of literacy in the Early Years, the very, very, very expensive cars—more expensive than I could ever afford—that turned up outside the private nurseries. These were the very, very, very expensive cars owned by the owners of these private nurseries who employed the teenaged likes of you and me on the cheapest rates of minimum wage possible to look after the maximum number of children they could possibly cram into their for-profit enterprise. Often, these minimum-wage workers ended up in these jobs by default. Failed by inappropriate schooling, the vital role of "carer" is degraded to something anyone can do if they can't do anything else. Inadequately trained, paid and valued, these teenagers who used to be the toddlers who looked at the world with love and expectation in the hope that the world would respond likewise, now, having been failed by their world, mind other people's toddlers so their parents can pursue careers and their bosses can make a very nice little profit, thank you very much.

Such a stupid, unimaginative and heartless way to treat these children.

The common mistake, of course, is to pretend that it is the children who are stupid, unintelligent. Since 1988, government policy toward the child has enshrined this mistake as a central organising principle in all of its legislation. The national curriculum's highly instructional teaching and learning model confuses the child's lack of experience with a lack of intelligence. Children have a naturally active intelligence that embraces experience, which they then reflect upon, learn from and make part of their understanding. Children are busy, active learners from birth, developing both knowledge and understanding and their individual characteristic skills, aptitudes and enthusiasms. Consider how much learning a young child gets through. Consider how quickly children learn—decode, make sense of, make their own—the languages of the variety of experiences they are encountering. Consider how difficult most adults find it to learn additional languages. Children have a much more active intelligence than most adults; the proper role of the more experienced adult should be to ensure that the child's experiences are as supported and conducive to the functioning of that child's intelligence as possible and to identify and encourage the development of the child's individual enthusiasms and particular skills, as keys to accessing as wide a range of further knowledge and skills as possible. Adults confuse their own relatively greater experience with superiority. Adults use this differential to assume roles of authority. But just as being trained to pass tests is in itself a meaningless index of anything other than a particular performance in a particular test, so accumulated experience is in itself a meaningless index unless it is used to positive effect. When adults assume automatic authority over children, this is often to the benefit of their own self-image rather than being of any benefit to the child.

Children benefit most in the process of applying their intelligence to their experiences and developing their individual skills, enthusiasms and attributes if they are supported by a positive environment offering a range of positive experiences and positive adult interaction, where the adult's experience enables them to smooth or facilitate or accelerate a child's access to learning and development.

This is why society evolved the concept of education and institutions dedicated specifically to learning, from kindergartens to universities.

Unfortunately, because, in practice, schooling is circumscribed by the weighted class nature of the political organisation of society in the UK, all too often children go to school to learn how to become stupid.

How else would you describe a system that tests five- and six-year-olds on their phonics skills and compounds the stupefaction by making them decode nonsense "pseudo"-words alongside real words? Where is there any *sense* or *meaning* in this? What is the point of making children learn what is pointless and meaningless?

This paradox has become more pronounced, as over the last thirty years the system of education experienced by the majority of our children has been subjected to the determined recuperation programme of the reformers. Learning about sines and cosines was pretty meaningless to me, and I am not sure there is any point to me having once known the sequence, names and fates of Henry VIII's six wives. However, learning about language by learning how to pass tests by decoding "brip" and "snorb" seems to me to deliberately exclude all point and meaning from the language of learning.

Them that's got shall get, them that's not, shall get tested on their phonics.

And the majority of those tested shall be failed too, because tests are really only intended to find out what the child doesn't know and can't do. They don't want to know about, let alone celebrate, all the amazing *stuff* the child might know and does do.

Franz Has Got a Plan

We're walking by the water, the waves move like the sea.
We're looking for a corner, I'm holding half a tree
Franz found in the water, like the red stone in his hand.
I don't know what I'm doing, but Franz has got a plan.

Franz has drawn the whole world, details he leaves to me,
The place where he plays football, the place we found the
  tree.
I draw Bad Frankenhausen, the zoo and Eng-er-land.
He may be only five years old, but Franz has got a plan.

He doesn't plan to be that old man who sits and shouts at
  his TV,
"You don't know what you're doing, referee".

Meanwhile outside our window, the gutters fill with stars.
Your satnav only tells you how lost you really are.
We don't know what we're doing, but we do the best we
  can.
I don't call this intelligent design, but Franz has got a
  plan. . .

Playfulness

Childhood is playhood.
—A.S. Neill

So far we have looked a lot at the ways in which the current conditions of schooling fail to meet the needs of the child and have also noted examples of how within the wider context of current social conditions the needs of many children are not being met by society. Perhaps if we considered what it is that would constitute an adequate response to the needs of children, as they move out of the small world of the family into the larger social world of the school, we would be able to hypothesise an environment that would not fail children. We might even use the characteristics of that environment to effectively reconstruct society to better meet the needs of both children and adults alike.

We have already identified the obvious importance of love and attachment. It is important that the child's positive attitude to the world be reciprocated by the world's positive attitude to the child. As A.S. Neill formulated it in *The Problem Teacher*: "The good teacher not only understands the child: he approves of the child".[1] Freire extends the importance of reciprocity to make it a central feature of good practice, with his insistence that education is a dialogue: "the teacher is no longer merely the-one-who-teaches, but one who is himself being taught in dialogue with the students, who in turn while being taught also teach. They become jointly responsible for a process in which all grow".[2]

The young child's learning is always a dialogue. At first the child engages in "lone" play, where the interaction, the dialogue, is between the child's senses and intelligence and the environment and its profusion of objects and sensory experiences. This solitary exploration of the immediate manifestations of an infinite universe is an important initial dialogue where the environment is a mirror that allows children to begin to define their uniqueness, to recognise the features of who they are and who they might become (and from time to time we all benefit from spiralling back to this moment, so beloved of classic film noir, where—as the private investigator lost in our own mystery—we confront and examine our image in a looking glass). The child then discovers their play is greatly enhanced, once it is shared with and is inclusive of others, once it becomes a reciprocating dialogue, a conversation. Others often give us the clues and the evidence leading to revelations we haven't yet managed to uncover.

Russian psychologist Lev Vygotsky, in attempting to analyse the constituents of "play," asserted that play has two essential components, imagination and rules. I am not sure "rules" is the correct word; I think "narrative" is a better description of the way young children understand play. A baby playing with those brightly coloured plastic objects that tend to get dangled above its head (or indeed playing with the natural objects some adults see as ideologically preferable) understands what happens as cause and effect, a consequence, essentially a simple two-part story. As children develop their autonomy along with their fine and gross motor skills, play becomes more prolonged and complex. As children learn to produce vocal sounds, they soundtrack their play. As language develops, children narrate and verbalise their play. My understanding of rules in play is that rules are always provisional and malleable to the *imagination* of the child and the intervention of other imaginations. Terms of play—rules—are generally in constant flux, subject to revision; it is the narrative that is the constant element. Anything can happen, and when anything does happen it is accommodated by narrative. As children become older, play becomes more formalised, and—like a game of chess—there are rules that limit the possibilities of narrative development. But unlike chess, interpersonal play is always amenable to negotiation, which will be accommodated by a change in narrative. Adults do this as well; their interpersonal interactions are also the province of imagination and narration that are reimagined in the retelling.

The significant element to children engaging in dialogue with the wider world is that although children are learning through their explorations and imaginations and their revisits and rehearsals, they are not dividing their activities into play or work. Work is a label they learn from adults, usually to describe an imposition, an activity forced upon you by someone else. This imposition, whereby learning is not owned by the children but directed by adult authority, replicates the classic description of the condition of alienation experienced by workers under capitalism, where you have no say or control over what your activity is made to produce. Carrying the analogy further, one could argue that since "reform" initiatives like the imposed curriculum and the publication of test results in league tables, children now endure a permanent state of alienation, not just because of their lack of agency over their learning, which has become imposed "work", but because what they produce is of more benefit to the institution, the school's standing and the head teacher's reputation than it is to the producer. The school enjoys the fruits of their labour more than the labourers themselves do. The number of parents who will testify that their child "used to enjoy school" but no longer does proves the validity of this analysis.

The anthropologist Pierre Clastres sees this concept of "work", something that is imposed upon you, and something that produces "surplus", something you the worker neither need nor enjoy, as a consequence of how European society has developed: "Two axioms seem to have guided the advance of Western civilisation from the outset: the first maintains that true societies unfold in the protective shadow of the state; the second states a categorical imperative; man must work".[3] We can see the overshadow of both the state and the imperative to produce as clear characteristics of current schooling. According to the *Guardian* newspaper, the average age for the onset of depression was forty-five in the 1960s but by 2016 it was fourteen. NUT general secretary Kevin Courtney wrote in a 2018 Facebook posting:

> School is now cited as the main cause of stress for 65 per cent of twelve-year-olds and 82 per cent of sixteen-year-olds. Natasha Devon, the ex–child mental health tzar, sacked for telling the truth about over-testing, reports that academic anxiety now tops the list of young people's worries, replacing bullying, higher than social media and body image concerns.

Courtney goes on to cite the 2017 GCSE maths test as an example of how the government's testing culture fails both children and their learning in every respect and is a major cause of mental health issues for children:

> Who can be surprised when many teenagers who got the equivalent of a C grade in their Maths GCSE last year scored just 17 per cent. The government made the tests much harder but did practically no preparation. To make it look OK to parents, they ensured that roughly the same number of candidates as last year got the equivalent of A*, A, B, C etc. So the mark equivalent to a C was seventeen marks out of a hundred on a paper. The government tells us you got a C, but they put you through a paper where you got 83 per cent wrong. How do you feel?

So looked at objectively, the way schools are currently run means they are unhealthy environments, antithetical both to learning and well-being. If we look at how young children's learning functions, learning that is not and has not yet been conditioned by somebody else's imposition of expected outcomes, we discover learning behaviour that is appropriate to the individual's needs and therefore the individual's well-being. Young children are fantastically successful learners; in the first five years of life, they have already learned motor skills, communication skills, and—with their brains 90 per cent fully developed—they will have learned how to be who they are, developing both consciousness and identity. This learning is the result of an innate active drive to explore and decode, the result of a delight in objects and experiences and the combination of action and reflection that ascribes meaning, makes connections and sorts, orders and arrives at understanding. Children are in dialogue with their environment; children establish relationships with their environment. Dialogue and relationship with others, particularly significant adults, greatly assists children's learning. The very best way to encourage the very best learning is by sensitive supportive engagement in children's explorations and reflections, by the right question at the right time, as well as by the right silence at the right time.

Children need to find things out for themselves and talk their ideas through. Children need to be allowed to play with reality and come to their own conclusions by testing their ideas in dialogue. Children need to be allowed to pursue their own interests in their own style—we know that biologically young children move, because they have to. They also rationalise and irrationalise, because intellectually they are equally animated by an energy that is part of their species condition. When they can do these things, their learning is secure, because it has been—all along the process—owned and meaningful rather than imposed, and their identity is secure, because it has been developed from within rather than imposed from without.

Adults can be significant partners in these processes.

The adult's significant role as "the other" when engaging in this playfulness with young children is to use their greater experience of interactions to enable children to move from exclusive solitary explorations into situations of dialogue (but adults also need to be able to recognise that sometimes children need solitary play, that children need everybody else to tactfully leave them to it, because, by and large, children do what they do, because they feel they need to do it).

Adults are most effective being in dialogue with rather than driving the play and the dialogue themselves. Being generally larger and stronger than young children, albeit nowhere near as energetic, adults can be effective supporters of learning and development by taking responsibility for ensuring that the children's environment is organised to meet their learning needs and maximises their learning opportunities (meeting children's needs not the adult's—this means going out in the rain and a lot of other places adults don't necessarily think they want to go, but which usually prove to be a lot of fun once you get there—that is the reciprocal part of the interaction). Also, adults need to learn to shut up. To be truly effective partners in dialogue, adults need to learn to stop always wanting to be right. Adults need to stop telling children what they think the answer ought to be.

The anecdotal account of Charlie playing in the mud that starts this book is referenced as a typical play event by A.S. Neill in *Summerhill* and used as an exemplar for what constitutes good practice. Although Neill can be a little confined by some of his contemporary attitudes (don't pick up a copy of *Summerhill* hoping for enlightening views on gender and race, for example), he is generally very sound on the importance of autonomy and self-regulation in terms of child development and learning:

> If a teacher sees children playing with mud, and he thereupon improves the shining moment by holding forth about river bank erosion, what end has he in view? What child cares about river erosion? Many so-called educators believe that it does not matter what a

child learns as long as he is taught something. And of course, with schools as they are—just mass-production factories—what can a teacher do but teach something and come to believe that teaching, in itself, matters most of all?[4]

That playfulness—exploration, reflection = dialectics!—and dialogue and supportive intervention within a rich, stimulating and supportive environment are the essentials of successful learning is demonstrated by the fact that, generally, the Early Years pedagogy is perceived as successful in scaffolding learning in formal schooling situations. Practitioners in the UK have always taken issue with the government's insistence on initiating more formal learning for children at the age of five, whereas most other countries, ironically largely with education systems *not* constantly being accused by government of "failing", consider the kindergarten stage of play-based learning that prioritises the development of social skills as something that ought to continue until the age of seven. Despite the largely welcome introduction of the Early Years Foundation Stage (EYFS) curriculum in 2006, practitioners often have to all but fist off the unwelcome attentions of school assessment coordinators who, having surrendered their professional integrity in the face of right-wing obsessions with testing, think that the best way to bump the school up the league tables is to make children read and write as soon as they skip happily through the school gates, by making them sit down quietly and do lots of reading and writing, when, developmentally, the children's learning priorities are elsewhere, to say the least. Again, the US provides us with an unattractive unadorned illustration of what happens when you have a system that wants to test children in the Early Years. Educationalist Nancy Carlsson-Paige writes:

> In recent years I have sat in classrooms where four-year-olds, who should be actively engaged in play-based,

hands-on learning, are sitting on chairs parroting back answers to teachers who are using a scripted curriculum that is aligned with tests. I have seen principals who enter kindergarten classes unannounced to make sure the teacher is teaching from the exact page of the curriculum at the exact right moment.[5]

In the UK, the play-based, hands-on learning and broad-based cross-curricular EYFS was proving such an effective way of supporting children's learning, that, by 2010, there were plans to continue its organisational features and its fundamental implicit child development pedagogy upward through the whole primary age range. Unfortunately, the election in 2010 allowed Cameron's toffs to weasel their way into power with the support of the Liberal Democrats (LibDems), and that put a stop to all that. It also put a pretty effective stop to the idea of further education for all, by hiking up student loans and student fees, something Nick Clegg leader of the LibDems, by this point deputy prime minister, had assured the electorate the LibDems were absolutely and categorically in principled opposition to.

The example of the general success of Early Years education has significant implications both for the subsequent stages of the school system and for the organisation of society as a whole. A successful model for social organisation, then, is one where individuals within it have ownership of their actions, and where their energies and priorities are recognised and reflected in their constructed environment, which facilitates their exploration and reflection, their learning and their sense of well-being. Learning and well-being are further supported by dialogue with adults, those whose age and experience—not expressed unhelpfully as intelligence or hierarchical position—means they have certain functions of organisational responsibility.

The characteristics of "reform"—imposition, testing, hierarchy, outcome, overproduction, alienation—have no place in this environment. My experience as a teacher of eleven-year-olds leads me to believe the values of successful Early Years education can indeed be translated appropriately for children throughout their schooling. My experience as a teacher of five-year-olds, however, leads me to believe these values need to be translated appropriately not only for children in schools but for people throughout society. These values need to be the reference points that describe the basis for the transformation of society, because these values, the values of playfulness and dialogue, are naturally and manifestly essential to the fundamental well-being of the human animal. "People mutht be amuthed", insists circus owner Sleary in rebuke to the utilitarian Gradgrind in *Hard Times*.[6]

The irrational yet characteristic human need for delight and enjoyment is a significant casualty of the model of "growing up" favoured by mass schooling.

> The genuinely positive social relations (those of cooperation, sharing, and aiding) prevalent in childhood are to be made distinct from the spectacle's vulgar interpretation/presentation: synthetic friendships, stories that applaud hierarchy and heroism, and adventures that only amount to transparent celluloid. We seek collectively to live out our dreams, while they seek to keep us stationary and entertained with cheap imitation thereof.[7]

What's the point in being taught how to grow up, if being "grown up" means there isn't any fun any more, or, rather, what fun there is to be had isn't really "yours" any more, just something somebody else makes up and sells you? We do grow, we get bigger, our stories become more complex, but maybe instead of thinking we are growing up in some outcome-related lineal model of progress, we should concentrate on spiralling outward, revisiting our narratives from different perspectives, reimagining possibilities and impossibilities, touching base with our previous selves and our previous insights, dreams and sundry other touchstones and retaining our capacity for delight, as we travel onward and circle outward.

A random unrelated observation of delight in action: my experience is, when young children build with bricks, and the building process is organised primarily by energy that is—on the gender spectrum—principally male, the bricks go up and up and up, with great endeavour and ambition, with children clambering on chairs and tables and stretching to put another brick on the tower, getting me to put more bricks on top of the tower—and then, somehow, it all falls down, we all laugh and clap with delight, and then we start again, and the process is repeated, only maybe this time the tower doesn't just somehow fall down, this time someone knocks it down, and the process repeats with increasing negotiation about when the knocking down happens and who does the knocking down. It is . . . great fun. When the building process is organised principally by energy that is—on the gender spectrum—primarily female, the bricks tend to go outward more than upward, and sometimes they even develop into constructions that represent functions, and there is a great delight in narrative, imagination, reflection and negotiation here too.

I always found that really interesting. And I delighted in being part of both types of play, and sometimes you even got both types of building going on at the same time. That did require a bit more negotiation, engaging ambition with imagination, laughter with reflection, balancing creation with destruction and recreation. But, hey, no one ever said it was going to be easy at the cutting edge of social progress.

James Dean and Sameena

James Dean loves Sameena, Sameena loves James Dean.
They both do lunch together and paint each other green.
They both like riding big bikes, they both hate unifix.
They'll marry when they're all grown up, or later when
    they're six.

Sameena wears an eye patch. Dad likes her brother best.
Dean wears his brother's old coat and chews and sucks his
    vest.
Dean's favourite game was doggies, till Sammy said, "Stand
    up".
Now, she makes me playdough dinners, and James Dean
    does the washing up.

When Warren throws a wobbler, Dean says, "My dad has
    moods".
Sam says ,"Mum says I'm Muslim, so books with pigs are
    rude".
Dean's dad don't like Diwali, but what Dean understands
Is, in English or Bengali, he likes to hold Sam's hand.

With me, her name was Carol. She had the whitest hair.
We looked all round the classroom cos God was
    everywhere.
We never did get married, not like how we planned.
We never found God either, but we held a lot of hands.

PART FIVE

GOOD PRACTICE

The Kreuzberg Sisters

Otto thinks he'll stop the rain
His thoughts are iron hard
He calculates the times of trains
And builds a house of cards
And when the rain falls anyway
Otto can't think why
But the Kreuzberg sisters catch the rain
One drop at a time

Adolph wants to build a wall
To keep the sparrows out
He orders snowflakes not to fall
And beer and sauerkraut
When the snow falls everywhere
Adolph can't think why
While the Kreuzberg sisters know the names
Of each bird in the sky

These old men raise an empty glass
To wars they never won
They say beneath my golden arse
You'll find the shining sun
And while they try to find their flutes
And both boots in the dark
The Kreuzberg sisters take their children
Playing in the park

And sure enough, step by step, taking half a chance
One by one and two by two, it turns into a dance

These sisters catch the Berlin trains
These sisters don't let go
They gather up the fallen rain
The sparrows and the snow

They make fresh coffee every day,
You old men say goodbye,
The Kreuzberg sisters turn the world round
One step at a time

A Brief Word about Best Practice

I was considering titling this part of the text "Best Practice", but then thought: accepting this idea of a constant rigorously paced drive toward superlatives is accepting the state's values and ideology, as well as accepting the triumph of the state's other great weapon of social control, the tabloid media's degradation of language. Now, "good" just isn't good enough. The idea of excellence carries with it an implicit hierarchy of value, while the overuse of superlatives renders language imprecise and judgements meaningless, intelligence-cleansing our social discourse of nuance and complexity. It might look like we've had nuance and complexity hammered out of us by the time we reach our late teens, but when you look at us when we start out, kindergartens are overflowing with nuance and complexity—and diversity.

There is also an implicit suggestion of uniformity, of conformity about the notion of "best" practice. If "best practice" can be identified and described, then a logical consequence would be that all teaching should conform to that model of education. But teaching ought to be about so much more than any systematised programme could ever describe. Teaching—education—is not like assembling flat-pack furniture or making a model aeroplane or following a recipe that promises to make an immaculate lemon meringue pie. It should be more than simply following the instructions.

Education happens because of the interaction between individuals. Individuals are a lot more complicated that flat-pack furniture, model aeroplanes or lemon meringue pies. Indeed, generally we have come to the understanding that the outward manifestation of that complexity, human diversity, is a good thing. Generally, when we look at the eco-systems that work well on this godforsaken lump of rock we find ourselves inhabiting, we have come to the understanding that, again, diversity is preferable to uniformity. So in terms of education, we understand that there is a diversity of learning styles and that different individual learners respond with differing degrees of engagement and understanding according to their particular learning style propensity. Effective teaching needs to take this into account but should not ignore the fact that teachers—educators—are diverse individuals with a suitably diverse range of skills and enthusiasms. Our old friends, the incontrovertible generalities of accountability and equality, are frequently employed by managers to insist teachers accept a particular "best practice" (usually nothing the teachers themselves have evolved) and apply it relentlessly in order to meet "the child's entitlement". The best way of force-feeding everybody the same centrally defined and politically determined curriculum according to a centrally defined and politically determined methodology is not, of course, the same as an entitlement to education.

Teachers—like children—work best when they are enthused by what they are teaching. To convey the idea that it is possible to feel passionate about what one learns, rather than to feel it is a means to the end of getting yourself a good job, teachers need to be able to operate as individuals, enthusiastic about a diversity of particulars. Their professionalism ensures they address all areas of learning, but their individuality ensures they also communicate the possibilities of enthusiasm and expertise. So there will be a diversity of good practice, and "best practice" ought to treasure and encourage that diversity.

The Road to Neverland

In 1978, for various reasons, I did a year of study for a Postgraduate Certificate in Education (PGCE). I was looking on this as possibly something to do until undertaking some postgraduate English literature study, while waiting for the songwriting career to take off. . .

It seemed like quite a good idea at the time. As a student in the 1970s, I would get a grant and play guitar a lot too. After three years studying English literature at Sussex University, I realised I was probably—again for various reasons—unlikely to be going back to selling carpets or cleaning the toilets at the Hounslow Co-operative's delightfully dysfunctional department store. Besides, after having worked as a teacher (untrained) for two summers in local authority–run schools for recently arrived East African refugees and troublesome indigenous characters who were better off if they were kept off Hounslow's streets for as much of the summer holidays as possible, I was surprised to find myself of the opinion that teaching was a pretty useful and socially positive thing to do: a good way of repaying my debt to society. The fascist National Front had regular stalls outside Holy Trinity Church on Hounslow High Street, with people queuing up to sign petitions about hanging muggers. (I asked if there was one I could sign in favour of hanging Nazis). During the two summer schools we somehow managed to create small worlds where Asian kids and dodgy white kids had a good time together and found out they had a lot more in common than they had expected.

The classroom seemed like a good space where good things could happen. I said as much in my interview at West London Institute of Higher Education: education was a good way to combat racism, and that was why I wanted to be a teacher. The lecturer who had previously been half-heartedly conducting the interview suddenly woke up and almost choked on the sandwich he was eating. "We don't say that sort of thing any more", he explained condescendingly. Playing guitar always looked like a lot more fun, obviously.

I finally gave up the day job when I hit sixty at the end of 2015, after thirty-five years of doing something to do that I had inadvertently soon come to feel very passionate about. I joke that teaching is like heroin; you think you can handle it, but it really screws you up. Or: if you bump somebody off you only get sentenced to fifteen years. I am still waiting for the songwriting career to take off, and because the pension is not the gold-plated guarantee of a life of ease the *Daily Heil* would have you believe it is, I still reluctantly sometimes do supply teaching in an attempt to stave off complete financial catastrophe. Teaching, even in the Early Years, is nowhere near as much fun as it used to be, and supply teacher rates, once the agency has taken its cut, are ridiculously low, but it does remind me that despite all the amputations (to quote Uncle Lou Reed), when you work with five-year-olds you are working with human beings at their best, and human beings at their best are just wonderful.

Things are so bad that I actually get better rates of pay playing guitar now than I do supply teaching. Nonetheless, I often think that it has been through working as a teacher rather than through playing guitar and writing and singing songs that I have been the more effective at changing, however insignificantly, the world for the better.

My dad, Ronald Walter Johnson, generally toward the bottom of the class at secondary school in the 1930s, then a pre-war solicitor's clerk, then an RAF navigator making complex dead reckoning calculations whenever the radar failed in order to get his mates and their special operations Liberator to where they were supposed to be and safely back home again, took the opportunity offered by the expansion of state education as part of the creation of the welfare state to train as a teacher, much to his family's surprise, I imagine. He proved to be an excellent teacher. Ex-pupil Clive Boursnell wrote: "No other teacher engaged with us kids as he did, not only did he teach facts but he taught us to *think. Thinking and working things out* was his inbuilt creed, all dished up on the biggest spoon of Love". When I started secondary school in 1966, my dad started working as a head teacher. And much to my surprise I also started work as a teacher thirty-three years after my dad did, for the London Borough of Hounslow, in September 1980. This was three years after Callaghan's inauguration of the Great Debate about education, with the ghost of William Tyndall School hovering like an awful warning in the background.

I am proud to say that Ron took me along to my first union meeting. The hall was packed. My dad pointed out the political radicals like Dave Sharp, who worked in "a special school", whose ideas, according to my dad, were best avoided. These leftist firebrands all nonetheless chatted to my dad with comradely affection and respect. My dad, possibly through both experience and temperament, favoured the politics of the post-war consensus, a common-sense socialism that generally put its faith in parliamentary democracy and local government authority. I have to say, I usually found the more radical arguments more pertinent when it came to formulating policy under and against the Tories. Ron retired two years later, and so was spared the first-hand witness of what the reformers did to his life's work. Who would have imagined when I started work that the "reformers" would eventually be so successful at normalising the unthinkable that the bad old days of payment by results, something my dad particularly snorted at, would come back to plague us dressed up in the slimy euphemisms of "performance management"? For a while, Ron refused to countenance the idea that Thatcher's agenda intended and was successful in inflicting serious, lasting damage to the achievements of state education, and to society in general. It was the very success of the welfare state generation of educators and their successors, like it was the success of the miners in bringing down the Heath government, that provoked such a determined and ruthless backlash.

In 1980, most of the primary schools in Hounslow were doing pretty much the same sort of decently caring job they had been doing when I had been attending one of them as a pupil over fifteen years previously. Radical education was something generally associated with schools in the Inner London Education Authority (ILEA). I was particularly fortunate, however, in that I happened by accident to get my first job in Hounslow's one and only flagship progressive lib-ed school.

Andrew Ewing Primary School, named after a local councillor who had devoted his life to the service of the people of Hounslow, was opened in 1973 by Tam Dalyell, later to be known as something of a radical Labour MP. It was purpose-built, open-plan, bright with big windows and pale yellow bricks in a snazzy honeycomb arrangement of octagonal shapes, with vertically grouped children and team-teaching teachers. It was known as the "do as you like" school, because children chose when they did what they had been assigned to do. Children were allowed to develop enthusiasms and become experts by focussing on their interests and to explore their learning at their own pace. Although they were encouraged to complete all their assignments, it was understood that simple coverage is the antithesis of genuine learning. And they moved about quite a bit. And, of course, we didn't have a school uniform. It was just brilliant: inspirational on all levels. So I was lucky to have had the opportunity to work in a radical environment that was committed to finding ways to benefit the development of each individual child, socially, emotionally and intellectually and to experience how effective a child-centred pedagogy can be—and how much fun too.

Andrew Ewing school's purpose-built, open-plan design facilitated cooperation and movement. The staff employed there when it opened were all committed to the progressive pedagogy the design encouraged, and, moreover, they were reflective and open-minded practitioners concerned to refine and improve their school's educational provision. What they *weren't* was a collection of politicised radicals. The junior head teacher was a welfare state socialist, but the staff were generally conscientious middle-class professionals, more radical in pedagogy than politics. It was a place you really ought to want to work; you probably needed to want to work in a team and without walls rather than expect to have your "own" classroom like the one you experienced as a child. I suppose it was an index of how rare such teachers still were at the end of the 1970s that I got employed there in the first place, as I had no such ambitions and commitments and really wasn't sure I wanted to get a job back in Hounslow anyway. Having been trained in middle school education and having failed spectacularly to get even an interview for a post as a English teacher in a middle school (one establishment suggested I learn to spell "limited" properly before applying anywhere else), I felt I had no choice but to get the train back down from Manchester, where I had been happily contemplating the possibilities of a vague career playing the area's abundant folk clubs, until my domestic arrangements insisted I get a proper job instead. So I returned to Hounslow where I had been offered an interview for a job in a junior school.

Reluctantly, I turned up on time at Hounslow Civic Centre for what I thought would be an interview. Not possessing a tie, I had resorted to a turquoise turtleneck sweater. It was a very warm July day, long past the usual date when school vacancies were filled for the next autumn term. Instead of an interview, the primary adviser Jean Evans explained that Andrew Ewing School needed someone as a matter of urgency for September to be a maths specialist for six- and seven-year-olds. I was a bit disconcerted, as, having just done an MA in Victorian literature, I felt that English (provided I avoided the tricky bits like spelling the word "limited") was my strongpoint. The head teacher would be formally interviewing me, Jean said. I was already working out my escape route. I explained that I had been trained in middle school education (even though there weren't any middle schools for miles around, certainly not in the London Borough of Hounslow) and so knew nothing what-soever about teaching six- and seven-year-olds. Furthermore, I added, I didn't really like maths. Jean nodded sympathetically. "Well, just go and have a look. If you don't like it, don't do the interview", she added reasonably. Feeling increasingly uncom-fortable in my turtle neck sweater but reassured that all I had to do was say no, I duly made my way to Heston. At the school office, I explained that I had been sent there about a job. The secretary called up the head, the indefatigable force of nature that was Irene Beach, who promptly appeared looking both energetic and mildly flustered, like she was "in the middle of something else", and who equally promptly threw her arms wide, suddenly beamed an infectious smile and declared, "Ah! Our new maths teacher! Come and meet your new class".

Somehow, I couldn't say no, particularly when she enthu-siastically introduced me to the children as "your new teacher", as if they couldn't possibly wish for anything better, this side of Father Christmas, than a new teacher in an inappropriate turquoise roll-neck sweater. Some of the children looked at me a little suspiciously, but generally they looked like they would give me the benefit of the doubt on Mrs Beach's rec-ommendation. Natasha and Sarah, already inseparable and supremely impervious to and dismissive of adults at the age of six, giggled, clearly unimpressed on principle. Natasha recently said "hello" via social media. She wrote: "Still great friends with Sarah, despite her living in the Cotswolds and me living in Hampshire! With eight children between us we don't manage to meet up more than a couple of times a year. . . . I remember teasing you on your first day because you wore a knitted tie! It's weird what you remember!!"

This was, of course, a very long time ago. No one gets jobs like that now, turquoise roll-neck or not.

Of course, Andrew Ewings weren't popping up like bluebells and primroses on every corner of the landscape of state education. More than most schools, Andrew Ewing was aware of the "awful warning" of William Tyndale. But after three years of "Sunny Jim's" Great Debating it felt like all that had been achieved was the unleashing of a quantity of wind and pontification that had apparently, so far, led nowhere in particular. Only in hindsight does it look like it simply opened the door for Baker's Great Education Reform Bill (GERBill). Meanwhile, despite the particular catastrophe of Tyndale, those ideas were still steadily percolating into the water supply. The revolution of everyday life was no longer the property and province of subculture, pop culture or Situationist theory: as well as the ambitions of the militant political revolutionary challenges—strikes, the Angry Brigade—schools were steadily effecting a social revolution of everyday life through comprehensive education and the application of progressive pedagogy to the state system.

Andrew Ewing was where I first realised Neverland was a possibility. I learned something I hadn't really noticed before; I learned that children were intelligent and independent, that reason works better than rules, and that adults work better by cooperating than by pretending they know and do everything on their own. I later learned that there are actually different ways to get to Neverland, because there are different environments and different circumstances where you have to locate Neverland. I also learned that often Neverland, because of the circumstances likely to be operating against it, can only be temporary. But pretty much all this learning came about through working in cooperation with other people, both colleagues and children. So really, these ideas are the product of lived experience and applied reflection, a dialectical process, rather than the result of research or critical reading. I was initially perplexed when PM Press suggested I add a bibliography.

As a teacher, the last thing I had wanted to do when not working was to read someone else's ideas about teaching. But in the course of writing and rewriting this book, I found myself not just fact-checking details on Wikipedia but also reading books that explored more fully some of the thoughts I found I had accumulated by experience. I read A.S. Neill properly for the first time and Paolo Freire for the first time. Paolo led me to Henri Lefebvre, and I realised through playing with their ideas about work and play I was continuing that lifelong learning journey educationalists now like to talk about. I found *No! Against Adult Supremacy* on a bookstall at the Tolpuddle Festival, in July 2018,[1] and was happy to see that lib-ed was alive and kicking in the twenty-first century . . . a friend of my son leant me Kozol's *Savage Inequalities*.[2] Then I found Chris Searle's autobiography in Brick Lane Bookshop and reconnected with the writing of someone whose activism and commitment to poetry I had long admired.

Thinking about it, I only learned that it was Neverland we would be talking about after all in my last year of working as a full-time teacher. It is the last hill that shows you all the valley. We were in the nursery. Ducklings Class had a real team-working ethos. For the adult team, there was variously Alex, Charlotte, Ella, Fiona, Gill, Sandra, Tara and me. For the children's team, there were the usual living legends too numerous to mention individually by name. It was Alex, however, who knew exactly who we were. We were, she said—collectively, children and adults—the People's Republic of Neverland. And so thanks to compañera Alex Brown, I now can give a name to and describe properly and exactly what I have really been doing in my thirty-five years of working as a teacher, and what this book is finally about.

Some Songs of Experience

Landing by accident in Andrew Ewing School, that infamous hotbed of progressive schooling in the London Borough of Hounslow, I have to admit that, for a while, I fell into the habit of vanguardist thinking prevalent among some of my colleagues, that Andrew Ewing represented the very cutting edge of educational progress, and so was the very paradigm of "best practice". Best practice, we thought, was therefore exclusively described by the characteristics that distinguished Andrew Ewing School from its neighbours. Best practice was open-plan, team-teaching, vertically grouped and committed body and soul to the concept of a child-centred education. It wasn't until I went off to see the world in 1987 in the capacity of a London Borough of Hounslow supply team teacher that I realised that good practice wasn't only the province of open-plan, team-teaching, vertically grouped and committed body and soul to the concept of a child-centred education. Indeed, while I did my best to interpret the principles of cooperation and child-centred education in classrooms and schools that had been constructed long before anybody had ever thought of open-plan learning environments and cooperative teaching, I also appreciated how important the physical reality of the environment is in facilitating or inhibiting education.

In my subsequent travels, I worked with colleagues who aspired to be inspirational within the confines of traditional classroom organisation. I also worked with colleagues who either metaphorically or literally were intent on sledgehammering away the structural inhibitions inherited with traditional schooling structures and traditional classroom organisation. But it was also obvious that a lot of good practice and good education was happening in places that had been built more in accordance with Victorian specifications than in accordance with post-war education radicalism. Although not always an insurmountable problem, the physical reality of the school's building conditions practice, and the existing economic reality of levels of funding limit options and possibilities for changing these conditions.

As a fairly typical example, the last school I worked in was built in the 1930s. It was an elongated L shape, originally with classrooms opening off a corridor that was open to the elements, with toilets situated unhelpfully at either end of the L. The corridor was eventually covered over, presumably as part of the post-war nanny state's pampering of the working class, and the air raid shelters were firmly blocked off when someone fell into one by accident. At some point, two temporary classrooms were tacked on at the end of the longer corridor, access to both involving another bit of covered corridor that was all stairs and steps, which had to be negotiated by children wishing to use the toilets, creating dead spaces both on the stairs, up the stairs and round the corner by the toilets, and dead space between the "temporary" classrooms that when I arrived generally served no purpose other than to offer opportunities for any child wishing to avoid adult supervision for the purposes of negative manifestations of imitations of unreconstructed patriarchy or bourgeois individualism. These were used to accommodate the reception classes, and despite regular occurrences of children injuring themselves falling up and down the stairs, particularly when it rained (the tarmac nursery outdoor area, being above the level of the dead space between the two huts, would leak pools of water through the brick walls into the dead space due to blocked drains), local authority health and safety bureaucrats repeatedly declared it fit for purpose for four- and five-year-olds, and so refused to give the school any money to do anything to make the space easier to negotiate. At the time, the generally laudable Early Years Foundation Stage (EYFS) legislation rightly made it a legal duty for schools to provide a positive, enabling learning environment, where children, rightly, have access to an outdoor learning environment—which we did. What the legislation didn't do, of course, was provide any funding to make sure these good intentions became a safe and secure bricks and mortar, grass and trees reality. So we had to make do with creative imagination that relied heavily on what we could scrounge—old tyres, beer bottle crates, palettes and an old piano. One hut was plagued by foxes living—and dying, and subsequently noxiously decomposing—under it and a roof that was too heavy, necessitating relocating that class of children to the school library for two terms while the walls were reinforced. As the school became more popular with local parents, successfully marketing itself as a small, child-centred establishment, the library disappeared, the space being needed for an extra classroom. The last Office for Standards in Education (Ofsted) report I experienced there was very positive, the only point of criticism being that the school lacked a library.

One of the many great falsehoods perpetrated by the "reformers" and imposed upon practitioners is that a failure to subscribe to their politicised notions of excellence is a failure to aspire to quality in the practice of state education. The intention in writing this is not to deny a faith in the possibilities of education but to restate that any faith is not in the state's agenda but in the tradition of libertarian education. Good practice is classroom practice located within the historical process of the people's struggle to "make a difference" to the conditions of their lives. In the Neverlands we are about to pass through, the values of "making a difference" through meaningful learning will be the good practice common to all.

The People's Republic of Neverland
(Or the Anti Childhood Tax Federation)

So here are some anecdotes of my experience of effective good practice. I reiterate that good practice, a bit like punk rock, is never about following fashions or expecting there to be a magic formula or a one-size-fits-all blueprint. It is all about attitude and a dynamic engagement with all the elements and realities of your environment. There are no rules. . . Well, no, there is one rule, which is more properly really a value, which I think we should come back to again later, best expressed for me by Deryck Whibley, guitarist and biggest ego in the post-punk metal band Sum 41, one of the greatest "coulda been a contender" bands you could think of. As Southampton Civic Hall, clearly not really acoustically designed to cope with the particular sonic frequencies favoured by post-punk metal, resounded to the frenetic clang, thud and rumble of Sum 41, and as half a hall full of post-punk metalhead Hampshire youth threw themselves enthusiastically at the stage and each other, Deryck and the band threw a pause, and in that frozen moment, Deryck uttered the immortal golden rule: "Hey, no one gets hurt, right?" He let the words hang for a couple of seconds in the silence, then threw a shape and whacked a chord out on his trademark Tele Deluxe, and at the same split-second moment the rest of the band piled in too and the clang, thud and rumble and mayhem and delight continued unabated, and no one got hurt.

Or, as A.S. Neill put it, "Each individual is free to do what he likes *as long as he is not trespassing on the freedom of others*".

The gender-specific pronouns aside, I am encouraged in my own beliefs when he adds, "And this is a realisable aim in any community".[1]

So let's start with my first experience of good practice, at Andrew Ewing Junior School, in the neatly tended, gently decaying 1930s suburb of Heston, 1980–1987, where no one got hurt, despite the non-existence of risk assessments for the annual school journey week away in Swanage.

And everybody wrote a lot of really good poetry too.

The People's Republic of Neverland, Heston

It took the bastards over forty years to shut down Andrew Ewing Infants and Juniors School. They had to use Office for Standards in Education (Ofsted), and finally bulldozers, academy status and a new name, before they had it finished off and wiped from the face of the earth, because unlike William Tyndale school, with which it had so many features in common, it didn't crash and burn in a blaze of notoriety but for nearly twenty years did a really good job of proving that a purpose-built environment and a staff committed to an ethos of child-centred team-teaching was very good practice indeed.

Here's, briefly, is how it worked. Children were vertically grouped. I worked in the Juniors, downstairs where Year Threes were together with Year Fours, while upstairs Year Fives were with Year Sixes. With sixty children in each year, these two teams were then split into four home base classes for registration and general pastoral purposes. As mentioned earlier, the "classrooms" for these home bases were four open-sided octagons grouped around a central general-purpose resource area. The teaching staff was a team of four teachers, each with both a home base to register, pastoralise and generally be primarily responsible for and a curriculum area for team-teaching. The curriculum was generally divided into maths, English, creative and humanities areas. The staff planned together, working with a topic-based approach, and generally worked out how to use the topic to cover teaching and learning for each of their curriculum areas, very occasionally having discrete weeks where teachers went off-topic to tackle particular learning needs, as well as determining how to shoehorn science into that curriculum arrangement somewhere somehow. Sometimes it was part of maths, sometimes humanities, depending on which teacher with which enthusiasm was responsible for which area that year. On Mondays, children would rotate as home bases round each of the four curriculum areas for an hour's "lead lesson" that would explain their learning assignments for the coming week. They wrote these into their assignment folders, then for the rest of the week they could choose where and when they worked to complete their assignments.

I could go into further and greater detail about this system, but the main thing I need to say is that it was extremely successful. I wasn't previously an enthusiastic proponent of radical education. At the West London Institute of Higher Education, we had experienced on the whole, Sylvia's philosophy of education course aside, a rather sedate course of instruction. We had tackled the perennial basics of literacy and numeracy and backgrounded our practice with the history and sociology of education. I think I probably took their insights for granted at the time but now realise that those insights were part of the backstory to this book too.

But it was my experience at Andrew Ewing that convinced me that this was a way of working that provided children with a very good education indeed. Andrew Ewing children were articulate, confident, skilled and enthusiastic, interested and interesting, responsible and responsive individuals. The school population was an interesting one too, if not necessarily the social demographic one usually associates with radical education initiatives. Mainly middle- and lower middle-class interwar semi-detached housing surrounded the school, garnished with some post-war additions that added elements of urbanisation to what had started out as a suburban idyll. There was, however, a good diversity that included children from the various Asian backgrounds and children from rented housing, nearby council estates with high-rise flats and Heston's only tower block, the lift shaft of which one of our Charlies managed to fall down during the summer holidays between leaving us and going to secondary school. He was passing the days hopping from the roof of one moving lift to another. The descending lift nearly severed his leg. Coming from a lively background and several other schools that didn't appreciate his cheery attitude, he had been doing more than all right at Andrew Ewing till that happened.

The diversity increased when midway through the 1980s the Thorncliffe Hotel, a concrete monstrosity built perched by the side of the M4 motorway and originally intended to house airline staff from not quite nearby enough Heathrow, was suddenly opened up to house families made homeless by a variety of circumstances. Initially it was used to house families from the Bangladeshi community who had been relocated from the East End of London, frequently having been the targets of racist attacks. Their kids pretty much all ended up in Andrew Ewing, and great fun they were too. As the 1980s wore on, however, more and more families were turning up at the Thorncliffe, because they hadn't been able to pay their rent or their mortgages any more.

There were also quite a few children who transferred to Andrew Ewing, because, like Charlie the lift-hopper, they had difficulty conforming to the confines of the more traditional schools that otherwise served the area, where the more aspirational middle classes sent their offspring. These dodgy characters all flourished at Andrew Ewing. Indeed, all types of children, from the waifs and strays to the those whose mums double-wrapped them in cotton wool every morning, in fact, everybody, flourished there, me included. I didn't give up the idea of being a songwriter, but, for those first seven crucial years, I would be saying goodbye to the brilliant Year Six children in July and I would look at the Year Five kids I had also been teaching that year and invariably think: you lot are pretty cool too; you lot look like you are going to have a brilliant final year here. I'll think just stay the one more year, then. . .

The success of Andrew Ewing depended to a great extent on the physical construction of the place—purpose-built for progressive education—but not entirely. The commitment of the staff and their belief in the vision of education that the school had been built to realise was crucial. When I returned there very briefly in 1997, that commitment and vision was a thing of the past. Both original heads had retired, and almost all of the visionary staff had left too. Teachers were appointed to fill vacancies regardless of whether they wanted to work in an open-plan, team-teaching, etc., etc. To be honest, there probably weren't too many of them about any more anyway, and I always wondered if I got appointed because Irene Beach, as an old school post-war socialist and National Union of Teachers (NUT) member, knew my dad was similarly inclined, so assumed his son would be generally sound too. Nonetheless, the crucial factor that did the permanent damage was the way the "reformers" had ruthlessly revised the values of state edu- cation in the intervening years. Andrew Ewing, if not quite William Tyndale in all its Inner London Education Authority (ILEA) radical majesty, was just the sort of place they hated on principle and their legislation had been designed to stamp out. I was there during its first Office for Standards in Education (Ofsted) inspection. The head inspector, a bumptious little man in Gestapo glasses, prowled suspiciously round Butterflies Reception Class. He glared balefully at two boys happily coop- erating on the construction of a wooden railway system, plan- ning, discussing their ideas, carefully fitting tracks together to realise their planning. "I'm not at all sure what they are learning here", he snarled at me with great disdain and implicit venomous disapproval. At the end of the first day's interroga- tions, the head held a meeting of all the staff, battered and browbeaten into various states of anxiety and self-doubt by the relentless negativity of the inspection process. She said she had managed to persuade them not to fail the school immediately by promising to buy into a genuine honest to goodness off-the-peg tried and trusted ready-made curriculum for us to deliver. She had settled on the one used in Cornwall. "We'll have to leave out all the bits about tin mining", she conceded. Did anybody have any objections? I was the only person to raise a hand. "Well, that's the way it is now. You either accept it or get out of teaching", she declared. The next day I resigned—again.

Staff morale was one of the key characteristics to the success or failure of Andrew Ewing. In the 1980s, the staff were trusted professionals, free to develop a curriculum that both addressed basic issues of literacy and numeracy and developed the whole child by utilising the child's own particular skills, strengths and enthusiasms. School was therefore intended to be an exciting, empowering learning experience both for children and adults. The commitment to child-centric values and the practice of team-teaching ensured that individual staff enthusiasms never achieved an overbearing predominance. Cooperation by adults as a model of education is, I think, very good practice indeed. It presents to children a positive paradigm of human interaction and avoids the pitfalls you face as a child when you are trapped in one room, for what at the time will seem an eternity, with someone you may—at extreme ends of the spectrum of possible responses—revere falsely as a divine authority or detest worse than yesterday's cold cabbage.

For adults, it is a good reminder that we are not the divine authorities we might be tempted to see ourselves as. Personally, I am happily only too aware that I have particular weaknesses, as well as the odd particular idiosyncratic strength. Working as part of a team, I have always enjoyed appreciating the strengths of my co-workers and have been grateful for the way they have compensated for my manifold inadequacies. The staff at Andrew Ewing enjoyed the complete trust and support of the head teacher. Irene managed the role of headship more in the spirit of coordinating chairperson, not so much democratically elected by ballot but by the democratically decided process of a local authority job interview. She accepted ultimate responsibility for the school, and she had her favourite saying, "Be reasonable, do it my way," which she occasionally exercised at the weekly Friday lunchtime staff meetings, where we all crammed into her office for half an hour. She would also engage in discussions over details of practice with staff and would be open to being persuaded that there might be ways other than hers of getting things done, without feeling her authority in any way qualified by having her opinion changed.

In terms of the implications for good practice with regard to teaching, the experience of working at Andrew Ewing taught me that it is teacher's professional autonomy that is essential to good practice, and that, of course, bears no relation to the mealy-mouthed shopping list of acceptable best behaviours contained in the current Teaching Standards document. At Andrew Ewing, staff likely often spent nearly the same amount of time each week dedicated to their work as teachers spend now dedicated to their paperwork, but it was time spent characterised by choice, enthusiasm, creativity and commitment to the children we were teaching, not by the disempowerment, frustration and anxiety induced now by directed time and governmental requirements.

In terms of implications for good practice regarding learning, working at Andrew Ewing taught me, surprisingly, that many of the elements that generate good teaching—enthusiasm, respect, autonomy—also generate good learning. I learned that if you take away as many walls and boundaries of time and place as you can, thereby trusting children as learners—and as human beings—you create an environment where people are free to learn. If you make the opportunities for learning exciting and engaging and directed toward recognising, responding to and meeting the particular interests and needs of the child, then you create an ethos that further engages the instinct of the young human to explore, play with and acquire knowledge, understanding and skills. This was, I think, something we evolved professionally through experience in our practice; now that buzzwords like "ownership of learning" have become part of our professional jargon, it is established good early years pedagogy and accepted as having a certain potency with older children too.

The assignment system also encouraged children to discover and pursue their enthusiasms, to develop their capacities, skills and interests as far as they could. And they did. I learned that if you give people responsibility, they will behave responsibly. Where I think Andrew Ewing may have differed from William Tyndale is possibly in the nature of the families that made up the school community. Andrew Ewing had a few grumblers but no organised, pain in the arse, articulate middle-class opposition. Having been built and opened as a purpose-built, open-plan progressive school, parents pretty much knew that they were in for an integrated day approach, so it wasn't something being imposed on their expectations.

But I also think that the school managed to put into effective practice an ethos of adult behaviour that enacted an approach to the difficult issue of authority that Irene summed up with her jokey little catchphrase about being reasonable by doing things her way. It was in Sylvia's philosophy classes that as student teachers we considered whether classrooms are intrinsically conflict situations. As I mentioned previously, at the time, I decided this was probably very likely. Thirty children who haven't chosen to be there are crammed into one room for most of the day and told to do things they haven't necessarily chosen to do by someone who has effective institutional control over every aspect of their lives for that period of time. I pondered how anyone could change those essential elements of a child's experience of schooling, which seemed inevitably to lead to conflict. My friend and adopted big sister Pauline, herself a teacher, had told me while I was a student that in the classroom: "You have to be more interesting than television". At Andrew Ewing I learned indeed that the more interesting you made things, the less conflict there was. But the emphasis on teachers as figures of responsibility rather than authority was also quite significant. Part of accepting that responsibility is the likelihood that as an adult who has furthermore trained to carry out the function of educator your experience may mean you have a more objective, informed, authoritative view of situations than children or parents, but an aspect of that mature professional sense of responsibility is, nonetheless, a willingness to engage in discussion, to make reason, along with people not getting hurt, one your primary values. Accounts often cite, with apparent tabloid-style shock and horror, William Tyndale head Terry Ellis's response to reports of junior children hurling milk bottles at children in the infants' playground. Terry apparently said it would help if the milk was in future delivered in cartons. This seems to me an eminently sensible attempt to tackle one aspect of the problem. I do not know at this distance in time if Terry then had a word with the hurlers, but I do know that Irene would have. She accepted that part of her responsibility and our responsibility was to ensure the well-being of children, and that children would understand that certain actions, irrespective of the relative potentials for harm of glass and waxed cardboard, are wrong actions in themselves and unacceptable because of their contravention of the golden rule of good practice punk rock that no one gets hurt.

The People's Republic of Neverland, East Berlin

I never actually taught in East Berlin. I went there in 1987 as part of the first formal delegation of London teachers to visit the GDR. We had a full programme of meetings and school visits, and I got to stand on the Wall at the Brandenburg Gate and look across at the wicked capitalist West I had temporarily absconded from for a week in the "workers' paradise" of actually existing socialism. Then one morning, we were offered a choice of visits: a visit to yet another secondary school or a visit to a kindergarten.

I chose the kindergarten.

It was something of an epiphany.

Purpose-built—again—it was literally a garden for children, with a schoolie sort of building in the middle where the children started off from and returned to after a while spent romping over the grass, under the trees and round the bushes, discovering the equipment and activities that the staff had set out for them. On their return, their more formal session involved sitting in a circle, having a snack and a chat for twenty minutes before heading off into the garden again for some more romping.

I was impressed.

I decided I wanted to make one of these happen back in Hounslow.

Since then, I have visited kindergartens in Belgium, and again in Germany, when gigging in Ilmenau. They have all been inspirational centres of child-centred, play-based learning. We should never tire of saying, as loudly as we can, the obvious truth. The "reformers" and the noisy reactionaries in our right-wing media are constantly complaining that our children are "not good enough", compared with children in "other countries". But instead of looking at how "other countries" educate their children to be "better than ours"—I mean, for a start off, nobody wears a stupid uniform to school in "other countries", do they?—we pay no attention to their pedagogy and insist on making our children do *more! more! more!* of what they are apparently not very good at, earlier and earlier in their young lives—and wear a stupid uniform while they're about it. Well, in "other countries", they generally have a kindergarten phase of play-based learning until the children are six or seven, and this takes place in buildings that are fit for purpose not tacked onto a school in a spare hut or run for profit in a barely converted basement, church hall, shed, etc. If you want to improve "our children", improve the start they get to their learning by making it more like the experience of those children who go to children's gardens till they are six or seven in those "other countries" where "children do better". And, of course, don't do it because you want to make "our children" better than everybody else; do it because all children deserve their quality time in Neverland.

The People's Republic of Neverland, Hanwell and Isleworth

I came back from Berlin determined to create children's gardens in Hounslow. Not sure how to achieve this, I decided I didn't want to carry on working at Andrew Ewing. Irene Beach had taken early retirement. Shirley Kember, the infant head had taken over, but things weren't quite so much fun as they used to be. The national curriculum was on its way, and Shirley was very concerned that we comply with the wishes of the Conservative government and kept going on about "accountability". The only accountability I ever wanted to feel was to ensuring the children I was working with had a really exciting and engaging educational experience that met their needs not anybody else's—and certainly not the requirements of the junta of Bad Queen Thatch. So I resigned for the first time on the day before the Autumn term started and set off to see the world and seek my fortune as a member of the London Borough of Hounslow official local authority supply teacher team.

In any event, I never really got much further than Hanwell, where I met 6B and ended up staying with them till Christmas. Hanwell was the wild west, the opposite end of the London Borough of Hounslow in all respects from the salubrious sought-after Chiswick end of the borough, which funnily enough I never did get to work in. The school served mainly a new estate of council flats backed up against the M3 motorway that was already showing signs of wear and tear and social failure. 6B had seen the deputy head of the school off on long-term sick leave within a fortnight, and the previous supply teacher hadn't lasted beyond lunchtime. They cheerfully considered themselves the Millwall FC of the school. "We're 6B", they declared. "Nobody likes us". "I do", I rather optimistically replied, and, as it turned out, I did, and we ended up doing a pantomime at Christmas for the whole school, much to everybody's great surprise. I also wrote possibly one of my better songs about them. It was a good way of getting fights to stop. I'd say I'd play the song if they stopped punching each other. And as time went on, it became an expression of their pride in themselves, sitting on the tables, swinging their kegs, singing along, and then back to doing a spot of learning. Here's the song:

6B Go Swimming

It always rains on Tuesdays, when 6B go swimming,
The sky's a grey wet blanket, the story of our lives,
You get the odd excuses, like Samantha's ears and Joanna's
    dog
Are always sick on Tuesdays, when 6B go swimming.
Dean's got no coat again, Lee twists and twists his plastic
    bag,
Michael's burnt on both his hands, and James has got four
    videos,
and Daniel finds some pink and white crochet for a baby,
A little piece of paradise, when 6B go swimming.

At Feltham baths the roof leaks, attendants shout and old
    men float,
And I collect the golden things that children wear instead
    of coats.
But when the unreal blue's kicked white and the laughter
    hits the water,
Davina's smile says it all, mega-bright, and 6B go swimming.
I've two degrees and I don't know how to be as happy as
    they are now,
I was always to shy somehow to dive in,
Now on the sides I sit and think: it's not a bad world, just
    badly organised,
You either swim or you learn to sink. . . 6B go swimming.

Free time and out, and I nag them through the showers
and back into their uniforms,
They flick their towels and they swing on the bars and they
jell their hair into hard spikes.
I help with chains and shoelaces, while Antony, King Rat,
King Tut,
Is last dressed, a little boy lost when 6B go swimming.
We rally round the sweet machine and thoughtful Trudi
tests her heart line,
Kina's last in line again, all her life, and she's lost 5p,
There's dog beneath the fallen leaves and my sense of
humour gets chewed and blown like bubble gum,
But diamonds also grow on trees when 6B go swimming.

No, I am not necessarily suggesting good practice consists of writing songs about the children you are teaching. I would suggest, however, that a careful and appropriate use of your personal skills and enthusiasms can be very effective in the classroom. But the main point is that good practice consists of liking the children you work with. Full stop. You like them as they are, not only if they are apparently as you would wish them to be. Good practice consists of finding opportunities and ways in which the children you work with can like themselves. Good practice consists of giving children opportunities and reasons to smile. These opportunities and reasons don't have to be major events or public occasions. The school said that 6B weren't allowed to use the sweet machine after swimming. This seemed a pointless piece of petty authority exercised over this bunch of very able, self-reliant, streetwise eleven-year-olds, so I decided they could, and they did. No problem.

Now, of course, this would be doubly objected to as a contravention of the current enthusiasm for "healthy eating". As an Early Years teacher, I have always thought that biscuits are a very effective educational resource. Not only do young children, like Winnie the Pooh, need a little something at eleven o'clock, biscuits are a nifty way of reinforcing maths concepts of shape, not to mention all manner of practical maths like sharing and counting up the chocolate chips etc. I also recommend biscuits as good practice—and making cakes, cooking pizzas, making great vats of mixed vegetable curry and vast bowls of spaghetti and noodles, and so on, and then sharing them. As a vegan, I am all in favour of a responsible diet, but I also subscribe to the idea that a little of what you fancy does you good, and so have taken a principled position of ignoring school edicts banning any foodstuff that isn't bona fide raw fruit 'n' veg, particularly as staff rooms are generally awash with biscuits, cakes, cupcakes, cookies, etc. deemed essential by staff to enhance their well-being and give them a little something to help get them through the trials and tribulations of the working day. And why not, I say. You need a little something to keep your spirits up as you glumly shovel phonics at a class of six-year-olds who would much rather be outside riding bikes.

Liking children and making sure that something exciting and interesting and relevant to them was happening were again useful resources of good practice when I ended up working at Worple Road School in Isleworth. Being a large, not to say overweight, child, the only sport I ever had any natural aptitude for—before I discovered rugby—involved floating on my back in municipal swimming baths. Hounslow had two Edwardian swimming baths, one slightly larger than a bath tub and the other slightly smaller. Both were so packed with chlorine, you felt another cupful and you would walk on the surface of them. Isleworth, however, had a very stylish modern swimming pool, next to a very stylish modern library. However, the Isleworth baths was also where the tough kids from the Worple council estate used to hang out. They terrified me with their uninhibited exuberance. So I thought it was another of life's little jokes when in 1992 I moved from teaching the generally amenable kids of Orange Class in Chatsworth Infants, the very school I had gone to as an infant child, to teaching at Worple School as the teacher responsible for special needs. I was promised work as a reception teacher, provided I took their Year Six class for their final two terms. Employing the good practice that had worked well with 6B gradually stopped the more excitable members of this new Year Six class I was in from running out of the classroom and having tantrums in the toilets or on the roof. I even managed one last school journey with them, a last hurrah in Swanage. And I didn't mind too much when on that rare occasion that I had £50 in my wallet to get the car through its MOT, someone lifted my wallet from my jacket pocket. The wallet turned up; the fifty quid didn't. Whoever it was, I knew it was nothing personal, and their need was probably greater than mine. I had the job, after all. The kids just had the estate and not a lot else to look forward to.

I also noticed that the classroom was dominated by the uninhibited exuberance and unruly tantrums of the boys who positioned themselves in every respect at the head of the class. But if you looked over their exuberant, not to say disruptive, energies, the rest of the class sat there quite keen to do something a bit more positive. I started pitching words and ideas over the disruptive unrulies and mentally rethought the class as being characterised by those individuals bored at the back and hoping something interesting might happen for a change not the ones who were likely to still be up on the roof at the end of playtime. Interesting things indeed started happening. The natural curiosity of the unrulies got them interested in what was happening behind their backs elsewhere in the classroom, and they stopped being quite so disruptive. The more they got engaged, the more their energies became cooperative. We had a real good time together. In July, this wonderful bunch moved on to secondary schools, and, in September, I finally managed to bluff my way into being a full-time reception teacher and effectively the Early Years coordinator, largely because no one else wanted the job. It was not an easy school to work in. The previous head had worked in the junior school I had attended. A darkly bearded individual, with a ferocious energy and essential deep kindness, he ended up spending his afternoons very drunk and distraught on Isleworth's park benches, eventually killing himself. He was a man I very much liked.

My new role presented quite a few challenges when it came to replicating an East Berlin kindergarten in West London. For one thing, the school field was the very far side of the very large tarmac playground. It also tilted at an alarming angle so that all water ran downhill and created a swamp that spread inexorably back up the gradient. Moreover, it was firmly reserved for the purpose of providing the school football team with a football pitch. But I was determined to get the nursery and reception children out into the best outdoor learning environment we could manage under the circumstances. I insisted that if we put a line of cones at a reasonable distance and asked the children not to go beyond that, we'd be okay. Besides, I said, we would be offering the children such an exciting and engaging range of learning experiences that no one would want to run away anyway. We did, and they didn't.

Writing this, I am aware that these were all initiatives undertaken well over twenty years ago, when I was younger, with a younger person's energy, zeal and conviction. I am not sure I could manage 6B nowadays so confidently. So you could say that good practice consists of having the energy and the sense of being fireproof that you find most manifestly in teenagers. But a general point might be that good practice is synonymous with energy and self-confidence, and you squander such priceless resources more quickly than through the slow attrition of ageing if you allow authority to a system expressly designed by the reformers to deskill and disempower workers, a system that accelerates the grinding effects of time unopposed. If you think you can avoid this attrition and get away with keeping your head down and crossing your fingers and playing the game, you're mistaken. The announcement via Chancellor Osborne that all schools would be academised whether they wanted to be or not, even if Ofsted could be used to twist their arms into submission, is surely clear evidence that playing the accountability game was never a sensible option. Accountability always seemed to fear the worst was likely to happen, that somehow your school might become the next William Tynedale. And then, surprise, surprise, the worst is announced as happening—to the undeserving poor and the deserving poor alike, anyway.

The People's Republic of Neverland, Hounslow and Hollingdean

It was my friend and jobshare partner Belle Martin who really came up with my involvement with what is possibly the single most radical initiative in education that I had most responsibility for. We were working in Alexandra Infants School in Hounslow. My mum had attended Alexandra Infants School as a child, when the infants' school was unaccountably situated up steep stairs and children had to walk back home for lunch and back to school again for the afternoon session. At the end of the 1980s, this venerable old edifice had been knocked down and replaced by the last school building Hounslow Council was ever to construct, on the old site of Hounslow Town amateur football club, where the infant Johnson had enjoyed watching execrable football on Saturday afternoons in the warm and congenial company of his dad and his grandad Harry.

I had ended up going back to teaching, despite the principled resignation in 1997, because I had finally become a father. Had I attempted to earn a living as a musician, I would have missed too much of being a dad. Being a dad is the best thing I have ever done, and I count myself so lucky to have done this, and lucky squared to have done this twice. At Alexandra Infants School I also managed to wangle myself formally into the role of Early Years coordinator. This was not so much a result of ambition as a way of defending the beliefs I had in the importance of play and outdoor access from the tendency of colleagues, panicked by their position in the league tables, to want to make young children sit down at tables and "ready" themselves for the avalanche of content that was awaiting them in key stage 1 once the national curriculum and SATs kicked properly in.

As the official Early Years coordinator, I reckoned I stood a better chance of telling them (politely) to piss off and get away with it.

Belle was a newly qualified mature student. She was a very good practitioner, with all the attributes you would want from a teacher of young children, and a splendid colleague. She didn't stay in teaching for long, leaving after a couple of years to do something much less stressful—running a pub with her husband. But she stayed long enough to make that significant difference all teachers are supposed to secretly dream of making rather than a significant income. We were working in the nursery. There was a pretty good purpose-built outdoor tarmac area, and all the classrooms were in a long open-plan line with easy access to the tarmacked outdoors. There was a wild area too, across the Key Stage 1 tarmac. We worked out a way of having the nursery children enter through a different set of doors, so we could set up the outdoors for them to use from the start of the day. We even got hold of some gloss paint and painted a rainbow around the new doorway to celebrate its elevation from the status of emergency exit. I had become accustomed to being called "teacher" or "you" or "mum" by the children, when suddenly out of nowhere one day Belle said "Isn't it such a mouthful for them, having to say 'Mr Johnson' or 'Mrs Martin'. Why can't they just call us Robb and Belle?"

Calling teachers by their first names? This was William Tyndale pure and simple. What a good idea, Belle. So we went to the head teacher, Alex Mitchell, and said this is what we want to do, and this is why we want to do it, and Alex (who had started her teaching career working in the school where my dad was a head teacher) said okay. We needed to discuss it with the rest of the staff though. Not all of the staff were convinced, and some of them muttered about loss of respect. I wondered if those who muttered about respect had ever noticed the magnificent levels of sheer outright contempt the average malcontented child could freight into their pronunciation of words like "sir" and "miss". But we arrived at a compromise. The Early Years team, with those epitomes of good practice, the National Nursery Examination Board graduates, or NNEBs, leading the way forward in terms of enthusiasm and commitment, as usual, were all in favour of this, and so, henceforth, were to be addressed by their first names, while everyone else remained respectfully addressed by title and last name.

It was lovely; I felt so much more of a person and a lot less of a pompous functionary. This change enhanced the relationships between home and school and supported the inclusive and friendly family atmosphere we wanted the children to experience. We wanted there to be no discontinuity of experience between the world of the child and the world of school, because we believed that to treat the world of the child with due respect facilitates the process of education, and that this is also an important statement that recognises our shared humanity. Educationalists know this is sound practice; it is the government that prefers to stereotype and dismiss as inadequate all parenting by those classes unlikely to read the *Daily Mail* and/or unable to afford a nanny. To use the few appalling deaths of young children to determine the way schools are supposed to treat the majority of the nation's families and children is an insult to the majority of the nation's families and children and an inadequate gesture to the suffering endured by the victims of abuse. Good practice is enhanced by genuine respect for the families you work with not just for those who appear to represent the values you hoped they'd represent, the nice middle-class values where children come to school already able to read, write, do long division, play the cello, speak Spanish and go on holiday in Tuscany that supposedly reflect the aspirations most teachers are expected to subscribe to. What we found at Alexandra Infants was that, on first name terms, respect increased, as relationships became more firmly established between real people rather than their roles of teacher, pupil, pupil's parent-carer. No one called me "mum" any more. Instead they used my name, and I knew it was me they wanted to talk to.

When we moved to Hove, and I eventually got a job in Hollingdean as the Early Years coordinator at Hertford Infants and Nursery School, I was carrying this experience of good practice with me. We solved most of the problems presented by the idiosyncrasies of the building, the dead spaces and the dangerous steps, by incorporating them as far as possible into our provision. We attempted to establish good practice in the reception that involved children being free to move between classes and to provide more than just a tired and smelly sand tray in the dead space between the classrooms. The space between the classrooms became both a space you passed through on your way to something exciting somewhere else (children only want to escape adult supervision when adults aren't offering them anything more interesting to do), as well as (variously and not necessarily at the same time) a quiet reading area, a noisy music area (we used to put the amps, electric guitars and drum kit there when we rehearsed for our annual Hertfest Rock Concert), the cooking area, the area for *BIG CONSTRUCTION*, and this spilled up the stairs when it became the area for extended construction and for ramps and wheeled vehicle racing. It became one of the variables of our planned provision. By including it in our thinking and planning, we turned a dead space into a valuable resource.

It was also the point of free flow access to the outdoor area. Some staff were initially reluctant to allow children into the garden—yes! here at last was a school that already had its own garden!!—because there was an abundance of shrubbery hindering direct oversight. Me and Sandra, who had arrived as a TA in reception at the same time as I did, stood looking at the problematic shrubbery. Sandra had been born in the GDR, so she knew all about what kindergartens were supposed to be like. I said maybe we could get the council to come along and cut it all down during the half-term holidays. Sandra nodded, and having been born in the GDR promptly engaged in a spontaneous working-class initiative and simply came in at the weekend and cut everything down on her own. So we now had outdoor free flow added to our good practice; free flow access to the great outdoors is probably the simplest and best way to eradicate all that imitated patriarchal and bourgeois individualist behaviour (or as teachers refer to it, bored boys—poor things, buzzing with energy and shot through with both testosterone and unhelpful images of masculinity usually involving violence and weaponry—being plonkers) that dead spaces encourage. The great outdoors is where they can have all the adventures they want, suitably resourced and supported, and afterwards, who knows, they might want to make a book about it out of the photos you and they take, and then make a story book about it, and then they might plan their next stories in advance and make books about them too. They don't have to, but they might want to. Who knows? Who knows what will happen when Charlie picks up a watering can and gives the mud a long thoughtful stare, appraising the possibilities?

We rotated staff round the different learning areas, so no one had to spend more than a week at a time being outside freezing in the winter, soaking wet in the springtime, etc., and we made sure that we engaged children in their own learning by planning topics that responded to their interests and needs, and we had prime time "first thing in the morning when you are bursting with energy" self-selection and self-initiated learning, and although there were adult-directed activities after snack time and our illegal biscuit maths sessions, children were still free to pursue their own learning, to continue their play, with or without adult support, as appropriate. We did our best to find ways for reception and nursery to share space and time, to function more as an Early Years unit and not as two separate year groups, despite the risk of children falling up and down the stairs.

I could go on and on and on, and even then some, about the details of good Early Years practice. Fortunately, there are lots of great books you can read written specifically about this.

More useful in the context of this book is to try to identify the essence of good practice rather than enumerate the way it is expressed through the different languages of the different chronological ages. Although the language of Early Years education is the one I am most articulate in, and through which I can often most clearly define these enduring characteristics of good practice, I think that there are core values of good practice that are common to the particular teaching and learning languages of all age ranges.

One of my favourite anecdotes involves Abderahman and a wooden train set. Why is it people in authority have such a problem with children playing with trains? Abderahman very much enjoyed playing with the trains. Otherwise a bit of a firework, when he was playing with the trains he was the model of calm focus. The head would occasionally sweep through the nursery, complain about all the toys being left on the floor, and invariably there would be Abderahman playing with the trains. After a while, the head started to comment pointedly that Abderahman was playing with the trains, yet again. But she never had the time to stop and look properly at his play, to observe his play with the due attention it deserved. It was not simply repetitive; it was spiral. Abderahman started off by joining the tracks in a linear way. Then his play constructed a circle. Then the circle spread outward, spiralled outward, enclosed space in more convoluted, ambitious, confident ways. Then Abderahman started including other children in his play, something he had hitherto found difficult to do. His play was complex, purposeful, a literal and metaphorical spiral that he worked through to help him revisit and develop his ideas, his imagination, his confidence and his social skills.

Again, the good practice is not to get everybody playing with a train set. Good practice is to look at what children are actually doing. Good practice respects children as learners, with the capacity to set themselves the challenges they need to meet their particular needs and to enhance their development. Good practice is having the professional confidence to allow them to pursue their learning and the good judgement to know when and how to intervene and when and how not to intervene. Good practice is knowing that if you want someone to learn something and retain that skill or knowledge as a part of their personality rather than regurgitate it like a parrot, you support them in the learning that they have chosen to undertake and in the discoveries that they make for themselves. Good practice is supporting autonomous activity, not pouring content into emptied pitchers. Good practice is *not* having to measure what a child does against anybody else's agenda.

Good practice is, as noted, creating and fostering an atmosphere of mutual and genuine respect.

So when an appropriate opportunity arose I told my colleagues at Hertford how we had used first name terms in a previous school and how successful that had been. The Early Years team were all very enthusiastic about this, so we approached the head who was sympathetic, but again said that it would need discussing with the whole staff. The response was very positive; it was decided that staff could decide how they wanted to be addressed, and before long, everybody was on first name terms, including the head teacher.

Hertford Infants and Nursery School had traditionally had a school community drawn primarily from the blocks of old council housing stacked up on the eastern hillside. Aspirational middle-class parents traditionally favoured the two primary schools located on the western hillside, the affluent owner-occupier "golden triangle" side of the Ditchling Road. But a couple of headships ago, to fill its empty places, the school had made efforts to present itself to the more well-meaning, less aspirational families both sides of the Ditchling Road as a small, family-friendly, child-centred school, concerned to develop the whole child rather than its place in the league tables (but hey—guess what? The school was actually doing okay in those areas too, all things considered). First name terms only deepened the inclusive family nature of the school and strengthened the quietly progressive ethos that opted for school values rather than school rules before it became fashionable to do so.

Is this good practice that impacts upon our measurable outcomes? In the current climate of obsession with measurable impact, the inclination is to state categorically: yes. This may well be the case, although we would presumably need a longer-term study involving control groups of similar children who use traditional forms of address to establish a scientifically valid conclusion. But that, I think, is not the point. Regardless of outcome, it seems to me to be good practice to treat people with respect, not to use the mechanisms of an institution to belittle them and reduce them to two-dimensional role players. My experience is that happy, secure children are better able to respond to opportunities for learning. An environment that generates genuine relationships based upon mutual respect is surely conducive to creating in children feelings of happiness and security. Treating each other with respect, however, also clearly locates us within a wider philosophical debate and, as an ethical position, is not so much "good" as "imperative" practice.

Oh, and I almost forgot to mention maybe the best good practice of all—having a sense of humour. Kids used to say to me when I was working at Hertford, "Robb, you're funny!" like they were surprised, although pleased, that I was, because, as an adult, that surely wasn't what I was supposed to be. "Good", I'd reply, and stick both my thumbs up.

I didn't manage to help get a popular movement going to get rid of the school uniform though.

The Constant Elementals of Neverland

Good practice is definitely not simply a utilitarian means to a measurable end, a way to produce an increased yield in terms of measurable outcomes, like you're hoping for a better bumper crop of turnips every year.

Good practice is definitely not at all doing what the government tells you to do. That sort of good practice is how well behaved, compliant and accountable citizens end up doing their best to produce an increased yield from places like Auschwitz every year, having started off just hoping for a better bumper crop of statistics to report next year.

Good practice is about providing a quality learning experience that responds to each child's needs and interests. That learning experience should be characterised by enthusiasm. It should, in a way, be an adventure, a discovery, and the relationships between all the individuals engaged in that adventure should be relationships of respect, trust and friendship. Adventures are likely to be enhanced by our ownership of them, where we choose the balance of risk and security, so good practice involves valuing children, valuing children's interests and supporting them in pursuing their own adventures, their own learning journeys. Needless to say, such journeys are the more difficult to pursue if you hem children in with real or metaphorical walls, so good practice involves movement not walls, open windows and open doors, both literal and metaphorical. Adults are likely to have accumulated experience and developed knowledge and skills that they can use to support the children's adventures and learning journeys, ensuring there are appropriate safety nets in place, and issues of well-being and security are addressed (rather than merely going through the superficial motions of health and safety tick sheets and risk assessments).

Through adults, children become aware of the vastness of humanity's accumulated experience, knowledge, skills, wit and wisdom. Adults should therefore not tell children lies and should be conscious of whose perspective of that vastness they are transmitting. This gets a bit tricky when it comes to things like Father Christmas, but if teaching is ever so reduced that it becomes a simple matter, a matter of manipulating meaningless clichés and spouting fatuous opinion, it is little better than the mere journalism that is the province of the likes of Gove and Osborne.

Father Christmas. I made myself and my two sons a promise when I became a dad. I promised I would never lie to them. If I didn't want to answer a question, I would say I don't want to answer that question, if I couldn't answer a question, I would say I cannot answer that question, and if I believed something, I would say it was my belief not that it was the truth. My son Arv says that during a "tricky bit" in the film *300*,[2] I told him that it was something he would understand when he was a bit older and not to worry about it now, so he didn't. So when it came to Father Christmas, I explained that once there was a man who was kind to children, who gave them presents, so each year at Christmas we celebrate that kindness with the character of Father Christmas. They both nodded; it all made perfect sense. A few years later they came home from school full believers in the existence of this old chap with the beard, the reindeer and a marvellous ability to travel down the chimneys of every child in the world, even when they have no chimney. Well, it was an adventure of the imagination they had chosen, so I decided my job was to support them. And when a few years later they checked with me that Father Christmas wasn't real, I supported them in that discovery also.

That is also how I think teachers should respond to the diversity of understanding and belief that they encounter in schools. We respect each other's journeys. I had always been pretty dismissive of Disneyland. We were having a week of activities and learning opportunities around the idea of journeys, because it was the time of the Hajj. I was talking about the journeys we make, and how some are particularly special. The next day a child came into the class more excited and animated than she had ever been. She wanted to share her book of her special journey. It was the book of her family's holiday to Disneyland. I looked through the photos, and they clearly showed a family having their best holiday together ever, and I felt duly ashamed of myself and my radical snobbery. I had a similar experience with regards to the loathsome McD*n*lds. During a reception class book week, we asked children to bring their favourite books in to share with the class. Next day, another Charlie proudly brings his favourite book in. It may have been his only book; it looked much loved and much used. It was a giveaway puzzle book from McD's.

Good practice recognises that children have rights. They have lives rich in vitality and experience—because every new experience vibrates and resonates for the child, whether it is going to Tuscany or Tesco's. They have the right to be themselves. They also have responsibilities, like the adults, to make sure no one gets hurt. Adults have rights too, including the right to be human, to have bad days, to make mistakes. They have the responsibility to make sure that no one gets hurt. Adults aren't perfect, they have the same rights as children to their emotions, which include anger, but they also have the responsibility not to hurt anyone. With children, adults have a great duty of care, and we should expect that with life experience comes a degree of emotional maturity. If we fall so short of perfect that we are clearly in the wrong, any of us should say sorry afterwards—and mean it. I don't think we have the right to administer punishment. That cold-blooded inflicting of pain or loss of privilege or systemised stigmatising, names displayed on the establishment's version of The Naughty List, seems to me an unacceptable act of cruelty.

Kindness, of course, is an important element to good practice. We should avoid the excesses of sentimentality; we should always remember A.S. Neil's insight that approval of children is vital to their happiness and well-being, and although it is a fact utterly ignored by "reformers", our experience proves to us the obvious simple truth that children learn best when they are happy and confident. Inhibitors of happiness and well-being—hunger, low self-esteem, conservative politicians—need to be removed from our learning environments, forcibly if necessary. But it is also important to recognise another obvious simple truth, that we can never be too kind to each other. There is a lot of nonsense spouted by old school Victorian-valuing sadists along the lines of spare the rod, spoil the child. They will always tell you, often with suspiciously alarming intensity, that it never did them any harm.

But it did, and it does, so kindness, for its own sake and with absolutely no strings attached, is by far the better way forward.

For what it's worth, my experience leads me to believe that children are essentially instinctively kind. Sometimes we can overcomplicate things. I think Adrian Mitchell's poem "The Baby on the Pavement" says this better than I could:

> People keep telling me about Human Nature
> and how vile it is.
> I have made up this story for them.
>
> There is a naked baby
> lying on the pavement.
>
> No, the naked baby
> is lying on a blanket
> on the pavement.
> (I find I can't leave it there
> without a blanket,
> even in a story.)
>
> Watch the first human being
> who comes walking down the pavement.
>
> Does he step over the baby and walk on?
> Does he kick the baby and walk on?
>
> He picks up the baby,
> wraps it in the blanket
> and tries to find somebody
> to help him look after the baby.
>
> Isn't that your Human Nature?

The People's Republic of Neverland and the REAL WORLD

One Tuesday night, we had this school meeting (these used to be called staff meetings, then I think they became in-service training, and at some point they mysteriously morphed into the continuing professional development [CPD] sessions—in short, staff meetings), where a couple of well-meaning men from a community education service set up by well-meaning men working in the computer industry turned up and kindly shared their computer industry knowledge and understanding of algorithms with us humble female infant childcarers.

Teaching infants algorithms seems to me to be a deliberate attempt to teach people not to be imaginative. Anyway, these two well-meaning men were absolutely adamant that this is just the sort of skill that infant children will need when they enter into something the two well-meaning men kept referring to with both enthusiasm and due reverence as the "real world". They kept on using that phrase the "real world" to describe where they thought they came from and where they thought the children ought to be heading once suitably trained by the unreal world of school. They used the phrase as a euphemism for commerce and to distinguish the practices and values of the computer industry from what happens in schools, which, to them, clearly was not real in any meaningful sense whatsoever.

Once the "real world" might have described the trafficking of people from Africa to work as slaves on the plantations of the New World or the labour required—or not—by the introduction of new technology into mass manufacturing processes. Now our well-meaning men understood the "real world" to mean the commercial application of information technology. Perhaps the well-meaning men would find the US charter school chains run by Apple and Microsoft a bit more acceptably "real world" than poor old benighted Hertford Infants School, kitted up with far too much of its budget spent on IT, in my opinion (we could have done with a library and a few more books—books tend not to go wrong as often as our IT equipment did) but mired nonetheless in the frankly messy occupation—hardly a proper job, really, not enough men in suits and ties in the workplace—of looking after even messier small children, hampered by local authority budget and quality control, and in deepest darkest Hollingdean too.

Nonetheless, what happens when a four-year-old builds a train track in a nursery classroom or when a fourteen-year-old engages in the school production of *Aladdin* is just as "real" as when men, well-meaning or otherwise, and indeed women, well-meaning or otherwise, make so much money working for virtual enterprises like Google or Twitter that they can effectively gentrify cities with their patronage. In San Francisco, they are happily expelling other, presumably less important, real worlds into the suburbs or onto the streets. Perhaps you are more real the more money you generate? Likewise the definition of "achievement" as the incontrovertible generality that I have seen used as a slogan from Hove to Brooklyn to define the purpose of education carries with it a subtext of valuation that excludes achievements—like train track building or appearing in the chorus line of the school musical—that are profoundly significant for the child deeply engaged by these activities but difficult to measure and largely an irrelevance if your idea of education is that its function is to produce individuals fighting fit for that "real world" of suits and ties that generates corporate and individual profits at the expense of those whose lives are not real enough in terms of their capacity for wealth generation.

The experience of the years 1939–1945 confirmed in vivid reality the idea of social interdependence that animated the theoretical fictions of Charles Dickens and the theoretical analytics of Karl Marx. That rich people owed their wealth and the ruling class their survival in the war to the efforts of the likes of you and me became an obvious if resented cornerstone of the consensus. The real world was one where all were accepted as contributing to the commonwealth. World War II was not won by Roosevelt in the White House, pursued to its conclusion by Winston's facility for speechifying, or won by the unreasoning brutality of Stalin but by the mobilisation of the energies of the people. And the people expected something better at the end of it.

The post-war consensus that financed the welfare state and the post-war realisation that indeed society is simply the sum of all its members has been replaced by the Victorian valuation that—despite what Cameron bleated in his initial justifications of austerity—we are not all in this together, and those who "have" are under no moral obligation to concern themselves with the welfare of those who "have not". I am, indeed, all right, Jack—or Dave, Boris, Gideon, Theresa, Donald et al. And no one nowadays cares to mention that your "having" only depends on others "not having", that your "having" is stolen from others, a theft that leaves more and more of those others homeless and pushing their world in shopping trolleys up and down Market all day and across the fine words of the United Nations Plaza all the way to the pavement outside Hollingdean Co-op.

So, realistically, this is what the real world really looks like nowadays.

I am sure the playful use of the term "Neverland" to describe the experience of education will provoke nothing but a negative response from the advocates of achievement. You can hear them sneering dismissively into their copies of the *Daily Torybastard*: "Neverland? Why, surely that's where children never grow up! This is exactly the sort of ridiculous millennial sixties thinking we need rid of, fulminate fulminate, overrun by migrants (again!!!) fulminate hurrah for the Blackshirts, etc., etc." Of course, using the term Neverland is partly a provocation, not quite a Situationist prank perhaps, but its use does assume readers value both an intelligent imagination and a skittish sense of humour. Of equal importance is the preceding qualification, "the People's Republic of", and, again, a sense of humour helps, but it does also signify a real, if playful, political position.

Of course, in reality, even in Neverland children grow— if not necessarily up—through their adventures. In our real world, whether train track building or chorus singing, the magical mystery that is the human child grows and progresses beautifully, in spirals, two steps forward, one step sideways, one step back . . . playfully purposeful and purposely playful. But it is the sad child whose sole aim in all this is just to grow up. Just as it is surely the sad adult whose sole aim in life is just to die.

Neverland represents a playful term that also questions the validity of both the hegemony of the concept of the "real world" and the necessity and the nature of "growing up". We have already noted reservations about what happens to us as we grow up. School can be seen as often the most direct and effective strategy to ensure we grow older without really growing up, that we are kept in a childlike state of stupefied dependency, but without retaining the positive attributes of openness and compassion and joy that are our innate human inheritance, because the schooling process has so disappointed our expectations.

As a substitute for the lived adventures of Neverland, we get the consumed spectaculars of never-never land. The society of the spectacle seeks to distract us with a succession of never-never lands, from Albert Square and dear old *Coronation Street* (the UK's premier purveyors of soap, where indeed no one ever grows in any sense whatsoever, merely circling round each other as interchangeable plastic plot devices in one of the many circles of hell Dante never quite got round to imagining)[1] through baking competitions to ballroom dancing circuses to "wars on drugs", "wars on terror", fifteen-minute celebs and five-minute hates. With their deliberate manipulations of presentation and language, the "reformers" have attempted to impose their never-never land perspectives on education practice too. The proposition that educating everybody to a particular standard ensures employability or that education is the way to eradicate poverty—these are never-never lands. The whole ragbag of hobby horses—testing . . . league tables . . . Ofsted inspections . . . selection . . . grammar schooling . . . phonics . . . Greek and Latin . . . academies and free schools—it is all never-never land.

Half a century ago, appalled at the prospect of actually existing democracy in education, the right published their Black Paper. Wikipedia will tell you that "today the Black Paper proposals for schools by and large are accepted by both the Conservative and Labour Parties in Britain".[2] They have now had over thirty years in power to achieve their aims, and in doing so they have had increasingly to dispense with the illusion of any notion of democracy or consent. Despite having access to support from powerful forces within British society, from the direct control exercised over education by government to the indirect control over political discourse exercised by the media, the "reform" never-never land remains just that, having continually failed both through the incompetence of its zealots and through the determined, principled opposition from education workers, parents and academics—from people who know what education ought to look like.

This militancy on behalf of our children, on behalf of the ideas of quality and equality inherent in our experience and expectation of good practice in state education, has frustrated the aims of the reformers for nearly fifty years. Indeed, despite the intense pressure schools and children have had to endure from anti-educational legislation, the increasingly incoherent testing systems and increasingly belligerent, inquisitorial inspection routines, the aims and practices of progressive education continue to be reflected not in the policies of major political parties nor in the editorialising of the mainstream media, often not in our schools as institutions, but in the day-to-day practice in many state school classrooms. These aims and good practices continue to animate the quality of the relationships and the quality of the educational processes at work and play in every People's Republic that aspires to ensure that every individual need and potential is addressed and each child goes home accepted, approved, justified, successful and happy.

Accepted by our society for who we are and approved of by our society, justified by our contribution to our society, and successful in our endeavours, and, therefore, at the end of the day, happy—I think that would be a good way for adults to end each day too.

A Very Small Piece of the Real World

Jodie's eating noodles, Happy Chinese New Year,
It's her third plastic cup full of noodles, and she grins from
    ear to China.
Everybody gets a lucky bag, there's noodles everywhere,
Even the class chairchuckers aren't chucking any chairs
My Lords, Ladies and Celebrities, allow me to present
This very small piece of the real world,

She's got two sisters and a brother, a dad who goes away,
A mum who doesn't listen when she's got things to say
Like: "Today we found this sparrow, mum, we don't know
    how it died,
And some little purple flowers, mum, what happens when
    you die?"
My Lords, Ladies and Celebrities, allow me to present
This very small piece of the real world,

Welcome to the real world. There's Jodies everywhere.
I know you're far too busy to answer every prayer
From every falling sparrow, chairchucker, waif and stray
Whose idea of seventh heaven is a Chinese takeaway
My Lords, Ladies and Celebrities, allow me to present
This very small piece of the real world,

You just closed down her hospital, sent her brother to Iraq,
It would be a good idea if both them came back, to
This very small piece of the real world.

PART SIX

A LONG HARD LOOK IN THE LONG HARD MIRROR

We have all learned most of what we know outside school. Pupils do most of their learning without, and often despite, their teachers.
—Ivan Illich

Ultimately the only thing I could do for him would have been to have found him a good lawyer. As a "teacher" I was impotent.
—Chris Searle

We learned more from a three-minute record than we ever learned in school.
—Bruce Springsteen

White people go to school
Where they teach you how to be thick
—Joe Strummer and Mick Jones

Toymaker

Tomorrow will be Monday, and like we always do, we'll sit
    round in a circle for the Red Class News.
I'll hear the sound of beating wings, I've heard that sound
    before, I'm busy opening windows
Someone else is locking doors
I thought it was a mission, it's only daily bread, I wish I'd
    been a toymaker instead

And then it will be Friday, I'll take out my guitar and sing my
    songs about Highway 5, between the gutters and the
    stars
And till they call last orders, we'll somehow muddle
    through
They'll want to hear what they want to hear, not always
    what I want to do.
I thought it was a mission, it's only daily bread, I wish I'd
    been a toymaker instead

If I was a toymaker, oh, I would make such things, I
    wouldn't deal in nightmares but in giving dreams their
    wings
Clowns that run on laughter, balls that bounce on air,
    wheels you can recycle and hearts you can repair
I thought it was a mission, it's only daily bread, I wish I'd
    been a toymaker instead
All those lost commandos, they were only in my head, I
    wish I'd been a toymaker instead

A Memory of Water

And sometimes, like every good film noir protagonist, you are bound to look in the mirror and find yourself confronting who you are and what you've done.

So when I look at the above statements, I am not sure I would immediately be able to disagree with any of them. If I look back at how I developed my adult identity, I did apparently indeed learn more about how I related to the rest of the planet from listening to music than I APPARENTLY learned from school. Through contemporary popular culture I learned a language that enabled me to make sense of the rest of the planet. I learned a language as a teenager I still speak today. Listening to Velvet Underground bootlegs looks alarmingly like my default setting.

As a working teacher, I have always been impressed by how much real learning happens in secret, as it were. The learning of the essentials of those communal languages like number and writing that enable children to decode experience and make sense of its stories has always seemed to me to be alchemy, a mystery bordering on the magical. I have looked out for those lightbulb moments when children process information and experience to develop the intellectual skills to be able to understand and express their ideas and experiences through those magical objectifying codes. As a teacher, and as a parent, I have to say that process happened . . . out of my sight or when I wasn't looking or when I was looking the wrong way or when I simply blinked. As a teacher and a parent,

I realised my function was not so much to "instruct" as to make sure there was the best possible environment, with the best possible range of supporting resources, wherein the magic could take place. Instruction is like memorising your lines, like theatre; learning is like understanding the meaning between the lines, interior and intuitive, like poetry.

Once the language has been learned the rest of the teacher's job simply becomes telling stories in those languages. Jack Stevenson, who clearly taught me enough German in four years to be able to interview the great renegade songwriter Wolf Biermann in German in Berlin in 2017, would always attempt to impress upon us his calculations of how little of our time was spent in his German class. That is probably why he was so keen to shift as many of the class as possible into the more meaningful context of a school exchange with Mainz and actually existing Germany, rather than leaving our learning up to a few textbooks in a classroom in a school in actually existing Isleworth. And if we learn so much outside of our formal schooling situations, and so much of it apparently in our first five years anyway, with diminishing capacity thereafter, the logical conclusion may well be that the function of schooling that is compulsory into your late teens is less to do with education and more about social control.

But if I am being really honest, throughout school I learned how to read languages and stories that have significantly contributed to my understanding both of the rest of the planet and my relationship to it. If left to my own devices, I don't think I would have read William Shakespeare's *King Lear* or Charles Dickens's *Bleak House*, and they led me all over the place. They have led me to borrow from school and never quite get round to giving back my prized battered old paperback copies of Graham Greene's *The Power and the Glory* and Charles Dickens *Hard Times* (the latter providing me, at seventeen, with a seminal perspective on teaching and learning that underlies the way I write about education in this text), which later led me to read Samuel Beckett's *Waiting for Godot* and George Gissing's *New Grub Street*. Had I not learned those languages, I probably wouldn't have learned how to speak Albert Camus, John Webster, Guy Debord and the Society of the Spectacle, Wolf Biermann . . . and these have made me as much who I am as listening to the Velvet Underground's "Waiting for the Man". It's always cool to say how much the Velvet Underground opened the doors of rock 'n roll perception for you (and no question about it, they did for me, and in walked radical noise mongers the Stooges and the Pink Fairies, and then a couple of years later Victor Jara and Bruce Springsteen did the same, only with added words too, and then the Clash turned up, and then Chumbawamba, and then. . .) but less cool to say how—in my case—the Two Brians (English teachers Brian Francis and Brian Weeden) opened the doors of literary perception for me. Not to mention the strange sociological role-playing game that history teacher Colin Davies tried to get us to play once. It involved each person in the class being handed a coloured shape that determined their life chances. It worked out that I got a coloured triangle that meant whatever I did I was going to lose. It seemed pointless to carry on playing, so, for the first time in my life, I went on strike and tried to persuade everybody else to stop playing such a blatantly rigged game too. It would also mean not mentioning Mary Clough, who taught me for two years in junior school; I met her when I was eighteen and selling carpets in Hounslow Co-op. She asked me what I was going to do. I said I wanted to be a writer. "Ah, yes", she said, "that was always on the cards". So—in retrospect, I have no hesitation at all in saying it is luck, or maybe social good fortune, that is writing these words as much as I am, because being no more special than anyone else, I had the good luck to have Mary Clough and Colin Davies and the Two Brians for teachers, as well as a dad who went out and bought me my first Velvet Underground single ("Waiting for the Man"), when he asked me if I wanted anything, because he was going out shopping down Hounslow High Street one Saturday morning.

I think everyone should be lucky like that.

But, of course, not all schools gave you good luck, not even during the high water marking of the libertarian 1960s and 1970s. And since 1987, all schools are driven by government legislation that is more concerned with curriculum imposition than with individual development, redefining "lucky" purely in terms of measurable outcomes. As we have noted, this imposition can be understood as a deliberate and conscious strategy to ensure the veracity of the Clash's allegation that schools are concerned primarily with the teaching of "thickness".

We might need to consider, therefore, if school is something generally best avoided. We have already referenced how looking at other cultures can provide an alternative perspective of issues of work and play. Anthropology will also provide us with alternative models of how societies not organised within the European and Western historical narrative transmit their wisdoms and values. These perspectives might help us feel we are closer to considering a more elemental, authentic, non-alienated model of the human animal. However, for most people likely to be reading this book, access to a more elemental, authentic, non-alienated practice is not a possibility. We are stuck with where we are, within that European and Western historical narrative. Alternative models may help us critique our alienated condition, but, to all intents and purposes, the alienation resulting from capitalism and all its discontents *is* our authentic condition.

Similarly, history can help us evaluate the value of schooling but cannot provide a reliable model for effective practice. Ivan Illich, that most entertaining and energetic opponent of school, positions school as a historical phenomenon and reinforces his polemic by reminding us that childhood is also a historical rather than a social phenomenon:

> We forget, however, that our present concept of "childhood" developed only recently in Western Europe and

more recently still in America. . . . Until the last century, "children" of middle-class parents were made at home with the help of preceptors and private schools. Only with the advent of industrial society did the mass production of "childhood" become feasible and come within the reach of the masses. The school system is a modern phenomenon, as is the childhood it produces.[1]

Well, yes, maybe so, but I for one am glad that in England the children of the working classes are no longer sent up chimneys or down mines or into the works of working factory machinery to mend broken cotton threads. I am glad that working-class families can love each other as individuals rather than simply economic units, like the bourgeois would be able to do if they hadn't generally favoured money over love and invented "public" schools where they could board their offspring out of sight and out of mind. I am similarly glad that black people are not sold as slaves, that witches and gay men are not legally burned alive, that women are not property and that Bedlam is not an entertainment. I am aware both that these liberties are not universally enjoyed and that they are sometimes subject to difficult issues of post-imperialism and cultural relativity. Even so, I look forward to the day every child born on this planet is entitled to a childhood and grows up to enjoy the rights previously only enjoyed as the province of stolen wealth and accumulated privilege. Full fucking stop.

The argument of this book is that in the post-war period state schools were beginning to fall under the control of the educationalists who worked there, and ideas of equality and libertarian, child-centred education were beginning to impact upon the schooling experienced by the unprivileged. This "Prague Spring" of education, state education with a human face, has since been subjected to a ruthless attack by the right, and the future of education looks pretty much like Orwell's vision of the future in 1984—"If you want a vision of the future, imagine a boot stamping on a human face—forever".[2]

There still seem to me to be very good reasons not to let this happen. I would argue that these reasons are of even greater importance in post-industrial societies where the people are disorganised by both poverty and unemployment and, therefore, the more likely to be organised along the tribal lines of race and patriarchy and the passive consumer distractions of media and spectacle.

First, I think that the experience of the institution that is school manages the process of transition from a member of a family to a member of society. As individuals, we are part of a family, a community, and of a society, but, above all, we belong to ourselves and to humanity as a whole. We have noted in the text how post-war state schools have been positioned as agencies of equality and opportunities for individuals to have needs met and abilities supported regardless of parental background, as well as to understand themselves as individuals who are part of the wider community of humanity. Generally, my experience is that all parents would say they aspire to love their children and would say they aspire to see them grow strong and capable. We also know that whatever parents say, there is also the likelihood, as poet Phillip Larkin once astutely observed:

> They fuck you up, your mum and dad.
> They may not mean to, but they do.
> They fill you with the faults they had
> And add some extra, just for you.[3]

We also know that hard times and deprivation make these parental good intentions and aspirations harder to realise. No one gets taught how to parent, and in my experience as a reception teacher, after 2010, the legacy of Thatcherism and the failure of Blairism meant that the classes I was working with contained more young children who were the victims not of deprivation, like 6B were, but of damage. School for those children luckless enough to be born in society's war zones may represent a less dysfunctional form of social organisation than their home circumstances, the only place where they have the opportunity to form meaningful and positive attachments. And where else has the potential to be the place where all us ordinary everyday people get to hear poetry? And where else has the potential to be the place where all us ordinary everyday people are likely to be given the opportunity to feel enabled, empowered and worthwhile not for what we do but for who we are? Where else are we all going to think and feel ideas and emotions outside the limited restricted tabloid codes of the media?

Schools are the places where the family's values get tested. School ought to be the secure space where you discover and decide who you really are. Your parents, with their inherited class politics, might have one view of the world: school ought to be the place where you find out there is more to life than reading the *Daily Bile* and watching *The Great British Bake-Off* on television—or supporting Manchester United when you live in Worthing. In *The Child and Its Enemies*, Emma Goldman notes:

> Great surprise is being expressed over the fact that the majority of children of radical parents are either altogether opposed to the ideas of the latter, many of them moving along the old antiquated paths, or that they are indifferent to the new thoughts and teachings of social regeneration. . . . Radical parents, though emancipated from the belief of ownership of the human soul, still cling tenaciously to the notion that they own the child.[4]

However much we love our children, they are not ours. Mikhail Bakunin probably says it best: children "do not constitute anyone's property: they are neither the property of the parents nor even of society. They belong only to their own future freedom".[5] We cannot be their best friends; we can only try to stay best friends. "The child, being fed on one-sided, set and fixed ideas, soon grows weary of rehashing the beliefs of its parents, and it sets out in quest of new sensations", as Goldman put it.[6] The experience of school provides the distance whereby children can view those beliefs objectively and differentiate the tensions between generations from the tensions between classes. Although a steadfast opponent of compulsory education, in "The Problem with Unschooling", Kathleen Nicole O'Neal admits:

> the idea of unschooling gives parents tremendous control over their children's lives. For all their problematic aspects, most traditional educational institutions allow young people something of a scope of autonomy (however limited) beyond the reach of their immediate families and they also provide youth with exposure to people of diverse backgrounds and belief systems of the sort their parents may not associate with. . . . Furthermore it is difficult for a young person who spends virtually all of her time around her parents (or those people the parents both know and explicitly endorse the child associating with) to develop a strong sense of independence. . . . Most disturbingly of all, unschooling gives the most dangerous parents even more scope for abuse of their authority whether it involves indoctrinating their child into questionable political or religious beliefs or allowing sexual, emotional, or physical abuse to occur with impunity.[7]

My friends who home educate their children all have interesting experiences and individual stories about this option. Sometimes they feel they have no option but to home educate, because school is—as schools now so often are—unable to adjust its rigid outcome-driven programme of curriculum delivery to accommodate their child's particular needs. Sometimes they later find they run out of things to teach, and their children need the social experience of school. In almost all cases, I think the problem lies with the school; it is that failure to be inclusive and the shortcomings of the industrial approach to education that "reform" has resurrected that means the institution fails to meet the needs of the individual child. These are the same failures that animate Ivan Illich's antipathy to school-based education, which he sees as instructional rather than meaningful: "Most learning is not the result of instruction. It is rather the result of unhampered participation in a meaningful setting".[8]

I think, on reflection, schools need to strive to become those meaningful settings again. I have worried, a little like Emma Goldman, that the child's natural instinct is to rebel, like Marlon Brando's biker in *The Wild One*, against whatever you've got.[9] If you have a school system run in accordance with the principles of equality, respect and autonomy, will children instinctively want to turn into fascists, merchant bankers and estate agents? I think this sounds neat in theory, but in practice. . .? Well, let's see, shall we? Let's see if irrational revolt or rational cooperation results from that kind of meaningful system. This is real life, after all, not a genre of culture produced by intellectuals in response to the absence of meaning caused by the death of a God, World War I and Auschwitz and Hiroshima. Enjoyable though noir existentialism can be, how long can you go on pretending 2 + 2 doesn't make 4? Or, to put it another way, I don't see a steady diet of reality TV producing a new generation of activists and advocates for social progress; the evidence so far is that in practice it produces the Trump presidency.

But, on reflection, all those years spent working for the state . . . was it just that, working for the state that wants to turn out kids that can walk on their hind legs without even thinking?

Then, obviously, you get the dissolve and the narrative flashbacks. . .

Well. . . there was this kid—we will call him another Charlie—I met when I started teaching. His elder sister had wreaked havoc on the school, and his younger brother was to do likewise. Mum was a bit of a character too. But Charlie was just a diamond; wise, funny, cheerful, kind, honourable, clever without being particularly bothered about school. I used to think—still do—that school is the place where we stand the best chance of breaking some of those vicious circles of deprivation and background. But I looked at Charlie's circles and options and wondered how his attitude and attributes would be received as he got older. So I decided that all I could be sure of was that every day I was teaching Charlie I had to do my best to make extra sure that Charlie had a good day, that when it was on my watch, as they say, the vicious circles were stopped from grinding round and round.

Years later, there was also Charlie who was a girl. Her background was a long slow car crash of low self-esteem and low self-esteem parenting, and no one could do anything about it. We all felt helpless. I tried to think that when Charlie was in the school we tried to make sure she went home having had a good day, that she went home happy with herself. I thought that what we were doing was like giving her a glass of cool water. Ahead of her was pretty much a desert. I think that is true for a lot of kids—well, the majority of us really. As we get older, we notice that both school and society care less and less about us. Self-esteem and support networks can help you through. Charlie wasn't good at networks. So all we could do was give her the water and hope it would get her as far as possible across the desert and give her a memory of what she might be looking for so she'd recognise it if she ever came across it again in the future.

And then I remember there was the Charlie, bright as Einstein but sad as a wet Sunday, who had trouble smiling, whose parents figuratively and literally preferred to speak a different language, who said, "I don't believe in God. I don't believe in Favva Christmas. I don't believe in nuffink", and that included herself . . . and there was Charlie who nicked the fifty quid out of my wallet . . . and then there was the one class with the Charlie, aged four, with the terrible backstory, who couldn't stop hurting people . . . and the Charlie, also aged four, with the terrible backstory, who hid under tables and hurt people too . . . and so on, and so on. . .

And all the other kids, not necessarily all called Charlie, possibly all for the purposes of this book called Phil to reference that Phil Ochs song "There but for fortune", that's maybe a bit hackneyed but nonetheless, nonetheless true, especially when Phil sings it himself—or Pip, to remind us we all ought to have the right to have great expectations—most of them, just like the rest of us, more or less okay, super confident, super shy, mostly maybe somewhere in between. They all deserve their good day and a memory of water to go home with too.

A.S. Neill says, "The aim of life is happiness. The evil of life is all that limits or destroys happiness".[10] At the end of the day, I think the minimum aim of teachers ought to include as a priority that all children go home happy.

It's not rocket science. It's not the full list of being accepted and justified and so on. Even in Neverland, there isn't a magic wand, but it is, I think, the least we can aspire to.

PART SEVEN

WHAT IS TO BE DONE?

There is no such thing as lost allusions!
—Raoul Vaneigem

Hands off Hove Park

Dear Mr Trimmer, dear Michael Gove
On behalf of the people of Brighton and Hove
We won't be bullied, bought or fooled
Hands off Hove Park School

Whose school? Our school, not yours Trimmer and Gove.
Whose school? Our school, keep it Brighton and Hove.

We like our school the way it is, cos it's a school and not a
    business
Privatisation just makes things worse, we want a school
    puts children first

Whose school? Our school, not yours Trimmer and Gove.
Whose school? Our school, keep it Brighton and Hove.

You put the con in consultation, cos we'd vote for state
    education
You keep things quiet while we shout loudly: no back room
    bungs from Apple or Saudi

Whose school? Our school, not yours Trimmer and Gove.
Whose school? Our school, keep it Brighton and Hove.

Hands off Hove Park...

Whose Schools? Our Schools

We need to reclaim our schools. We need to reclaim our schools for our children and our communities by refuting the priorities and values imposed on schools by the exhausted "reform" project. As a first step, at the level of daily classroom practice, teachers have the opportunity to "make a difference" in the way they manage and respond to the state's increased assault on the idea that education should be a meaningful process.

At the level of the classroom, teachers can start to reclaim our schools by actively looking for opportunities for children to reclaim their learning from the learning that is imposed on them by the state.

Schools already have a historical tendency to favour pointless activities. There has been a fondness for fabricating systems of competition, with children arbitrarily divided into houses—you get a sense of the enduring potency of this nostalgia with the way it is uncritically presented as a central feature in J.K. Rowling's Harry Potter novels. This kind of random organisation of children is often linked to a system of extrinsic rewards—house points, stickers, marbles in a jar—while individually children are policed by reductive one-dimensional systems of public judgement. In infant schools, you get individually named pegs clipped according to "behaviour" on representations of the sun or a dark cloud. In secondary schools, you get your photograph displayed ranked according to how well you are doing at meeting your progress rate targets. Human complexity is again reduced to a simplistic score. In England, nearly all schools have traditionally insisted on children wearing a school uniform, a meaningless but effective distraction strategy. Children can thereby be terrorised by the requirement to conform, or they will expend their energy subverting the uniform rather than questioning what they are learning. The excuse often offered that the uniform is a great social leveller is nonsense, because affluent children wear pristine versions, while children from poorer homes wear hand-me-down versions. However, since the initiation of the "reform" agenda, the tendency toward eviscerating meaning from education has become the dominant characteristic of the system. The purpose of school and study is primarily presented as the imperative to learn to pass tests not to understand or enjoy or see meaning and become expert in particular areas of knowledge. In the case of primary schools, reformism has resurrected the strict division of learning into subject areas. Cross-curricular connections, topic work and joined-up thinking are discouraged by these artificial borders of knowledge. Young children learn not to read for meaning but to decode words correctly. At General Certificate of Secondary Education (GCSE) level, schools berate children and their parents with self-serving utilitarian outcomes—good results are good for the child's future employability and for the school's reputation—that eclipse the idea that the purpose of studying history, for example, might be to provide an individual with a toolkit of particular and active knowledge that will empower their understanding of how the world works—or simply be a set of stories and insights they might enjoy.

This absence and/or perversion of meaning is compounded by the way adults manipulate language to impose the state agenda onto what takes place in schools. As we have noted, children no longer work in schools; they no longer even play in schools. They *LEARN*. Their very experiences are defined by language that asserts the values and goals of the state. They are not allowed the language to express their experience of school as an imposition—I mean, really, how many children would not find the experience of "pace and rigour"—the hackneyed term favoured by the Office for Standards in Education (Ofsted) as their criteria for good classroom practice—hard work? An approach to language that dismantles your organic language acquisition and reconstructs it in terms of graphemes, phonemes, segmenting and blending similarly is surely downright hard work. Children are being denied their experience of real free play by adults insisting that it is only of value if it is governed by learning outcomes. Children are constantly badgered by adults telling them exactly what they are doing, which therefore defines the play and drives it toward particular outcomes, because adults are driven by the state to meet particular targets. Play has become the province of adult intentionality.

Just as cardboard boxes, plastic bottle tops, lolly sticks, bits and bobs of this and that, and rolls of masking tape and pots of glue now often find themselves supervised by clearly written signs declaring, "I am learning to attach two surfaces together", "free" writing areas and opportunities now need to appear justified by similar signs announcing, "I am learning to form my letters correctly". Am I? What if, instead, I am actually making an alien spacecraft, or cutting up paper furiously, simply because I am pissed off with always being told what I am supposed to be doing, or just because I want to see what happens when I do, or writing the word "poo", because it writes as good as it sounds when you say it, and I can't write the word "fuck" yet, and/or I am writing the word "love", because it is the most important word in the universe.

It probably still is, even when you're eighteen and can write "fuck", no problem. Indeed, although your "playing" soon becomes completely annexed within the terms of the word "learning", you are probably subjected to an even greater degree of totalitarian adult control over your explorations of your experiences. No wonder you're even more pissed off by the time you're eighteen. Adults—teachers—define and control the correct answers. When play has become the province of adult intentionality, the child is denied the right to playfulness and play for its own sake; teachers have surreptitiously abandoned their supportive partnership role and become authoritarian representatives of the state, conscripting play and learning to suit those purposes and priorities defined by the state's insistence on desirable and measurable outcomes. Yet it needs to be emphatically stated—to a child *all* play is purposeful. It is an end in itself.

We will need to consider more fully elsewhere the link between the play of children and the leisure choices of adults. Half a century ago, A.S. Neill was moved to wonder "if the great masses who watch professional football are trying to live out their arrested play interests by identifying with the players, playing by proxy, as it were".[1] While football matches are ostensibly a spectacle organised around essential elements of competition and outcome, the processes and the rituals of watching football are often as significant to the participants as the final match day score. Closely observed, most adult leisure activities are processes undertaken for individual idiosyncratic reasons, where outcomes are outweighed by the pleasurable experience of participation.

Obviously, all experiences have outcomes; the two great errors imposed on schools by the reformers are the insistence that outcomes are all-important and processes aren't and the narrowing of the educational experience of children to value, promote and produce particular state-sanctioned outcomes. Having lumbered the nation's schools with a national curriculum, the state then set to telling teachers how they had to "deliver" it. The language tightened its grip on what the children were allowed to learn. From identifying possible learning outcomes, it moved through desirable learning outcomes to simple learning intentions. The teacher, like a well-trained sheepdog, only had to bark its little flock of sheep into the designated sheep pen. Children were not to be allowed to deviate from this trajectory, and any other learning or skills were forbidden and not to be taken into consideration. Ken

Loach captured this hilariously in a perfect metaphor in his 1969 film *Kes*.[2] Billy is rubbish at football, so he gets put in goal. He is rubbish at goalkeeping too, but while he's waiting in the goalmouth, he passes the time by swinging on the crossbar, and shows himself to be a naturally talented gymnast. But that is not a skill the game or the teacher are in any way interested in.

Effective education therefore needs to return ownership of learning to children, which will return meaning to learning. Meaningfulness is not the imposed intended outcomes of the curriculum, as managed by the teacher; it is what is meaningful to the child that is important. This requires an environment that facilitates three processes: first, the process of the child exploring an environment that is conducive to and supportive of the child's development; second, the process of adult observation, with the adult noting what the child considers meaningful and, on reflection arranging opportunities that will enhance the child's learning based on the child's interests—someone really ought to have noticed Billy swinging on the above-mentioned crossbar and worked on finding ways to make this a key that unlocked meaningful future development for him; third, the process whereby children's voices are heard within the education space, where it is not just the teacher who notices interests and enthusiasms but where children do too. Children are self-aware, self-confident and able to articulate their ideas, interests and perspectives and to have agency over what they do and what they think. The educational space becomes a meaningful experience for them when their actions and ideas are valued.

However, since the 1980s, teachers in England have found themselves increasingly coerced into valuing only what the state deems valuable. When SATs and league table publication started off in the 1990s, I was working in the London Borough of Hounslow. Hounslow had a teachers' centre, and state schools in Hounslow generally took a justifiable pride in their commitment to children and their commitment to the profession of education. No school "taught to the tests", so Hounslow appeared somewhere in the top half of the bottom half of the table, the sort of mid-table position often favoured by our local football team, Brentford. The elected councillors— it was a Labour council—went ballistic. Hounslow teachers were letting Hounslow's children down, particularly working-class children. Intimidated, schools starting teaching to the tests. The league table position edged up into the top half of the table. Hounslow council preened at its achievement. My friend Marilyn, a Year Three teacher and National Union of Teachers (NUT) local secretary, complained that now children arrived from the infants unable to work together, play together or manage basic social skills like sharing. But they could pass more SATs, apparently.

Meaningful education, on the other hand, would be "teaching" to the child not the test.

The lunacy of the league table approach to teaching and learning becomes even more farcical when you look at the nonsensical notions it has slipped into common acceptance in its wake. Schools—and therefore individual teachers—are expected to make year-on-year improvements. This frenzied state of permanent forward-driving reminds me of the sort of feverish activity fascists like Benito Mussolini employed to distract the people from the practical bankruptcy and failures of the fascist state. In reality, of course, not only do children vary, so do cohorts and classes of children—you are somehow expecting schools to increase output regardless of the nature of the raw materials involved. Children—people—are nothing if not an unknown quantity! Everybody is also expected to be "above average". Just think about how that proposition would work in reality, along with results that are expected to show year-on-year improvements. You might have a class of Einsteins one year and a class full of stand-up comedians the next, regardless of the more realistic likelihood that the human species is unlikely to evolve significantly in the course of a couple of years, and one bunch of seven-year-olds will likely inhabit the same spectrum of abilities as another bunch of seven-year-olds.

Meaningful education, on the other hand, would focus on and delight in the individual development of every individual character making up every individual bunch of seven-year-olds—and seventeen-year-olds.

The obsession with measured outcomes means children are increasingly not educated in complex, three-dimensional bodies of knowledge but dog-trained to pass as many tests as possible. The idea that an examination system assessed skills and aptitudes to present a summation of both learning and of the individual—if you liked history but were bored witless by physics, you did well in history exams and crashed in physics exams, or vice versa—has been replaced by a fanatical drive to shovel as many children as possible through as many exams with as many good grades as possible, regardless of whether they really "learn" anything, and retain for its own sake whatever they have been trained to regurgitate in exam conditions. The "liberal education" idea that graced education for so long like a vague yet delightful perfume, blooming in the philosophies affecting mass education in the 1960s, the ennobling cultural aesthetic of learning for its own sake, for enjoyment, the child's delight in whole-body, whole-being play developing further into intellectual playfulness, has been well and truly banished from the utilitarian functionalism that the state again wants its schools to administer.

Meaningful education would return us to that idea of liberal education, that there is an endless landscape of thought you can play with, all manner of trees of knowledge you can choose to enjoy fruits from, to make sense of, as you explore what it might mean to be you. And it might all mean nothing, but that will still be a whole lot more meaningful sum of nothing than the miserable pittance the state now has in mind for you.

To get people to comply with unpalatable directives, authority often sugars its orders, presenting people with good reasons for doing bad things. With state education the narrative used equates better exam results with increased employability. However, the state under the control of the right, has promoted the interests of profit and business over the interests of employees. Euphemisms like "flexibility" and "competition" have been used as a cover for dismantling ideas of job security, and with the imposition of "austerity" conditions the state has mounted a full-scale assault—paid for by the people—on the institutions and practices that existed to ensure the security of society's vulnerable members. Young people are now growing up in a social landscape decorated by an endless plethora of consumer commodities but characterised by insecurity and scarcity. Thatcher did not abolish society—humans are animals that only survive by grouping together and working together in societies—but the interests she represented have succeeded in making society deeply dysfunctional. The lack of those characteristics of human social groupings that had come to define human society because they met the complex needs of this complex animal, i.e., compassion, empathy and inclusion—the attributes of community—mean that our dysfunctional society fails to meet the needs of a significant number of its members. There are no safety nets, assurances or "jobs for life". Instead, there is capitalism's misapplication of a simplified Darwinism to somehow justify the struggle for employment.

Meaningful education should respond to this abolition of the state's social responsibilities and the monetarisation of social identity by developing both our understanding of community and our skills of mutual cooperation, as well as our capacity to operate as confident, autonomous individuals.

The state's rationale for getting schools to enforce measurable outcome education, the sweetener, the sugar-coating that is used to get teachers to swallow the bad medicine that confuses rising test results with good practice, is "employability", the idea that this empowers young people in the job market and makes them more likely to get the good jobs—because there are no longer enough good jobs to go round, no matter how many tests you have passed. Unfortunately and increasingly, there are not enough jobs to go round that provide workers with an income that adequately meets basic needs. Families with parents in employment are living in conditions that even the state recognises as poverty. Pay is below subsistence levels, and more and more of that politician's favourite, "the hard-working families", are forced to resort to food banks to feed their children.

Meaningful education would stop pretending that everything will be okay if you get good test results.

Schools, or, rather, school managers (they used to be called head teachers), are the real short-term beneficiaries of this testing culture. Reputations are enhanced, which in the case of senior leadership can and often does lead to increased income—the real sweetener: rising test results increase the senior management's employability. Good scores empower senior management in the job market and make them more likely to get the good jobs—the bigger schools, the bigger incomes. Children are in all respects sold short by this model of education—their work is well and truly appropriated to create profit for others. School becomes a succession of potentially stressful hoops they are pressurised to jump through, and opportunities for genuine education are narrowed by increasing time spent training children to jump through these hoops, as the tests determine the curriculum . . . outcomes are valued over processes, and achievement is used to rank children according to performance in a narrowing curriculum that favours those able to perform well in traditional academic terms. Teachers—and some schools—make heroic efforts to maintain a concern for the child as a unique individual with individual needs and individual abilities, but they are increasingly constrained by bad legislation that drives schools toward bad practice. Schools are often awash with the verbiage of good educational intentions. Buzz phrases like "creative curriculum", "ownership of learning" and "learning to learn" abound. But, in reality, the overwhelming pressure of measured performance and outcomes overshadow the teacher's classroom practice and priorities.

The state has prioritised the bad practice of teaching to outcomes over learning with meaning. Teachers therefore need to resist with good practice that reverses this valuation.

Good practice is learning that is meaningful for the child. Good practice is a dynamic response by autonomous, properly trained, qualified and funded educationalists to the needs of each individual child. Good practice is interested in the unique needs of the child not the shiftable, shifting and shifty needs of the minority of powerful people who all too frequently take control of the state. Each teacher needs to decide whether they are going to side with the needs of the child or the needs of the state. It is a question of integrity. Teachers need to reassert their integrity, to remember that they probably became teachers in most cases to make a difference. We also need to reassert the idea that the role of teacher is a complex one, so children deserve to be supported by people who know what they are doing. I can turn a tap on and off, even work a shower and drive a car. That doesn't make me a plumber or a mechanic. A plumber or a mechanic can become parent, but that is not the same as becoming a teacher. Don't ask me to service your car or mend your plumbing, those aren't my skills. But give me a class of four- or five-year-olds, and I know what I'm doing. Conversely, don't insult our children by using cut-price non-professionals or people doing cut-price on the job training schemes instead of properly trained and qualified workers who actually know what they're doing and why they are doing it.

Parents and activists need to be vocal in their support of good practice. The wisest parents want their children to be happy with themselves and with their friendships. Parents should refuse to accept their child or any child being reduced to a score. Expect the school to talk about the children not about their statistics. Parents should insist their child, every child, is known as an individual whose attributes are recognised and welcomed, whose well-being is supported.

The state's strategies of competition, outcomes and selection support the existence of a system of social privilege that not only serves the particular interests of the ruling elite but also creates a culture of stress and anxiety. The state's strategies of deregulation and privatisation support the existence of a system that configured individual needs not as priorities to be met but as an opportunities for profit. Ofsted inspectors, some settings and schools and managers, and even some teachers and parents, collude in these strategies that produce healthy statistics and unhealthily depressed and alienated individuals. The culture of atomisation and competition is the politics of divide and rule. None of this is good practice. It's toxic nonsense. Don't touch it with a barge pole.

Reclaiming our schools is made a lot likelier by cooperative collective action. "Whose school? Our school" was one of the chants of choice of the 2014 "Hands Off Hove Park" campaign, opposing Hove Park School being turned into an academy at the whim of the head teacher. I think it was probably me that started it up as the first demo at the school gates was winding down. It worked so well because it was both a challenge to hierarchical authority and an assertion of collective vision. The head, who was so keen to turn the school into an academy, liked to travel first class when accompanying children—who were travelling second class—to prestigious events in London, had a fondness for brand new cars paid for by the school and expenses paid jaunts to Saudi Arabia in term time and sent his own child to a "public" school. Legally obliged to "consult" with parents and the school community, he insisted consultation didn't involve a ballot and showed us a PowerPoint presentation about Plato's Cave and all the extra money the school might get if it converted to an academy. He explained his reasons for wanting to turn the school into an academy to the local press: it was not because the school was failing (it wasn't), but because academy status would gift him with more freedom and more power. At that time, you could count successful anti-academy campaigns pretty much on the fingers of one thumb. Nonetheless, the campaign mounted by the parents and the local NUT and school workers (the teachers went on official strike, and the pupils staged spontaneous demonstrations), supported by the community, some of Brighton and Hove's Green Party councillors and MP Caroline Lucas, was successful. We had marches, pickets and picnics. We convinced the local authority to ballot parents—this produced a 71 per cent vote against academisation. We discovered the head had somehow allowed the four parent governor places on the governing body to remain vacant. In legally required elections, four anti-academy parental candidates were overwhelmingly elected, jeopardising the head's ability to command a compliant majority of governing body votes.

Later, we were the subject of a Department for Education (DfE) briefing analysing how we won, to warn other heads what to watch out for. Needless to say, the DfE analysis was laughably incorrect. Our campaign was successful because of a combination of factors, most of which the DfE didn't seem to have noticed. Even Education Secretary Gove proved unexpectedly useful, by having a second name that rhymed with "Hove". This helped no end with the song writing and the slogans (I think it was Natasha's daughter who came up with the nifty "Hove Park not Gove Park" slogan). NUT School representative Compannera Liz Ritson was one of those factors, energetically and efficiently organising in the workplace and utterly impervious to management intimidation. And the energetic and efficient self-organisation of the parents, the "Hands Off Hove Park" campaign coordinated by Sarah Arjun, Sharon Duggal and Natasha Wiseman, moved the debate from a defensive response to a proactive and effective challenge. Being self-organised meant parents weren't as circumscribed as organised labour. Being self-organised also meant we weren't psychologically conditioned to being as circumscribed as organised labour. The DIY punk rock can-do attitude was infectious. I had to do a phone radio interview one day, being the only person available probably. The interviewer's last question was: "What will you do if (the subtext being 'when') the campaign is unsuccessful?" As a trade unionist, I was used to this sort of thing; ever since the Miner's Strike, we'd done a lot of being unsuccessful. But I wasn't speaking here as a union member, I was speaking as part of the punk rock "Hands Off Hove Park" campaign. So I said the question was irrelevant, because we weren't going to lose. The parents of the school community and the people of Brighton and Hove weren't greedy, selfish or stupid, so this academisation wasn't going to happen. And when it didn't, I was trying to think what it felt like and decided it felt a bit like it had felt when Apartheid ended, only—being more personal—even more so.

Collective action: you can't beat it. It is local organised collectivity that stops your local school being academised, just as it was national organised collectivity that stopped Trump poncing round London in Her Majesty's golden coach in 2018. Globally organised collective action by school students resulted in an estimated one million pupils walking out of school on Climate Strike in March 2019.

Organised collective action by some teaching unions has opposed the centralising, politicising agenda of the state and effectively slowed down the process of "reform". In 1988, Kenneth Baker was making statements in favour of deregulation of pay and conditions and of making strikes by teachers illegal. Thirty years later, the Teachers Pay and Conditions Document still refusing to ratify Gove's nasty little plans to dismantle the principle of national pay and conditions, the government is reduced to attempting to sidestep this with the policy of enforced academisation, thus legally allowing head teachers and their academy bosses to pay whomever they like whatever they like. As we noted in part two, collective action by parents who took their kids out of school on a Kids' Strike Day put a stop to that too.

The state seems to gamble on being able to ignore us most of the time, whether it is ignoring two million of us marching through London to oppose an illegal war against Iraq or the thousands of people signing petitions to oppose baseline testing for four-year-olds. Nonetheless, when it looks like popular and very public opposition might find ways to access decision-making or even just win a vote somewhere against the state's policies, the state becomes nervous. Sometimes the state responds with proactive repression, but at other times it responds by removing the cause for the widespread complaint. Gove got unceremoniously shifted from his job as minister of education just before the 2015 election, because it was obvious even to Prime Minister Cameron that, despite some pretty stiff competition, Gove is indisputably far and away the least popular and most ridiculous minister of education ever. Similarly, after the shambles of the first year of a recommended trialling of baseline tests for four-year-olds, the government quietly announced the tests had become very optional indeed.

Perhaps because they feel they have less mediating control over the possible modulators of opinion, schools are a little warier of public opinion than governments. Governments, of course, have a greater degree of power and societal authority and a greater capacity to control media and manipulate opinion. Also, sadly, they don't have voters' evenings like schools have parents' evenings, and they don't let you make an appointment to talk over your concerns, so they are a lot more distant and are a lot less vulnerable. Sadly, smug toffs never seem to get the custard pie smack in the well fed piggy pink snout they so richly deserve. As we have seen, the media takes great delight in vilifying state education in its headlines, whether it is William Tyndale Juniors or Little Ducklings Nursery. With the annual very public publication of test results in league tables and the publication of Ofsted, schools have become even more vulnerable to media attention and "public opinion".

But this proximity and daily contact can and often does work in teachers' favour, because parents can easily appreciate the realities of school life and recognise the very real

dedication most teachers have to that idea of making a difference for children, of making a difference in terms of their children's development and learning. Good practice will make it
manifest that teachers and parents share a common interest in
the well-being and the development and learning of the children they are both responsible for. Speakers at the Kids Strike
rally in Brighton made it clear that the strike was in support
of their children's teachers—placards proclaimed: "We love
our teachers!" My experience is that whenever teachers go
on strike, the majority of the letter writers and the pundits
spitting bile and thundering outrage in the media aren't actually parents. Parents tend to support teachers, the more so
when teachers and schools operate a good practice open-door
policy of honesty and respect. It is inevitable that teachers and
schools will encounter parents with whom serious and significant disagreements emerge. My more extreme examples of
disagreement have included a member of the National Front
and a very fundamentalist Islamist. But, even there, while
agreeing that we very much disagreed on quite a few core
issues, we could establish a workable relationship, because
we established that we both shared a commitment to the well-
being and development of the child.

Maybe I was lucky. The extremity of parental opinion that
I worked with never mounted up to the same kind of "angry
sizeable minority" that the teachers at William Tyndale had to
put up with. I would also have to be honest and admit that—
certainly since I left Andrew Ewing School in 1987—I have
always also been part of, sometimes the entirety of, the radical
progressive minority. Which is actually not something I mind;
I like democracy, and I quite like the idea of consensus, of
individuals contributing their perspectives toward a collectively agreed upon understanding. I would say that my aim in
writing this book is not to assert the primacy and inviolability
of any ideas it might express or espouse but, rather, to contribute a voice that has been increasingly sidelined to a debate that
has been increasingly shut down by the state's assumption of

the inviolability of the agenda of "reform". The state has done away with dialogue. This book thinks that vital social relationships depend on interaction, involvement and discussion. You stand up for what you believe in and engage in discussions with those who don't agree with you. You influence people, and sometimes they influence you. In some discussions, there are some points upon which you will not compromise, but there also may be areas where it is possible to arrive at a shared agreement in order to arrive at a workable consensus. This is not the paradigm that the "reformers" favour. They don't compromise and debate, and they are not interested in consensus. They are always pathetically right.

Their opportunism and hypocrisy are breathtaking. They turn "Sunny Jim's" Great Debate into the naked complete control of the national curriculum, and they turn Phoney Tony's cheapskate academy sticking plaster into a full-blown privatisation zombie apocalypse. They dress greed and self-interest up in nostalgia and "British Values" as a distraction from neoliberalism's commodification of state education, which—bizarrely—turns schools in post-industrial England into exam factories.

As teachers and parents, we need to recognise the intentions of the state's priorities for what they are and recognise how they fail to consider the real needs of our real children. We need to insist we get state schools that both recognise and meet the real needs of our delightfully real children, because we know some delightfully real children come from homes where, thanks to the Thatch's abolition of society and the ubiquity of capitalism, they are not going to get the support they deserve or come from homes that may well not be able to afford—even if they wanted to—to send their children to a nice, progressive "private" school. So we need to make sure our schools are orientated toward benefiting all the children who attend them.

Children benefit most when engaged in the process of applying their intelligence to their experiences and developing their individual skills, enthusiasms and attributes. Their learning and well-being are enhanced if they are supported in this process by a positive environment offering a range of positive experiences and positive adult interactions, with the adult's experience enabling them to smooth or facilitate, consolidate and extend a child's learning and development.

This is why society has evolved the concept of education and the institutions dedicated specifically to learning, from kindergartens to universities. The 1989 United Nations Convention on the Rights of the Child not only recognised the right of the child to education but also declared in unequivocal terms what that education should be directed toward. Article 29 states: "the education of the child shall be directed to ... [t]he development of the child's personality, talents and mental and physical abilities to their fullest potential".[3]

No ifs, no buts, no government cuts.

Not according to the wishes of a wise parent. Not according to the interests of the neoliberal market.

Children have the right to be educated for their own sake.

The teacher's job, therefore, is surely to ensure that that is what happens.

Meaningful education.

Full stop.

Alchemy, Trust and Politics

> You really can't inspect Summerhill because our criteria
> are happiness, sincerity, balance and sociability.
> —A.S. Neill

In reclaiming our schools, we need also to evolve a road map of what we would like them to look like in the future. If the current schools replicate the current view of society endorsed by the state, can we reverse this process and envisage schools that might anticipate a view of the individual and social relationships we would wish to see realised in society? This was clearly the aspiration of much progressive education before it got closed down by the Thatcher government, that schools would create citizens who would ameliorate the future characteristics of the state.

So far, the tendency of these arguments would seem to suggest the formulation: the child = good, the state = bad. There is a fine tradition of thought that views the state, in whatever way it organises itself, as by its nature a negative and repressive social construction. Historically, the state, the political expression of social government, has been the organising and legitimising principle behind actions that if undertaken by individuals within society would be seen as pure and simple criminality. European liberal democracies slaughtered and plundered the world with their empires, and the totalitarian regimes of the last century cannibalised those subjected to their rule in concentration camps and gulags. The state is an organisation that can easily be turned into a weapon whose main effect is to do damage to the people on a monumental scale. State education, as we noted earlier, was historically conceived as a social strategy that would further the interests of the state. However, within that history there have also been examples of education being reconfigured in opposition to the interests of the ruling class, moments and movements, individuals and professional organisations, that have attempted to wrest control of teaching and learning away from the state, insisting that teaching and learning are the proper responsibility of an autonomous profession of educationalists who prioritise education rather than training and the child's needs rather than the state's. It has sometimes even been recognised that children themselves have ownership rights over their learning. These are the models of education we need to rediscover, because they position education as a strategy for social progress. These are the models of education that existed before Baker's "reform" bills of the late 1980s came into force.

The model of state education in Britain was very much influenced by the ideas and opportunities of the post-war consensus of the 1950s, and later by the libertarian blossoming of the 1960s. The state was understood to be the welfare state, which, in turn, was understood as having the welfare of its people as a central priority. This idea provided the opportunity for teachers as a group of workers to evolve and implement an educational praxis that effectively had the welfare of children, the needs of the whole child, the needs of the future citizen—and, therefore, the question of the nature of the future society—as a central priority. The consequence of theories of liberal education and the democratisation of comprehensivisation meant that state education no longer prioritised simply fitting classes of people for ready-made social functions.

Teachers, as a profession, started to develop a pedagogy to meet the real needs of real children, often drawing on progressive theories of education that were able to operate outside the agenda of the state, because they served the children of the socially privileged. This pedagogy recognised the importance of the concept of development in understanding how children learn and grow into competent individuals. Any objective observer of children will come to the self-evident common-sense view that children—people—are all very different, and their commonality is these shared differences. We are different sizes and shapes, have different attitudes, aptitudes, skills, perceptions. . . and all of these differences evolve and develop at different rates.

Reclaiming our schools means advocating a non-lineal approach to learning. Our schools will need to have less of a timetable for teaching and more opportunities for the development of learning.

In England, the teaching of the formal literacy skills of reading and writing has always seemed to attract particular attention from people who know nothing about it. In the context of this book, it also offers a clear example of the distance between the "reform" priorities of the right-wing state and the pedagogy evolved by practical experience.

Government, media and many unwise parents are convinced that the quicker you can get a child reading and writing the better. This will somehow be better for the nation when it comes to competing with its economic rivals and better for your individual child when it comes to competing with its classmates. This is nonsense; no research shows that making young children learn the formalities of reading and writing in the Early Years has any long-term benefits whatsoever. Quite sensibly, teachers, who by the 1970s were starting to understand child development, would talk about "reading readiness" in children, aware that in most countries children experience play-based learning until the age of seven, by which time they are generally developmentally able to engage with the challenges of more formal areas of learning, like reading. But although there are these generalisations, times where you could expect certain developments to be taking place at particular chronological ages, as with the spectrum of gender tendencies, each of us will find ourselves at our own point, moving at our own pace within these generalised time frames.

The formal skill of writing needs to be embedded within the child's overall language development. First of all, children need to feel they have something to represent through mark-making, something to write about means having something to say, some personal particular purpose. Children also need to have developed the necessary muscles that will be controlling the tools of mark-making—in boys, the muscles responsible for fine motor control actions generally develop fully at about the age of seven, several years later than in girls. It is therefore both counterproductive and not a little cruel, setting boys up to fail at an early age, if schools expect boys to write neatly when they don't have the muscle development to do so. Joined-up handwriting is a particular waste of time and energy in this context, without even mentioning that no one outside of the classroom ever uses it as a form of communication.

Instead of being faced with opportunities to fail, children should be in the kind of supportive environment that allows them to be successful, that allows them to be who they are and learn as they are. I have already admitted that although I spent many years teaching reading professionally, as it were, I remained mystified by how children managed the process of learning to read—it seemed that they all somehow contrived to have their lightbulb moments when I wasn't looking. When I became a parent, I thought that at last I would be able to so closely monitor and observe the process that I would be able to catch the moment when the jigsaw of reading skills clicked into place. Nope, I missed it again. Twice. All I have learned is that it is alchemy, magic, and all you can do to support it— indeed, all you should do to support the acquisition of reading skills—is provide as wide a range of different experiences and strategies as possible. Literacy skills are language skills and need to be embedded within language development. Children need to develop their spoken language before and as well as they develop the decoding and coding skills of reading and writing. They need opportunities to talk and listen, to talk and be listened to, in order to explore idea, emotion and imagination. And they need books and stories, but they deserve real books and real stories not just godawful soul-destroying workbooks and reading schemes, because a diet of such outcome-orientated pap will more than likely kill the appetite for literature and act as a disincentive to decoding print, by making it not worth the effort. But books and stories that provoke an emotional and intellectual response, and there are some absolutely brilliant writers producing witty, articulate, eloquent books for young children, and these include favourite books and favourite stories you can return to and consolidate your skills and gather new insights or just simply more enjoyment from—that's the stuff to give 'em; the rest is the child's right to their own alchemical processes.

No one seems to find it odd that, according to the media, children in Britain still somehow manage to lag behind children in other countries, despite thirty years of government legislation and raised standards in hind leg peripatetics. It is not simply that education has to cope with the incompetence of the government's pedagogy; the process of developing language skills is made more uphill by the fact that it has to take place within the historical context of an increasingly illiterate society. Social communication has been gutted by image and slogan; pop music's adolescent inability to articulate and the traditional stereotypical restricted codes of the working class have been used by the ruling class since the mid-1970s as handy standards to limit social discourse. Newspapers became tabloids, and then texts became tweets. Media mogul Rupert Murdoch, whose flagship best-selling tabloid the *Sun* never ceases to impress with its daily redactions of language, thought and meaning, is both the government's greatest supporter and the greatest promoter of illiteracy, which would be funny were it not for the bile, stupidity, greed, racism and sexism that he promotes as well.

Commerce has also plugged children into more restricted languages; children are sold Xboxes and Fortnite, where they would once have bought the weekly print comics; compared with current tabloids The *Scum* and the *Daily Star*, the old *Beano* and *Dandy* look positively Shakespehearian in their use of wit, imagination and characterisation.

Nonetheless, schools are expected to maintain a velocity of lineal timetabled progress in these increasingly uphill conditions, wherein a twenty-first century president of the United States is unable to express himself through anything more complex than a tweet. This process of forward movement is to be characterised and indeed driven by the Office for Standards in Education (Ofsted) inspectorate's old favourite phrase, "pace and rigour". There is to be no pause, no let and no lateness. Successive governments, so fond of announcing their commitment to "the family" and the values of "the family", have nonetheless shown a zeal more often associated with the Stalinist regimes of former Eastern Europe in prising children away from their parents and making sure they spend more time in the hands of the state, which, of course, now also means there is an increased likelihood they will be spending more time in the hands of and making a profit for the private sector.

The question for teachers is simple. Who do you trust? Do you trust the state, an institution that voted enthusiastically in 2003 for an illegal war against Iraq, insisting that it had weapons of mass destruction, when, in fact, none existed, that insists that the global economic crisis of 2008 must be paid for by the poor and the socially disadvantaged rather than the rich elite who caused it, that consistently fails to meet its own stated economic targets and that for the last thirty years has treated state education not as a public service but as a deliberate blunt instrument of ideologically motivated social control, on the one hand, and an opportunity to make a nice little earner for the business-minded, on the other? Teachers, do you trust the state's "great reformers", a succession of privileged (mostly) white males, with no background in education or experience of state education? Or do you trust yourself, your instinct to "make a difference", your training, your colleagues and your collective experience of the work that making a difference entails?

Lastly: Do you trust children? Do you trust their potential? Do you accept that each child has innate unique potential that is expressed best through an exploration of their particular individual skills and abilities? I suspect most teachers, however deskilled and devalued the state may have made them feel, would rather trust their children than the state. So I would suggest, brother and sisters, that what we need to do is put that trust back at the centre of what we do, not just for a moment of theoretical consideration, but full-time as the prime cause of everything teachers do and education does. We must put the individual child back at the heart of our schools and make the child's needs not the state's our priority.

But we also need to look honestly at the power relationships within schools. If experience teaches that "reform's" authoritarian agenda is the antithesis of genuine education, we teachers should take care not to impose such a structure on the children we are hoping to educate. We should also take care not to exchange "reform's" set of grand desirable outcomes for our own slightly more liberal set of grand desirable outcomes. We have seen how "Sunny Jim" Callaghan's amiable Great Debate about what a wise parent might want for their child created the conditions for the 1987 Education Reform Bill, where the wise parents had become Mad Maggie Thatcher and Smoothiechops Kenneth Baker. That is why I tend to favour consideration of educational liberationists writing before the "reformists" seized power. Recent debate seems—like the confused substitution of social mobility for social justice—to have had its terms defined by the utilitarianism of "reform". Education is unquestioningly presented as a means to improve *society's* outcomes and to further *society's* growth. "Creativity" and flexibility of thinking are only

desirable now because we think they will be of use to our continued growth as a leading nation in the digital age. People are
serving systems—again. In the case of liberationists like Paulo
Freire, Emma Goldman, Ivan Illich and A.S. Neill, although
they often speak in their particular historical contemporary
language, the aspiration at the heart of their writing is a set
of shared beliefs and values—"that school fit the child," as
Neill put it,[1] that systems serve people, that meaning is vital
to learning and that a healthy society is only realised through
autonomous individuals not automatons, through educating
the whole child not by outputting increased outcomes. This
is a direct challenge to the authoritarian nature of the state
and just the sort of dangerous subversive thinking those "wise
parents" Thatcher and Baker sought to stamp out before it
started infecting the children of the masses.

Putting these radical ideas into practice isn't necessarily
easy, and it is even harder when, as a worker, you find your
job description apparently entails having to implement lunatic
government policies and, furthermore, provide convincing evidence that you have been doing good implementing whenever
the Ofsted vultures turn up. Operating a system of teaching
that is characterised by pressure and stress is bound to have
consequences for the quality of social relationships within
that system, as the pressure and stress of teachers is translated
into the pressure and stress of those supposed to be doing the
learning. Children accustomed to being on the receiving end
of adult authority don't always immediately respond reasonably when offered systems based on respect, cooperation and
reason. Our classrooms aren't going to be reclaimed overnight.
But values rather than rules and dialogue and reason rather
than decree and obedience are attributes that are both worthwhile in themselves and conducive to genuine education.
Classrooms need to become spaces of equality; they need to
become playgrounds and workshops where every individual
is of equal importance and every individual's needs are met.
Everybody needs to go home happy. The teacher's particular

role is to make sure this happens. Teachers need to stop pretending to be god almighty and try being more like democratically elected coordinating chairpersons. Teachers need to be able to see themselves as fallible and human, to recognise they might be mistaken and to apologise when they make mistakes. A.S. Neill is a forthright and convincing advocate of honesty in the relationship among those involved in the alchemical processes of education. He understands that children are naturally tolerant of adult moments of grumpy temper, as well of each other. However, his writing is circumscribed by the historical context of a gentler more traditional liberal state when he insists that he never expressed his personal political views to his pupils. Now, and in retrospect, we can see that the very existence of an institution like Summerhill and the pedagogy of child-centred education represents a political view very much in opposition to the politics of the ruling class, particularly as those politics have developed since the collapse of their gentlemanly liberal façade.

The contradictions between the developmental needs of the child and the political priorities of the state become more marked the more marginalised and excluded the child's community is. The most vulnerable children are the children who invariably suffer the most from the centralised state's market-orientated agenda. Working in economically deprived Stepney, Chris Searle observed in *This New Season*:

> The child becomes divided against himself. The anticipation of his ordeal makes him see himself merely as a unit for successful or unsuccessful consumption by a society solely geared to examination results. His humanity is degraded and broken. The "nervous desperation" to achieve adds to the confusion of adolescence. Like the teacher, the child quickly recognises and chases his career prospects and gets on with the job. He has no share in the government or decision-making in the life of his school. That is taken care of by

other, higher people. His education is not for participation or democracy, but for consumption. He will make profit for someone else, and a salary for himself. This is the vision of life school offers him, and no matter how lovingly his teacher treats him, unless he committedly opposes this situation by political struggle in the schools, he is in absolute collusion with this future.[2]

Although written in 1973, these are the societal and educational conditions still grinding away at children's life chances nearly half a century later. State schools and their pupils are in a constant institutionalised state of anxiety over examination results. Schools and pupils have no sense of having a voice in their own futures, and as government funding is ruthlessly cut year-on-year, support for those pupils least likely to achieve the necessary exam scores, the most vulnerable and most challenged individuals who deserve the most help, is stripped away in a ruthless triage system. As academies have greater control over their own admission policies and provision, children with special education needs are finding themselves increasingly—sometimes literally—excluded from mainstream education to preserve finances and ensure the highest possible examination scores.

As the "reformers" have made manifest, education is never politically neutral. The right will insist you should silence yourself and let them carry on indoctrinating children unhindered or insist on the "right to freedom of speech" if you try to shut them up. Just because being political in opposition to these unscrupulous, cynical, hypocritical, censorial advocates of the "rights of greed and privilege" isn't necessarily easy doesn't mean you should censor yourself. Legislation isn't politically neutral. Curriculum isn't politically neutral. Pedagogy isn't politically neutral. Teachers shouldn't pretend to be politically neutral either.

Educational Privilege and the Ruling Class: Unfit for Purpose

> We're the hammer and the nails, we're the needle and
> the thread.
> You couldn't find your own elbow with an A to Z.
> —Robb Johnson, "Win, Lose or Draw"

We find ourselves in a country that in all respects of measurement features as one of the wealthier geopolitical entities on the planet. This is also a country where more than four million children officially live in conditions defined as poverty, and head teachers can take home salaries of £200,000. Them that's got just keep getting. . . When we look at who has been in government, particularly for the last thirty years, it is apparent that we have effectively had government of the privileged, by the privileged, for the privileged. As a matter of record, we have been governed by the following leading lights of educational privilege: Margaret Hilda Thatcher received a scholarship to a grammar school and went on to Oxford (surely the best argument against social mobility anyone ever needs); John Major is another grammar school product (no university but a career in banking); Anthony Charles Lynton Blair went to a prestigious fee-paying "public" school, followed by Oxford (to all intents and purposes, he lied both to Parliament and the public to pursue an illegal war against Iraq that has had disastrous consequences both for that region and for the wider world, providing the circumstances for the rise of terrorist militancy, and for whom "sorry" seems to be the mildest word); Nicholas William

Peter Clegg attended a couple of "public" schools, Cambridge University, and then the University of Minnesota, followed by a master's degree at the College of Europe (a LibDem Quisling in Cameron's 2010 coalition government); even Nigel Farage, the UK media's favourite armchair fascist, went to "public" school and then on to a career in banking. But, of course, the absolute epitome of government by privilege was the Cameron government, at the centre of which was a cabinet drawn over-whelmingly from the same privileged background: very pres-tigious "public" schooling followed by Oxford University. Their arrogant sense of entitlement was surely only matched by their sheer incompetence. This was a government that responded to a massive global economic crisis caused by the irresponsi-ble practices of the banks by—bizarrely—declaring economic war on the nation's public service workers, the disabled and the very poorest members of society, who successive govern-ments had consigned to an existence dependent upon state benefits. This was a government that consistently failed to meet its own economic targets, that presided over increasing poverty levels and increasing dependence on food banks, that even failed to win its own referendum over Britain remaining within the European Union, in a cynical attempt to stem the haemorrhaging of support from its own right wing toward the more far-right UKIP party (figureheaded by ex-Conservative Party member Nigel Farage). Their legacy also includes the shameful destruction of civil society in Libya, the catastrophic consequences of Cameron's own little militaristic adventuring.

Educational privilege is synonymous with ease of access to positions of social privilege, positions of authority and gov-ernance. There are particular establishments that guarantee greater chances of access to privilege—there is hierarchy within the hierarchy; it is not merely "public" school and uni-versity that ensures access to continued and further privilege. Eton, then Oxford University, and moving within the circle of the Bullingdon Club was the predominant background characterising the Cameron cabinet. Not only is the essential inequality of this system morally unacceptable, it is, moreover, an objectively ineffective way to run a country. Cameron made much of "broken Britain" in his initial election campaign, yet his government's policy of austerity simply increased the damage being done to individuals and communities—so we must logically conclude he was either a hypocrite, an incompetent or both. The Eton and Oxford educated Bullingdon Club member Boris Johnson has a public record of racist and xenophobic remarks, and in the wake of the referendum on EU membership he was appointed foreign secretary. Again, objectively, this appointment of someone from a privileged background with personal attitudes and skills that appear directly to conflict with the function of their public office suggests either hypocrisy or incompetence, maybe cynical politicking that demeans further the integrity of the state, or perhaps it's just a post-modernist populist joke, beyond satire. It is surely an index of the utter exhaustion of the neoliberal attempt to recuperate parliamentary democracy to see Boris Alexander de Peffle Johnson finally clambering his porcine, privileged, mendacious populist bulk into 10 Downing Street as prime minister in 2019. Even his Bullingdon Club chums had done their best to keep his hands off any sharp implements for most of the preceding decade, happy to see him sidelined in vanity projects like appearances on the BBC's smug celebrity comic substitute for political satire *Have I Got News for You* or buffooning about as Mayor of London, with union flags, unfeasible plans for unbuildable bridges and a variety of stereotypical blonde females.

The conclusion is obvious: the privileged elite are rubbish at government. Over the last thirty years, privilege as a selection process has produced government after government that is not fit for purpose.

"Education reform"—or "education, education, education"—has always been presented as a high-profile public vote-winning policy focus of those governments. The "reform" project is now clearly exhausted, its initiatives having failed to achieve their stated aim of "improving" state education. Despite lavish government support—no question here of standing on your own two feet—free schools continue to fail at a much higher rate than any other type of school. They also tend to be primarily set up by faith groups. Academies provide no significantly better education than do the schools that remain with the local authority. Academies that the Office for Standards in Education (Ofsted) deem inadequate are six times more likely to stay inadequate than state schools similarly categorised, while even the *Daily Telegraph* was concerned in January 2014 to discover that "taxpayer-funded Academy chains have paid millions of pounds to businesses with personal links to their directors and trustees".[1] As a strategy to transform state education, academy status has in reality only succeeded in transforming schools into opportunities for private enterprise, the thin end the Global Education Reform Movement (GERM) agenda.

The reintroduction of ideas of utility and competition in education has spawned an attendant culture of private tutoring and cramming. Parental support for education has become skewed into parental pressure on children to pass tests. Learning has been ruthlessly monetarised, even out of school hours. Children's bookshops now feature not only children's literature but also shelves groaning under workbook after workbook purporting to enhance your child's chances of achieving success in national curriculum tests. In a perverse way, this supports what educationalists have always asserted and successive governments have denied—that access to education is enhanced by access to resources. Of course, access to resources and the quality of those resources depends upon your economic ability to purchase them. Therefore, the more affluent you are, the more able you are to afford better resources, and, therefore, the more likely you are to achieve better results in test situations.

In September 2016, the bankruptcy of the reformist project was again made clear when unelected prime minister

Theresa May, imposed into office by the Tory Party after the disastrous performance of Cameron and his clique in the referendum over EU membership, declared that her government would be reintroducing secondary modern education. This is the old obsessive nostalgia for the pre-comprehensive school that tested and selected children at eleven years of age. As always, the wording used when competition over an artificially created scarcity of desirable outcomes is involved focuses attention on the winners rather than the losers. The winners in the selection lottery would be going on to receive the privilege of the bright child, a grammar school education. At the time, the figure of 20 per cent was used as an estimate of the proportion of children likely to be selected for grammar schooling, based on the proportion of children who received grammar school education when the system was in widespread use in the 1960s. This means 80 per cent of children not able to afford to purchase their privilege outright by attending fee-paying "public" schooling will be receiving a second-class education service.

All that legislation, all those initiatives, free schools, academies, all that rhetoric about entitlement and improving standards and every child matters and closing the gap . . . swept to one side. The last pretence of "reform" is the sentimental wish that all would be well if the clocks would simply be turned back by fifty years.

The 2016 announcement dressed itself up with some vague modifications intended to combat concerns—there were to be places at grammar schools specifically reserved for "the poor". Again, this is in itself such a bleakly revealing statement; "the poor" are, it would seem, an accepted part of Britain's political landscape, and only the deserving few will be airlifted out of the abyss, if they can prove they merit the rewards of social mobility. Decades ago this triage system was shown to be an invalid mechanism, because as any fule kno children develop at different rates, some people do not respond well in formal testing situations, tests only test what is being tested, etc., etc. Again, there are vague assurances that children can be retested at regular intervals and so presumably we will have children relocated between schools thanks to what—a thirteen-plus exam, a fourteen-plus exam, a fifteen-and-a-bit-plus reassessment? Will there be an exchange system perhaps, with any underperformance in Latin leading to relegation from the higher realms of academe to the lower slopes inhabited by the hewers of wood and the drawers of water? Such simplistic, "back of a champagne napkin" notions are nonsense, the fantasy of a political ideology without even the slightest attempt to reference reality or, indeed, common sense.

Fundamentally, the affluent buy success, while the less affluent, the working class, the non-working class, the underclass—*the poor*—the four million or so twenty-first-century Timothy Winters in their rented accommodation and bed and breakfasts in Kabul Streets that no amount of government redefining of what constitutes poverty can manage to massage away, find themselves in families that can't buy anything of any quality whatsoever, and that includes their children's education. So that is why we need to have comprehensive schools, your lordshits and ladyshits, because social mobility is the wrong answer to the wrong question. The question should not be: How can we help the deserving children of the deserving poor? The proper question is: How can we end such poverty? In asking that question, we need to ask how such poverty was created, and we will inevitably conclude that our problem is not with *the poor* but with *the rich*.

A February 2016 *Guardian* article comparing private and state school inspectorates noted: "At my school, the most passionately discussed item on our 'ISI [Independent Schools Inspectorate] is coming' agenda was what cake we should provide".[2] It is clearly high time we closed these breeding grounds of entitled incompetence down.

Sunflowers, Playgrounds and Schools

> Grow gardens and hospitals on every street, sunflowers,
> playgrounds and schools
> Where you do what you like cos you like what you do...
> —Robb Johnson, "Be Reasonable"

Sunflowers, of course, are predominantly tall and yellow. Ideally, playgrounds and schools, however, ought to be harder to tell apart.

We need to be more vocal advocates for a pedagogy that prioritises children and the developmental needs of children. We need to be advocates for a pedagogy that considers the state's greatest asset to be the people, the true constituent of its identity. The state needs to be understood not as some mystical narrative of privilege like the monarchy and not as an opportunity for plunder and exploitation, a monster that can only feed on its own children, but as an arbitrary, historical and geographical practicality that is in a constant state of becoming, being the sum of all the people it serves. The true purpose of the state is the practical task of attending to the well-being of people, the well-being of the individuals within its parameters.

And then it can wither away, thank you very much. We can replace the totalitarian hierarchy of centralised state control with a more effective and more participatory federation of democratically constituted local collectives and communities.

As noted earlier, we arrived at a point where nationalism, as an expression of the character of the state, was being replaced by the values of democracy, inclusion and equality. These are not "British Values", although they should be the values of the geographical area encompassed by the term Britain. These are human values. These are values much more in keeping with the instinctive human values that children naturally tend to express in their behaviour and attitudes, that they recognise as important characteristics of a successful, happy society.

In many respects, our task should be less challenging than the task that the "reformers" undertook. We have already won the argument. The "reformers" have expended vast energy in an attempt to make clocks run backwards. Only now do I think that perhaps I should have more accurately called them "deformers" all along. The disastrous consequences of such an illogical idea are to be seen very much in the shadows that threaten our children, the threats of failure, poverty, home-lessness, war and terror. Since Thatcher trumpeted a return to Victorian values, and the education deformers trumpeted their return to basics, we have witnessed both society and edu-cation turned into a shambles. Whatever disguise they dress their politics up in—"privatisation", "austerity"—the conse-quence for most of us is that the quality of our lives is wors-ened. We need to trust the validity of our experience again. The media chatters happily at us each morning, dazzles us with its celebrities dancing for us each evening, but in between, in reality, we experience nothing but the failure of the state and its reforming initiatives to meet our daily needs. We have, all of us, experienced what works, our own Neverlands, and we need to use these experiences to animate and direct our progressive aspirations. And we, all of us, have experience of what doesn't work, and we need to use this knowledge of the state's failures as the shadow that sharply defines our vision of progressive and positive alternatives.

We know that we experience time as lineal progress and understand our lives in terms of trajectory, but we also know that when we have our deepest moments of existence we experience time differently, and these deeper moments are often cyclical, repeated and explored in spirals. We also know that since the Industrial Revolution, the fetishisation of lineal technological "progress" by the accumulators and the owners benefiting from the material outcomes produced by technology encourages the idea that technology determines social progress. The ruling elite's cynical abdication of responsibility for the consequences of its use of technology to generate their short-term material gains has resulted in significant environmental degradation. This is not progress; this is simply a more complex form of oppression. So what we do not want is schooling that mimics that paradigm of heedless progress, that harries us toward outcomes, that defines development in terms of acceleration, that insists we always set and then exceed targets.

We want an education process that allows us to play, that explores diversity, that takes its own time, that trusts us to develop at our own pace, in our own spirals. Returning to Victorian values returns us to notions of rapacious acquisition, imperial conflict, the survival of the fittest and the punishment of undeserving poor, to the inevitability of the mutually assured destruction that was World War I, when "they" needed the likes of us, but only to power their factories, bloat their profits and fill the trenches and the cemeteries. Now, though, they have moved their factories overseas, and they fight their wars by proxy or with drones. There is the uneasy feeling that, despite having turned the clocks back, back to the century of Empire and Privilege, they no longer need us, and so history, which they like to claim has ceased to exist, has arrived at a point of paradox. We would do well to note this, as they strip away even the "benefits" they allowed us when they stripped away our jobs and reclassify us as fit to work, when there is no work to be had. They don't want us any more; their reforms now work on behalf of corporations that salivate over the prospect of getting their teeth into our public services, because our only use now is as assets that allow access to public service budgets. They reduce our lives to the statistics of accountability and accountancy.

But our lives continue to be so much more complex than their reductions—and so much more beautiful. Each one of us unique, the centre of the universe. However we get here, by love, by accident, by whatever, we get born, we grow, we unfold, we exist, and history also keeps stubbornly unfolding. Slowly, generation after generation, we have been wising up. Our gods and masters have responded by stuffing us with their facts, teaching us to be ugly and stupid, diverting us with bread, circus and spectacle. It's all just wolfing down the cheap fast foodstuffs while watching the far distant galaxies play football on Sky TV, after all. If teachers want to make a difference, and why else would anybody really want to do this job, it is a difference that is so much more than the national curriculum could ever test you on. In our current post-industrial media-mediated wasteland, it is a difference that perhaps constitutes a truly significant threat to the hegemony of the ruling class.

Having gambled on destroying both the jobs and the communities that opposed them, the ruling class has attempted to hammer its nails into our coffins by rigorously controlling all forums of public discourse and creativity, education, journalism . . . culture. By destroying our jobs and our communities, they hammer away at our capacity to organise politically. By enforcing their ownership of the means of discussion—whether imposing their values on popular culture or what happens in our schools—they hammer away at our capacity for autonomy. The thing is, though, while they can oversee who gets what access to what job, who gets what access to which media, who gets to be a celebrity, they still need more workers than they are able to easily police, or even provide and control, to person the state education system. They haven't yet managed to plug every child into internet learning, and, actually, internet learning isn't really going to work, because algorithms are not how children operate. The ruling class doesn't want all those untended children and malcontented adolescents inhibiting their strategies for getting people back to work for peanuts. They want parents off benefits, but they definitely don't want their offspring bored shitless and hanging about the UK's high streets and street corners. They need to send our children to school. In England, they have been sending our children to school since 1870, so they can learn to be stupid. School is where everybody has to go. And that, brothers and sisters, is our great opportunity to "kick out the jams", as the MC5 once used to say. Where else are all our children likely to learn that they belong only to themselves and to each other? Where else now are they guaranteed the opportunity to learn about ideas and emotions they are not being force-fed by the right-wing media or the echo chambers of social media, which—as we are now noticing—like any other media, are susceptible to the manipulations of the monied right, in any case? In state school classrooms, where, as workers, we care more about each other than all the carrots and sticks of the centralised state, that's where. That's where we make a real difference. That's where our children can get their fair share of poetry and motion. That's where our children can learn to fly.

Despite all their legislation, their triumphalist speechifying and declarations and denials and diktats, the deformers can only cripple and maim. All children born are born anarchists. All children born are born with wings, their own wings, looking for their fair share of the sky. Children will play, children will learn, and children might well go on climate strike, and so tomorrow will happen, eventually, anyway. They close the windows, they lock the doors, they reduce the play and the learning to hoops to jump through, to meaningless lumps of sanctioned, sanitised content to be consumed and regurgitated, and then they constantly blame schools for the catastrophe that is the society they have governance over. In their exam factories, they try to stop up the ears and the eyes and the mouths of learning and questioning with "Right Answers", like they would hold back the very hands of time.

And it hasn't worked. It doesn't work.

Our task is to let the clocks run forward again.

EPILOGUE

A Brief Character Sketch and a Recipe

Who Was That Man?

On the field of Hastings, 1066,
Normans storming up the hill, arrows thick as bricks,
Who was it told King Harold to hold his head up high?
Harold holds his head up, gets an arrow in his eye.

Who was that man, lost in history's groves?
Who was that man? His name was Michael Gove.

At the conference in Munich, 1938,
Chamberlain meets Adolf to settle Europe's fate.
Neville asks his ministers: "Should this peace treaty be
    signed?"
Who was it said to Neville: "This means peace in our time".

Who was that man, that bungalow in Hove?
Who was that man? His name was Michael Gove.

In all of history's cock-ups, one factor's always true,
When someone puts their foot in it they get Gove upon
    their shoe.

So when the ConDem government came in in 2010,
They handed all the big jobs out to the Eton toffs again,
But when it came to education, they hadn't got a clue

So they gave the job to someone completely clueless too.

Who was that man, his favourite colour: mauve?
Who was that man? His name was Michael Gove.

Who was that man, the floater in your swimming pool, the
    bloater on your stove?
Who was that man? His name was Michael Gove.

Who was that man who loved state education like
    vampires love garlic cloves?
Who was that man? His name was Michael Gove.

How to Shape the Future with Play Dough

Here is an index of how bad things have become. Back doing
supply work again, the reception classes I have been in so far
are able to boot up colourful but terminally dull phonics programmes for kids to gawp at on the classroom massive white-
board computer screens, but they have forgotten how to make
play dough.

Can you believe it? We learn through the use of all our
senses, and here we have Early Years Classes doing away with
three senses, replacing touch, smell and taste with watching
the spectacles on a giant television.

Play dough is the Molotov cocktail of the Early Years, a
great provoker of collective social interaction and individual
well-being. Everybody loves play dough. And guess what—
though its outcomes are always only temporary . . . you can
sometimes measure them!!!!! Temporarily, of course.

This is the easiest way to make it, but you can add colours,
glitter, scents, textures and durability with only a little refinement to the recipe.

Try it out with your Year Ten class too when things get
really desperate.

1) mix 4 cups of flour with 1½ cups of salt

2) add 2 tablespoons of oil
3) add 1 cup of water, a little at a time, mixing as you go
4) maybe add more flour if it is sticky, more water if it is dry, till you get it all gathered up into a nice smooth ball of dough. For colouring, you could add food colouring, cocoa powder or powder paint

Job done. No cooking, and no need for bourgeois luxuries like "pesky hard to come by at the local corner shop at the last minute" cream of tartar either. Remember, as Huey Newton once might have said, for working people to be free, they must seize control of the means of production. Seizing the means of production requires a firm grip on the political realities of the moment. Play dough is great at developing your first firm grip skills.

CODA

1: A Song of Infant Sorrow

Egg Soup for Breakfast

This is how you have egg soup for breakfast
It gets the kids to school by ten to nine
Lateness will be punished by a letter
Absence will be punished by a fine
The school will turn the children into data
By teaching them the tests they'll never pass
While all you have to do is boil some water
Providing you saved money for the gas

This is how you have egg soup for breakfast
Providing you saved money for the gas

It's not a simple matter having egg soup
You have to choose what you're not going to do
You run the risk your kids will be excluded
If you buy the cheaper black school shoes
Egg soup needs a pinch of private landlords
Egg soup likes a lot of private gain
Then you add in universal credit
And queue up at a food bank in the rain

This is how you have egg soup for breakfast
And queue up at a food bank in the rain

You boil the egg five minutes in the water
Dad eats the egg before he goes to work
Mum puts salt and pepper in the water
This is how kids have egg soup
the sixth richest country on the planet
Where head teachers take two hundred grand a year
For measuring the measurable outcomes
While four million childhoods disappear

This is how you have egg soup for breakfast
While four million childhoods disappear

2: Two Songs of Infant Joy

The Glue Factory Strike Song

Welcome to the Glue Factory, we like the windows shut,
So we can tick the boxes in case Ofsted turns up.
We've done a risk assessment, and our targets have been
    set,
We've analysed the data, and our targets have been met.
Welcome to the Glue Factory, we like to lock the doors,
It helps us with our learning, turning children into scores,
There's such a lot of learning, it's like shopping list,
But if it can't be measured, of course, it can't exist.
David is a good boy, see him wag his tail,
He clearly learned his phonemes, while you just learned to
    fail,
But sometimes David wakes up in the middle of the night,
With the nightmare when he wakes up, the factory's gone
    on strike,
Singing: open all the windows, open all the doors,
We won't send our children up your chimneys any more
Let's unlock the sunlight, let's break out the sky,
Give every child a childhood, where no child ever fails to
    learn to fly. . .

Welcome to the Glue Factory, the goalposts have been
    moved,
All imagination has been surgically removed,

Our good is now not good enough, we have been
    reassessed.
We have to boil more bones up and be tested on our tests,
But Boris is a good dog, see him wag his tail,
He's learned his British values, while you just learned to fail,
But sometimes Boris wakes up in the middle of the night,
With the nightmare when he wakes up, the factory's gone
    on strike,
Singing: open all the windows, open all the doors. . .

Now David went to Eton, and Boris went there too,
And then they went to Oxford, and all their chums did too.
They never went to factories where they turn you into glue,
Where they boil away your dreams until there's nothing left
    of you,
And you, you're just a good dog, see it wag its tail.
Die for your country, go from jail to jail,
Surplus population, and when the ends don't meet,
You're just another homeless someone else's son or
    daughter on the streets. . .

Welcome to the Glue Factory Academy,
The CEO is happy with his brand new MGB,
The teachers are all qualified in cleaning MGBs,
The children are all learning how to fail GCSEs.
Theresa she's a good girl, see her wag her tail,
She's also went to Oxford, that's why she's the prime
    minister,
And one day when she wakes up in the middle of the night,
She'll find it's not a nightmare, the factory's gone on strike,
Singing: open all the windows, open all the doors. . .

That's Not Fair

No one likes a bully, bullying isn't cool,
That's why we don't want bullying here at Hertford School.
You think you're big and clever, you can throw your weight
  about,
You try that at Hertford, hear the kids all shout,
That's not fair.

Don't pick on us cos we're little,
Don't pick on us cos we're small.
Pick on someone your own size,
Brighton and Hove Council.

You say we going to have to have one class instead of two,
You say you've got no money, and there's nothing you can do.
The council's all important, the kids must do without,
With a half-price ticket up the i, hear the kids all shout,
That's not fair.

Don't pick on us cos we're little,
Don't pick on us cos we're small.
Pick on someone your own size,
Brighton and Hove Council.

Warren punches Darren in the dinner queue,
I didn't want to do it, but Theresa told me to.
Eenie meenie minie mo, the little one loses out,
You try that at a Hertford, hear the kids all shout.

Dear Father Christmas, I know you're really busy,
What we'd like for Christmas is our school left as it is, we
Don't want council Humbug, and if they don't desist,
You'll have to put those Scrooges on your naughty list,
Ho ho ho ho ho.

Don't pick on us cos we're little,
Don't pick on us cos we're small.
Pick on someone your own size,
Brighton and Hove Council.

ENCORE

To teach children to love and respect others, to inspire
in them the love of justice; to teach them as well that
their instruction is undertaken in view of the interests
of everyone: these are the moral principles on which
henceforth communal education will be based.
—Poster, Paris Commune, May 1871

We carry with us
The work of our fathers
The strength of our mothers
Their faith in a future
That works for the millions
Not millionaires
Where each shall be valued
And all will be shared

Here on this street, here in this union,
Here in our hearts, hear in our hands
The future starts here

These are our streets, this is our union,
These are our hearts, these are our hands
The future starts here
—Robb Johnson, "The Future Starts Here"

Never Trust a Neoliberal
(A Post-Borexit Postscript)

Perhaps we shouldn't wonder at the uncanny tenacity with which capitalism manages to hang on like grim death to its power and privilege. Whatever it calls itself—late capitalism, neoliberalism, dot.com capitalism, Sky Sport or Virgin Care—it has been regularly buying itself and its unscrupulous ruling class a new lease of half-life since Marx formulated its apparently inevitable demise through its own inherent contradictions over 150 years ago. At moments of crisis, turkeys vote for Christmas and workers rush to enlist for the nation state rather than the class struggle, and rather than vote for a properly funded health service, a care service, an end to food banks and homelessness, an economic strategy that addressed climate change and a national education service with no more high-stakes testing or punitive inspection regimes, enough of the UK electorate instead vote to Get Brexit Done and so lumber us with Boris Johnson's far-right Tory government.

Total control—both direct and remote—of the media, of the marketplace where workers have to sell their labour and of the institutions that transmit knowledge and values, is something of an asset in this miraculous process. The neoliberal state has turned much of the traditional working class into a non-working class, replacing collective community with atomised anxiety. Without the commonality of the workplace, with its opportunities for daily interactions that develop a shared and owned understanding of the world, individuals now have understanding imposed upon them by the spectacular media. Children, of course, still have opportunities for community—they attend schools, which is why the right has been so intent on imposing conditions on that community with its reforms. For many adults, however, opportunities for community are reduced to the outward significations of tribal identity. Ordinary people start using the divisive language of tribal exclusion—"my people", "our people", "my country", "our borders". The superficial official narrative suggests we've happily turned the clock back to somewhere approximating an idealised nostalgia for 1913, plenty of flags and no bothersome working class to spoil the regatta, just sturdy peasantry doffing their caps to their betters and the economic miracles of unleashed enterprise. Underneath this, the reality is the clock tends to get stuck at twenty years later, plenty of flags and hurrah for the blackshirts.

Turning the clock back is seen as perfectly acceptable in the national media, as long as it is the ruling class doing the turning, steering us back toward generally understood periods of national greatness. During the 2019 general election campaign, however, one of the tropes used to castigate the Labour Party was that it wanted to return us to the 1970s, generally understood in the media as the decade representing the dire high-water mark of British socialism, and therefore a Thoroughly Bad Thing, culminating—according to the officially media-sanctioned national memory—in a Winter of Discontent with mountainous black bags of rubbish and unburied dead piling high on every street corner due to striking council workers, etc., etc., etc. I suppose, in a way, the same could be said about the argument of this book; a good place to reset education would be the 1970s, before Callaghan's Great Debate made the right's moral panic about schools respectable. By the 1970s, theories of education that favoured the needs of the child rather than the agenda of the state were starting to translate into classroom practice. This book believes that if you are interested in education being provided for and accessed by all citizens, then you would look to taking up again those progressive pedagogical initiatives that had steadily been moving education provision forward, particularly in the twenty years following World War II. If you are interested in education, then you will understand that what happened next, the right's "Reform", is anti-education, an interruption in the timeline of progress. "Free schools" run by enthusiasts and zealots rather than trained workers (anybody fancy visiting a "free dentist"?) . . . teaching young children Greek and Latin . . . making them bark phonetically through meaningless non-words . . . implementing policies that only value measurable outcomes and marketising opportunities. This is not credible pedagogy; these are the dead fingers of privilege wagging at our children: sit . . . wait . . . beg . . . roll over . . . die for your country.

I think it may well be a bit more uphill now, though, than I was anticipating when I first finished the "What Is to Be Done?" section. Brexit, of course, is the right playing their joker. Whatever they try next, and it won't be pleasant, they can't play that particular "get out of jail" trump card again. Sooner or later, the people who voted to Get Brexit Done will work out they've been had. Meanwhile, of course, the right will be trying to do us serious damage, and—analogous to the analysis that finds a close correspondence between the 2020s and the 1930s—we will need to make every street Cable Street. Unfortunately, although the Borexit government appears only too happy to publicly pursue the distractions of populist flag waving, they are also continuing to impose their tired old policies of anti-education. Baseline testing for five-year-olds remains a government policy, despite no one who knows anything about five-year-olds having a good word to say for it (but they would be more of those pesky experts Gove said we shouldn't listen to. Why listen to head teachers worrying in the *Guardian* when you can read a column by Mrs Gove about her husband's class A drugs use in the *Daily Mail*?).[1] A 2020 government review of the Early Years Foundation Stage (EYFS) prompted the British Association for Early Childhood

Education to state: "We believe that the proposals are problematic and need significant further changes to ensure the revised EYFS is an improvement on the current version rather than a backward step."[2] Unsurprisingly, one of the elements the review proposes to remove from the curriculum is "understanding" in language development.

Nonetheless, determined collective action can still derail the policies of neoliberalism, whether nationally in France—popular militancy saw off Macron's attempt to impose a dose of neoliberal austerity on the nation's pension rights with the longest strike action since 1968—or locally in East Sussex. In June 2019, Moulsecoomb Primary School, serving one of Brighton and Hove's larger housing estates, got graded "inadequate" by an Ofsted inspection that many of those who experienced it felt was deliberately hostile. This was supposed to lead to automatic academisation. The school community, however, with the support of the local council, were having none of it, and, so far, have seen off any academy company showing any interest in taking them over. The parents staged a *Game of Thrones* inspired funeral march to welcome one lot of prospective buyers and picketed the car parts warehouse (!) owned by another prospective buyer. The school is also hoping for another inspection; the "inadequate" judgement was based on a narrow focus on the results of a particularly challenging cohort. The new Ofsted framework implemented in September of that year would have been able to recognise the excellent broad-based educational opportunities experienced by children at the school. Previous Ofsted guidance relied heavily on high-stakes testing outcomes. Ironically, schools that have enthusiastically turned themselves into successful exam factories to ensure best possible test scores now find themselves being criticised for a lack of breadth in the educational opportunities they provide. It would be nice to think that somehow Ofsted had enjoyed an epiphany and realised its culpability in promoting anti-ed exam factory farming. You would, of course, also be forgiven for thinking they just changed the rules to catch schools out over what they are not doing anymore, the good practice that schools have abandoned to achieve the very, very, very best test scores they could ever possibly get.

Never trust a neoliberal.

Unfortunately, many education workers, having been undereducated by the national curriculum and then badly trained by Teaching Standards, cannot imagine finding themselves anywhere other than trapped in a plot by Kafka reading from a script by Orwell. Parents and students and interested members of the general public might also think that after over thirty years of neoliberalism this is the natural condition of state schooling (although Extinction Rebellion school strikes do suggest that some students are not as susceptible to neoliberalism's delusions of authority as the state would wish them to be).

I would hope this book might assure them that Kafkaesque bureaucracy and Orwellian doublethink are not inevitable characteristics of state schools. Schools have been and can be places of education rather than training. The distractions of Borexit cannot disguise the reality that the right's programme of school reform has ground to an unsuccessful standstill. I hope this book reminds readers of alternative models of education that, once rediscovered, provide us with effective reference points for our schools in the future.

State education provides a good context for starting to challenge the orthodoxy of the right. With organised labour threatened by anti-union legislation, and individual workers intimidated by increasingly casualised employment practices, you could argue that schools are one of the few places left where people experience an organised community whose intrinsic values are capable of contradicting the values of the dominant neoliberal state. It is, after all, a context within which the majority of us do some significant developmenting, both as individuals and as social beings. From this perspective, it therefore becomes vital that we reclaim our schools from the complete social control intentions of the state and

reconfigure them as opportunities for individual development and empowerment. We know we are more than mere
measurable outcomes, more than someone else's economic
opportunity. We know we want all our children to be more
than outcomes and opportunities too.

Our task is still to let the clocks run forward again.

Glossary

A.S. Neill—teacher, author, founder of Summerhill, the UK's most enduring libertarian education establishment, his work is animated more by an understanding of psychology than an interest in economic conditions.

Anthony Charles Lynton Blair—Labour Party prime minister of Britain from 1997 to 2007. He insisted his priority was "education, education, education", then appointed a series of ministers—including David Blunkett and Ed Balls—with no background in education and a vision that endorsed the conservative utilitarian nature of state education (that it serves the interests of the state) and the Conservative legislation that enforces this model of education (that it is enforced by the diktat of the centralised state). The Blair government's enthusiasm for private finance initiatives also opened the door for the later Tory attempts to privatise state education, with the creation of "academy" status. Initially a knee-jerk quick fix to parachute private finance into schools identified by the Office for Standards in Education (Ofsted) inspection process as being in difficulty, the Tories recognised this as an opportunity to enforce wholesale privatisation of state education school by school.

Baroness Margaret Hilda Thatcher—initially famous for stopping free school milk ("Maggie Thatcher, Milk Snatcher" was possibly the first slogan I chanted on my first demo), she was indeed the carefully calculated thin end of the right-wing attempt to destroy the progress made by generations of ordinary people toward a society that attempted to meet the needs and aspirations of all its members not the greed of the privileged toffs at the top of the economic food chain.

Borexit—the noun representing the unfortunate conjunction of Britain leaving the European Economic Union (Brexit) with the latest in a long line of old Etonian prime ministers you wouldn't let run a Lucky Dip stall unsupervised at your school's summer fair, let alone have in charge of your country (Boris) being responsible for "Getting Brexit Done".

Boris (Alexander de Pfeffel) Johnson—a US passport holder until the US insisted he pay them some taxes, he crops up from time to time in the text and is the very epitome of all that's wrong with government by large amounts of money and privilege. At the time of writing he is currently the latest in a long line of old Etonian prime ministers you wouldn't let run a Lucky Dip stall unsupervised, etc., etc. Hides in a fridge during general elections when faced by unwelcome questioning (https://youtu.be/Lp9XoiFbZcI). No relation.

Chris Searle—teacher, writer, advocate of poetry, working-class children and social change. Effectively sacked in 1971 by the school he worked at for publishing a book of poetry written by the children he taught—the school wanted chirpy cockney sparrows, the poems voiced challenging social realism—he was eventually reinstated thanks to pupil strike action, National Union of Teachers (NUT) support and a judgement (presumably through gritted teeth) by the Conservative education minister Margaret Hilda Thatcher.

Emma Goldman—author, anarchist, proto-feminist, advocate of individual liberation, with the distinction of having been deported by both the US and the Soviet

Union. Like Victor Serge, an international and inspirational troublemaker.

England—the big bit in the middle of the United Kingdom, the small land mass shaped like an old man located off the coast of mainland Europe that usually votes in Conservative governments. The writer George Orwell presciently calls Britain "Airstrip One" in his 1948 satire *1984*.[1] We do still have more US bases, not to mention expensive US-made nuclear weapons, than are actually good for us. This is where most of this book takes place, apart from a quick but significant visit to East Berlin in 1987.

Grammar schools and secondary modern schools—a local curiosity, rather like the bizarre obsession with forcing children to wear embarrassing and demeaning school uniforms. The idea is that children are to be tested at eleven years of age, and those who "do well" are assumed to be academically gifted and go on to grammar schools to receive a top-quality education that leads to university and glittering careers in the middle classes. Everybody else—about 80 per cent—gets kept off the streets for a few years until they are old enough to join the workforce and compete for low-paid working-class jobs. Common sense appeared to prevail around 1974, when they were supposed to be replaced by non-selective comprehensive schools. Diehard Tories keep trying to bring them back from the dead, whenever they can't think of anything else to do.

Ivan Illich—writer, philosopher and Catholic priest, responsible for the seminal *Deschooling Society* (1971).[2] Chris Searle, in *Isaac and I: A Life in Poetry*, writes of meeting him: "He told me that the main problem with education was schools and teachers—that the 'school' was a deformed institution and that teachers working within the state system were like 'good prostitutes'. . . . There was much to agree with in these ideas, but much to take issue with too. . . . Was teaching in a school like Sir John Cass [the school that had sacked Searle] like selling yourself, serving an institution that was so clearly misconceived, unjust and full of scorn for its majority? Not if you thwarted it from the inside, impeded its reactionary objectives and made its learning spaces classrooms of resistance. . . . He shook his head as if I were a lost cause to him, and we shook hands and smiled at each other as if we were never going to fully agree".[3]

James "Sunny Jim" Callaghan—Labour Party prime minister of Britain from 1976 to 1979. He is generally perceived as having travelled politically from the left to the right, ending up as Lord Callaghan of Cardiff. His public response to the clash of pedagogies and politics at William Tyndale School, to call for a public debate about education, effectively legitimised and opened the door to the reactionary "reform" project, with its imposition of a national curriculum in 1988, accompanied by standardised tests at the ages of seven, eleven and fourteen.

Liberal education—a pedagogy that provided the philosophical framework for state education's more progressive tendencies in the 1960s and 1970s. Liberal education sees education as of intrinsic value. Rather than training children for particular social functions, it aims to develop the individual's capacity to make rational choices. You could see this partly as a response to the mid-century rise of totalitarianisms, and you can also see why *neoliberalism* wouldn't appreciate such ideas circulating among the children of the masses, as this might well cause them to object to being simply used as disposable marketing opportunities in neoliberalism's free-market new world order. Love me, I'm a neoliberal . . . like the right's use of the word "reform" instead of a more accurate term like "reaction", the deliberate perversion of meaning in the use of words like "liberal" and "free" and the current staggering negation of meaning in a term like "fake news" is breathtakingly Orwellian.

London Borough of Hounslow—the geopolitical area of England I grew up in and where I spent twenty-five of my thirty-five years of working life. Visitors to the UK arriving at Heathrow airport will be travelling through Hounslow on their way into London. By car, you will most probably be travelling east either along the M4 motorway or along the A4, the romantically named Great West Road. There will be the nice part, Osterley. If you are on the A4 you will pass a large phallic structure called Gillette Corner. Then there's Brentford, which is where my dad started teaching in 1948, and where Brentford FC play. If you go by underground, you'll be taking the Piccadilly line eastwards, and you might be surprised to find that Hounslow has not one but three underground stations—Hounslow West, Hounslow Central and Hounslow East. This might well tempt you to assume that anywhere that has three underground stations one after the other must be worth a visit. Hounslow has indeed had much to recommend it. From being largely a collection of coaching inns on the road that ran west from London to Bath and Bristol between the old parishes of Heston and Isleworth, it blossomed into a residential commuter suburb in the first half of the twentieth century. Both my parents moved there in the 1920s. At the end of the 1920s, the Great West Road became studded with new light industry factories. In the early 1950s, while Heathrow airport was growing a little bit to the south, slightly further west, British trad jazz, and thereby also skiffle, and thereby also British rock 'n roll, was being genetically engineered in the back rooms of pubs in Cranford. In the late 1960s and 1970s, Hounslow became multicultural, and thank goodness for that, because by the time I reached adolescence it was obvious that there was nothing more mind-numbingly dull than the endless stagnant respectability of the Sunday afternoon monoculture I was growing up in. There also turned out to be quite a lot of pub rock there too, which also helped no end. Throughout the 1980s Hounslow generally had a Labour Council and a May Day family fun day that always culminated in an old school white rock 'n roll act that could usually trace its lineage back to skiffle—one year we even had the King of Skiffle Lonnie Donegan himself—followed by a band of local bhangra heroes—after Lonnie came my favourite bhangra merchants, Premi. We left in 2006. We had two young sons, and with the new millennium, the slow collapse of capitalism had caught up with even the cheeriest of West London suburbs, and it was not a happy place to be. Homes that were once built to house a modest 1930s family got chopped up by greedy landlords into hutches for the impoverished. The alley opposite where we lived became inhabited by those consequences of free enterprise, your unfriendly neighbourhood teenage drug dealers. Even Pizza Express closed down. We now live in Hove. That's okay. I had eight really great years teaching in Brighton. My wife Meeta sometimes asks me if there is anywhere—apart from Paris, obviously—I would like to move to. I say Hounslow, in 1999.

Michael Gove—nobody likes Cameron's ministers of education either, and the prize buffoon here, of course, is Michael Gove, secretary of state for education from 2010 to 2014, with his absurd enthusiasms for teaching Greek and Latin and his habit of pouring taxpayers' millions into daft and dysfunctional "free schools". Zealot of testing, performance management, deregulation and privatisation, with a degree from Oxford and a background in journalism, if you can call working for the Murdoch press "journalism", Gove is probably the most unpopular education minister ever, (a real achievement there, considering the competition). He was followed by a succession of nondescripts; like the Tory education ministers namechecked in reference to the initial "reform" legislation put through in the Thatcher years, they are really only remarkable for how little they know about education, often combined with what large amounts of money and privilege they have. In the text, there are various other dubious characters—their particular claims to ill fame are detailed in context, so I don't think we need to list them here.

Mikhail Bakunin—possibly the most archetypal romantic anarchist troublemaker of all time. He was charismatic and invariably able to come up with a correct analysis and a nifty aphorism. It's a pity his visionary genius couldn't escape dismal standard-issue nineteenth-century anti-Semitism.

National Union of Teachers (NUT)—once the most active of the teaching unions, often at the forefront of campaigns to effect social progress through education. Now amalgamated with the smaller Association of Teachers and Lecturers (ATL) into the National Education Union (NEU).

Ofsted—the Office for Standards in Education, the central government inspection body, operated by private sector providers. The central government's goon squad, their "judgements", along with the government's publication of national curriculum standardised test results in school league tables, became the mechanism by which state schools could be privatised as "academies" under the 2010 Cameron government. Nobody likes them.

Paulo Freire—writer, philosopher, Workers' Party São Paulo municipal secretary of education, responsible for seminal *Pedagogy of the Oppressed* (Portuguese 1968; English 1970).[4]

Public schools—in the UK, schools where people pay fees to the school so their children can attend that school are called—bizarrely—public schools, even though the overwhelming majority of the "general public" don't go to public schools but go to state schools instead. In the US, these establishments are more sensibly called "private schools". In the UK, these are places where no matter how clever or clueless you are, if your parents can afford the fees, you're in, and after that you can go to Oxford or be a pop star, actor, media something or other, prime minister, whatever you fancy having a go at. To avoid confusing any of our North American readers, we shall put scare quotes around the word "public" whenever we refer to these dreadful old bastions of privilege.

School uniform—Another bizarre feature of education in the UK, this deliberate infantilising remains a significant characteristic of state education in the twentieth century. It is an anachronism that references the outward signs of hierarchy found in military, security and paramilitary organisations. Traditionally, "public" schools favour smart, distinctive/stupid looking uniforms. The Batman gowns that referenced the "higher" levels of university learning may have vanished from state school corridors, but, in the UK, adolescents are generally still forced to wear a school uniform that emphasises conformity and strict gender division, as well as referencing traditional preadolescent forms of school dress. Grown men and women assert that school uniforms:

A) make all children look equal (this is nonsense; Daljit from the flats will be wearing a cardigan with sleeves her two brothers have already chewed through, while Tarquin with the leafy garden will be modelling something crisp from the official school-approved school uniform shop).

B) prevent arguments with their parents over what Daljit and Tarquin want to wear to school in the morning (rather than engage in meaningful dialogue, some parents invent spurious shibboleths of authority, like school rules or the Elf on the Shelf Rules, probably because that's how they were cowed into submission when they were young).

C) instil a Sense of Collective Identity and are A Great Aid to Maintaining Discipline. (Daljit would rather wear an Avengers T-shirt, because she has decided she wants to save the planet and is already looking forward to the next Climate Strike day, and Tarquin wants to wear something purple, because that's his favourite colour. Instead they have to wear a stupid blazer and tie that look like something you see in a 1950s black and white film where Norman Wisdom runs amok in a toy department.[5] But while they're thinking about how to subvert things like sock colour and skirt length, the school congratulates itself that they won't be asking awkward questions about the boring and meaningless curriculum.)

Sir Rhodes Boyson—headmaster, disciplinarian and organising principle behind the deeply reactionary Black Papers (a series of publications that gave disgruntled authors and academics the opportunity to pretend whinging represented pedagogical debate), Tory MP and government minister. His mutton chop whiskers and deeply authoritarian attitudes appealed to that element of British working-class culture that considers itself poor but loyal and likes nothing better than to be ordered about and to send its sons off to ensure some corner of a foreign field is forever England.

State schools—funded by taxation, free and open to all, as opposed to "public" schools, which is what state schools are called in the US. "Public" schools in the UK are not free and are only accessible to the filthy rich and the upper middle class, with enough scrimping and saving. State schooling is generally divided into two stages, the primary stage and the secondary stage. These also have their own subdivisions. . . . Your school year is the academic year (September to September) in which your birthday falls, for example, the year you have your seventh birthday in is Year Two. Obvious, really. The primary stage includes the early years—nursery (four-year-olds), reception (five-year-olds)—the infants—Year One (six-year-olds), Year Two (seven-year-olds). Then the juniors start with Year Three (eight-year-olds) and ends with Year Six (eleven-year-olds). Secondary schools start with Year Seven (twelve-year-olds) and end with Year Elevens

(sixteen-year-olds)—and then you have what is still generally referred to as the Sixth Form, made up of seventeen- and
eighteen-years-olds.

TAs and NNEBs—criminally underpaid adult co-workers in
schools, they are usually expert practitioners at working with
and relating to children and quietly keep the wheels running
in most classrooms. Teaching Assistant and National Nursery
Examination Board qualifications aren't quite as academic as
traditional teaching qualifications, which is why these workers
get paid fewer peanuts and are the first to have their conditions
worsened when the school budget is having trouble funding its
often non-teaching senior management team.

Tony Benn—Labour politician, resolutely left, MP for forty-
seven years, left parliament in 2001 "in order to spend more
time on politics". I borrowed this when I took early retirement
in 2015, saying i was giving up teaching in order to spend more
time on education.

Victor Serge—journalist, anarchist, Bolshevik, convict, exile
. . . if there was anything kicking off in the name of social progress in the first half of the twentieth century, Victor was generally there.

Welfare state—the post-war (here post-war is always
Anglocentric shorthand for post–World War II) commitment
by the British state to provide appropriate and equal cradle to
grave care for the well-being of all its citizens, except for the
rich who could carry on their privileged lifestyles through
elite institutions like fee-paying "public" schools and private
health care. The welfare state was built on the cornerstones
of the 1944 Education Act and the 1948 National Health
Service (NHS). Not nearly as exciting a progressive social
experiment as the Paris Commune, it nonetheless lasted a
lot longer.

William Tyndale Junior School—the very significant mid-1970s collision point between the increasing professional self-organisation of rank-and file-teachers and the gathering strength of the organised right-wing authoritarian backlash.

Selected Bibliography

Primary sources for most of this book are personal experience, memories and ideas, and interaction with pretty much everybody I have ever worked with—adult co-workers, children and parents. My interactions with my father Ron Johnson and the first head teacher I worked with, Irene Beach, were particularly important. They were first and foremost teachers, "those obscure soldiers of civilisation".[1] Headship was not a career move but an added responsibility you undertook as a teacher. Their principled commitment to the absolute importance of the job of education and the absolute importance of every kid they taught was inspirational. Some co-workers already feature in the text; I won't, in fact, can't, name everybody else who helped shape this book—the list is too long—but have to say particular respect to Alex Brown, who, among so many other giftings, gave the book its title before leaving the planet in July 2018. If we worked together, then thank you. If we went to National Union of Teachers (NUT) meetings, strikes, marches and demos together, held the Hounslow NUT banner together, went to East Berlin together, then thanks for the solidarity and comradeship, and particular thanks and maximum respect to those underpaid expert practitioners, teaching assistants and nursery nurses, who have forgotten more about education than most senior managers nowadays ever manage or bother to remember. Thank you to my family, who generally and kindly put up with any inconvenience caused by my bewildering enthusiasms and random absenteeism, and thank you to Ramsey, James, and Michael at PM Press, who did like-wise, and who also actually read the bloody thing and made supportive noises and practical helpful suggestions.

Office for Standards in Education (Ofsted) inspectors, on the other hand, and anybody else colluding with the state over the last thirty or so years, can generally just fuck off.

I've used the internet to check remembered detail and confirm some of the more ludicrous aspects, antics and pro-nouncements of government and media. Books, however, are always so much more substantial than pixels on a screen, I think. The following books and writers should be thanked for their influence, however indirect, on the text.

Biddulph, Steve. *Raising Boys in the Twenty-First Century*. London: HarperCollins Publishers, 2018.

Bourne, Richard, and Brian MacArthur. *The Struggle for Education, 1870–1970*. London: Schoolmaster Publishing, 1970.

Camus, Albert. *The Myth of Sisyphus*. London: Penguin Modern Classics, 1981.

Dickens, Charles. *Hard Times*. London: J.M. Dent, 1920. Accessed December 27, 2019, https://ia800302.us.archive.org/8/items/hardtime00dick/hardtime00dick.pdf.

Ellis, Terry, Jackie McWhirter, Dorothy McColgan, and Brian Haddow. *William Tyndale: The Teacher's Story*. London: Writers and Readers Ltd., 1977.

Farren, Mick. *Give the Anarchist a Cigarette*. Dorset, UK: Pimlico, 2002.

Featherstone, Sally, and Ros Bayley. *Boys and Girls Come Out to Play: Not Better or Worse, Just Different*. London: Featherstone Education Ltd, 2005.

Freire, Paolo. *Pedagogy of the Oppressed*. New York: Bloomsbury Academic, 2018 [1968].

Goldman, Emma. *Red Emma Speaks*. Edited by Alix Kates Shulman. London: Wildwood House Ltd, 1979.

Hagopian, Jesse, ed. *More Than a Score: The New Uprising Against High Stakes Testing*. Chicago: Haymarket Books, 2014.

Illich, Ivan. *Deschooling Society*. New York: Harper and Row, 1971. Accessed January 23, 2020, https://archive.org/details/DeschoolingSociety.

Jones, Owen. *The Establishment: And How They Get Away with It*. London: Penguin, 2014.

Leeson, R.A. *Strike: A Live History, 1887–1971*. London: George Allen & Unwin, 1973.

Lefebvre, Henri. *Everyday Life in the Modern World*. London: Bloomsbury, 2016.

Levy, Shawn. *Ready, Steady, Go! Swinging London and the Invention of Cool*. London: Fourth Estate, 2002.

McGough, Roger. *Strictly Private: An Anthology of Poetry*. London: Viking, 1985.

Neill, A.S. *Summerhill: A Radical Approach to Child Rearing*. Oxford: Hart Publishing Company, 1960. Accessed January 21, 2020, https://archive.org/stream/Summerhill-English-A.S.Neill/summerhill_djvu.txt.

No! Against Adult Supremacy. London/Bristol: Dog Section Press/Active Distribution, 2017.

Rogers, Dave. *Singing the Changes*. Coventry: Bread Books, 2005.

Rosen, Michael. "Phonics: A Summary of My Views" (blog), January 3, 2013. Accessed January 13, 2020, http://michaelrosenblog.blogspot.com/2013/01/phonics-summary-of-my-views.html.

Ross, Kristin. *Communal Luxury*. London: Verso, 2016.

Searle, Chris. *Classrooms of Resistance*. London: Writers and Readers Publishing Cooperative, 1975.

Searle, Chris. *Isaac and I: A Life in Poetry*. Nottingham: Five Leaves Publications, 2017.

Searle, Chris. *This New Season*. London: Marion Boyers Publishing, 1973.

Searle, Chris, ed. *Wheel around the World*. London: Macdonald, 1983.

Seifert, Roger V. *Teacher Militancy: A History of Teacher Strikes, 1896–1987*. New York: Falmer, 1987.

Serge, Victor. *Anarchists Never Surrender*. Oakland: PM Press, 2015.

Shakespeare, William. *King Lear* (1606). Accessed January 24, 2020, https://www.folgerdigitaltexts.org/download/pdf/Lr.pdf.

Suissa, Judith. *Anarchism and Education*. Oakland: PM Press, 2010.

Vaneigem, Raoul. *The Revolution of Everyday Life*. Oakland: PM Press, 2012.

When I started to write this book, I thought about its physical reality, how long it ought to be. *The Myth of Sisyphus* has always been one of my favourite books of philosophy in all respects, so I roughly estimated how many words it had, and decided that if I could manage 40,000 words that would be an acceptable sort of shape. Camus is also one of my favourite writers and thinkers, and his work probably backgrounds my writing and thinking. Also providing the cultural background: Levy, Farren (what would a bibliography in a book referencing twentieth-century culture be without the presence of the late, great Mick F?), Seifert and Vaneigem (again, what would a bibliography in a book referencing twentieth-century culture be without a Situationist?). The books by Hagopian and Ellis are truly inspirational accounts of particular key struggles, and I included Dave Rogers, because, searching for where I knew what I know about Saltley Gate, I found his song was the reference that sprang most readily to mind. Owen Jones is very, very good at tracking how the right changed the post-war consensus. I can't say I ever extensively read books about teaching—a bit of a busman's holiday, I always thought, reading about the job you did—but I once heard Ros Bayley talk about gender, and I liked her talk and her book very much. My dad had a copy of *The Struggle for Education* when it first came out in 1970. Forty-eight years later, attending the NUT annual conference (the last one before the "great amalgamation" with the Association of Teachers and Lecturers [ATL]—but that's another story), I was happy to find it both reprinted and highly informative. At the 2018 conference, I also heard about children having egg soup for breakfast, austerity in action. Dickens tells you all you need to know about how dreadful Victorian values were (he should know, he was there), and with Mr M'choakumchild he perfectly shows us how dreadful the current pedagogy of reform is. Shakespeare, in *King Lear*, tells you all you need to know about how dreadful—and pathetic—authority and power are and, indeed, how precious and transient Life is. And the cultural workers: there's Billie Holiday, Ken Loach, Phil Ochs, George Orwell and Bruce Springsteen, all providing background context, insight and a soundtrack, and the poets Billy Blake, with his French revolutionary hat on, Charlie Causley, *Timothy Winters* always one of my dad's favourite poems, Rodge McGough, whose anthology *Strictly Private* was my main resource book of poems when I was teaching ten- and eleven-year-olds, while Chris Searle's anthology *Wheel Around the World* still remains my favourite, the late, truly great Adrian Mitchell always will remain one of my favourite poets, and Joe and Mick, public service announcements *WITH GUITAR* . . . well, what would a book about education be without a little bit of culture and a whole lotta poetry going on?

Playlist

Some additional notes about the songs featured in the text.

Charlie
(CD album: *Man Walks into a Pub*, 2010) This is a true record of a true story. US jazz-folk singer compañera Barbara Dane sometimes sings it (she also sometimes sings *Be Reasonable*).

All You Need Is Love and Comprehensive Schools
(CD album: *Ordinary Giants*, 2018) Sometimes in performance at some point I feel the need to add after the "and" the words "properly funded and democratically locally controlled".

Oliver Twist
(CD album: *The Big Wheel*, 1998) Does anybody remember literacy hours? This was another temporary hobby horse. First the children had to sit on the carpet for twenty minutes while you told them what the correct answer was. Then they had to go off and do some simple mechanical tasks that proved this was the correct answer for maybe twenty-five minutes. Then before they started finding (a) loopholes in the correct answer, (b) something interesting out or (c) they have an overwelming urge to start chucking chairs about, they had to come back and sit on the carpet for a plenary session, where they all agreed you'd been right about the right answer all along.

In Buttercup Class We Smile
(CD album: *Invisible People*, 1997) True stories. I only changed their names.

Orange Class News
(CD album: *Overnight*, 1991) Orange Class were a Year Two Class. Like many of us, they always had a lot to say to their co-workers when they arrived in the workplace, so we invariably had a circle time after the register at the start of the day. This was a pretty true snapshot of what was likely to happen. Circle times and "show and tell", where children augment their narratives by bringing an artefact to share with the class, are absolutely essential strategies to show children the respect they deserve for their lives and their worlds. Dog training pitcher fillers hate this sort of thing, and children love it. Your role is the job of any good chairperson, to make sure no one gets hurt, Matthew's stories don't go on and on and on for too long and the individual's right to silence is always respected.
At the Siege of Madrid*
(CD album: *21st Century Blues*, 2000) "Barcelona" would be more historically appropriate, but "Madrid" sings better.
Goalkeepers
(CD album: *Ordinary Giants*, 2018)
Little Vinnie Jones*
(CD album: *Some Recent Protest Songs*, 2011) I changed his name. Some audiences start looking a little uncomfortable when we get to the lines about not liking the rich.
Franz Has Got a Plan
(CD album: *Bring Down the Moon*, 2013)
James Dean and Sameena
(CD album: *The Lack of Jolly Ploughboy*, 1994) I changed the names. There is quite a bit of normative gender stereotyping here, I know, but that's how it was. Sometimes you just can't quite get all the radical politics you need to into the one song. Fred Small does a pretty good job of managing this on "Everything Possible" though, which you should listen to to make up for my shortcomings here.
The Kreuzberg Sisters
(Vinyl and CD albums: Eurotopia, 2020) Spending more time on education meant I got to do some work for the Equalities

education charity, Persona Doll Training. I attended a conference organised by German, Czech and Slovak educators in Berlin in January 2019. The conference was both inspirational and in Kreuzberg, hence this song.

6B Go Swimming*
(Cassette album: *Songs for the New Jerusalem*, 1988, and most subsequent CD anthologies) Also sung by folk legend Roy Bailey.

A Very Small Piece of the Real World
(CD album: *Man Walks into a Pub*, 2010) Inspired, as they say, by real events.

Toymaker
(Officially unreleased, 1999) I always really liked this song but never quite knew what to do with it and only found a demo version of it again in 2018.

Hands Off Hove Park
(Officially unreleased but available via the Hands Off Hove Park website, 2014)

Be Reasonable*
(CD album: *The Big Wheel*, 1998, various anthologies and the title track on the PM Press 5CD box set *A Reasonable History of Impossible Demands*, 2016) Possibly the current greatest non-hit.

Win, Lose or Draw*
(PM box set *A Reasonable History of Impossible Demands*, 2016) Written after the 2010 election, it first appeared on YouTube and on a limited run demo CD.

Who Was That Man?
(CD album: *Us & Them*, 2014) One of my more popular songs.

Egg Soup
(Officially unreleased, 2018)

The Glue Factory Strike
(CD album: *Songs from the Last Seven Years*, 2017) I think I can detect the influence of my friend the great Leon Rosselson in this song.

That's Not Fair

(Officially unreleased, available on Bandcamp and as a limited run CD to raise funds at the school Christmas fair for local homeless charities, 2017) The "i" in verse two is the particularly ugly and pointless "i360" steel phallic erection Brighton and Hove council got a massive government loan to build on the Brighton seafront that Brighton and Hove residents are allowed to access at reduced rates. This song features the wonderful voices of the Hertford Community Quire, including members of the Hollingdean National Ballet cooperative workshop. Brighton and Hove council attempted to cut its education budget spending by halving the two classes per year provision at Hertford Infants School. This would effectively soon close the school by starving it of funds. Larger schools in obviously more middle-class areas nearby weren't even considered for cuts. The council mistakenly thought that because Hertford was a small school in a more working-class area with a high number of children on free school meals they could send a couple of suits down with a PowerPoint, accompanied by a couple of councillors, and the community would quietly roll over. We didn't. Hertford remains a two form entry school.

The Future Starts Here

(CD album: *My Best Regards*, 2016)

All songs © Robb Johnson; all released versions on Irregular Records unless otherwise stated.

* indicates songs available on *A Reasonable History of Impossible Demands*, 5CD box set (PM Press 2016).

Notes

Prologue

1   All songs quoted in this book are written by Robb Johnson, unless otherwise stated.

Remote Control

1   Victor Serge, "The Religious or the Secular," in Mitchel Abidor, ed., *Anarchists Never Surrender: Essays, Polemics, and Correspondence on Anarchism, 1908–1938* (Oakland: PM Press, 2015), 49.

2   John Gatto, "Against School," *Harper's Magazine*, September 2003, accessed January 25, 2020, https://www.cs.mcgill.ca/~abatko/ interests/teaching/essays/Against_Schools.

3   Alexander Inglis, *Principles of Secondary Education* (Boston: Houghton Mifflin Company, 1918), accessed December 27, 2019, https://archive.org/details/principlesofseco00ingliala.

4   Gatto, "Against School."

5   Emma Goldman, "The Social Importance of the Modern School," Emma Goldman Papers, Manuscripts and Archives Division, New York Public Library, Astor, Lenox and Tilden Foundations, accessed December 27, 2019, https://theanarchistlibrary.org/library/emma-goldman-the-social-importance-of-the-modern-school.

6   Emma Goldman, "The Child and Its Enemies," *Mother Earth* 1, no. 2 (April 1906), accessed December 27, 2019, https://theanarchistlibrary. org/library/emma-goldman-the-child-and-its-enemies.

7   See Mark Bray and Robert H. Haworth, eds., *Anarchist Education and the Modern School: A Francisco Ferrer Reader*, trans. Mark Bray and Joseph McCabe (Oakland: PM Press, 2019).

8   Rudolph Steiner, *Rudolph Steiner in the Waldorf School: Lectures and Addresses to Children, Parents, and Teachers*, Catherine E. Creeger, trans. (Hudson, NY: Anthroposophic Press, 1996), 7.

9   Rudolph Steiner, *The Foundations of Human Experience*, Robert F. Lathe and Nancy Parsons Whittaker, trans. (Hudson, NY: Anthroposophic Press, 1996), 43.

10   A.S. Neill, "Love and Approval," in William Ayers, *On the Side of the Child: Summerhill Revisited* (New York: Teachers College Press, 2003).

11   A.S. Neill, *Summerhill: A Radical Approach to Child Rearing* (Oxford: Hart Publishing Company, 1960), accessed January 21, 2020, https://archive.org/stream/Summerhill-English-A.S.Neill/summerhill_djvu.txt.

12   Mikhail Bakunin, "Revolutionary Catechism" (1866), in Sam Dolgoff, ed. and trans., *Bakunin on Anarchy: Selected Works by the Activist-Founder of World Anarchism* (New York: Vintage Books, 1971), accessed December 27, 2019, https://www.marxists.org/reference/archive/bakunin/works/1866/catechism.htm.

13   Nic Maclellan, ed., *Louise Michel: Rebel Lives* (Ocean Press, 2004).

14   Randhir Singh, *Marxism, Socialism, Indian Politics: A View from the Left* (Dehli: Aakar Books, 2008), 12.

15   Roy Bailey and Michael Brake, eds., *Radical Social Work* (London: Hodder & Staughton, 1975).

Workers' Control

1   R.S. Peters, *Ethics and Education* (London: Allen & Unwin, 1966).

2   Chris Searle, ed., *Stepney Words I and II* (London: Centerpiece Publications, 1973).

3   Chris Searle, *Isaac and I: A Life in Poetry* (Nottingham: Five Leaves Publications, 2017).

4   Ibid., 184.

5   Chris Searle, *Classrooms of Resistance* (Lanham, MD: National Book Network, 1981).

6   Searle, *Isaac and I*.

7   Ibid., 259.

8   Terry Ellis, Jackie McWhirter, Dorothy McColgan, and Brian Haddow, *William Tyndale: The Teacher's Story* (London: Writers and Readers Ltd., 1977), 123.

Great Debates

1   James Callaghan, "A Rational Debate Based on Facts," Ruskin College, October 18, 1976, Education in England, accessed February 23, 2020, http://www.educationengland.org.uk/documents/speeches/1976ruskin.html.

2 John Gretton and Mark Jackson, *William Tynsdale: Collapse of a School—or of a System* (London: Allen & Unwin, 1976).

3 Stephen Daldry, dir., *Billy Elliot* (London: Universal International Pictures, 2000).

4 Stuart Maconie, "The Privileged Are Taking Over the Arts," *New Republic*, February 7, 2015, accessed December 27, 2019, https://newrepublic.com/article/120996/mumford-sons-coldplay-other-privileged-musicians-taking-over-arts.

5 Mikhail Bakunin, "Revolutionary Catechism" (1866), in Sam Dolgoff, ed. and trans., *Bakunin on Anarchy: Selected Works by the Activist-Founder of World Anarchism* (New York: Vintage Books, 1971), accessed December 27, 2019, https://www.marxists.org/reference/archive/bakunin/works/1866/catechism.htm.

6 Emma Goldman, "The Social Importance of the Modern School," Emma Goldman Papers, Manuscripts and Archives Division, New York Public Library, Astor, Lenox and Tilden Foundations, accessed December 27, 2019, https://theanarchistlibrary.org/library/emma-goldman-the-social-importance-of-the-modern-school.

Complete Control

1 Richard Lester, dir., *A Hard Day's Night* (Beverley Hills, CA: United Artists, 1964).

2 Quoted in David Marquand, "The Paradoxes of Thatcherism," in Robert Skidelesky, ed., *Thatcherism* (London: Chatto & Windus, 1988), 165.

3 Quoted in Robert Eccleshall, *English Conservatism since the Restoration: An Introduction and Anthology* (London: Unwin Hyman, 1990), 247.

4 Margaret Thatcher, "Mrs. Thatcher Follows Tough Line," Finchley Press, February 1, 1980, accessed December 27, 2019, https://www.margaretthatcher.org/document/104297.

5 Charles Dickens, *Hard Times* (London: J.M. Dent, 1920), 2, accessed December 27, 2019, https://ia800302.us.archive.org/8/items/hardtime00dick/hardtime00dick.pdf.

Zealots and Their Hobby Horses

1 *National Curriculum—Children, Schools and Families Committee*, www.parliament.uk, April 2, 2009, accessed January 13, 2020, https://publications.parliament.uk/pa/cm200809/cmselect/cmchilsch/344/34402.htm.

2 "Early Years Foundation Stage," gov.uk, accessed January 13, 2020, https://www.gov.uk/early-years-foundation-stage.

3 Michael Rosen, "Phonics: A Summary of My Views" (blog), January 3, 2013, accessed January 13, 2020, http://michaelrosenblog. blogspot.com/2013/01/phonics-summary-of-my-views.html.

4 Quoted in Christopher H. Tienken and Carol A. Mullen, eds., *Education Policy Perils: Tackling the Tough Issues* (New York: Routledge, 2016), 44.

5 Billie Holiday and Arthur Herzog Jr., "God Bless the Child" (New York: Okeh Records, 1941).

Goon Squads and Thought Policing

1 See Camilla Turner and Phoebe Southworth, "School Funding Campaign Criticised for Claiming 91 Per Cent of Schools Face Funding Cuts," *Telegraph*, January 17, 2019, accessed January 15, 2020, https://www.telegraph.co.uk/news/2019/01/17/teaching-union-criticised-claiming91-per-cent-schools-face-funding.

2 Nicky Morgan, "Letter from the Secretary of State for Education, Rt Hon Nicky Morgan MP, to the Chair of the Committee on 7 July 2016," www.parliament.uk, accessed January 25, 2020, https://publications.parliament.uk/pa/cm201617/cmselect/cmeduc/674/67404.htm.

3 Michael Rosen, "SATs: Literally Failing," *Guardian*, August 21, 2008, accessed January 15, 2020, https://www.theguardian.com/commentisfree/2008/aug/21/earlyyearseducation.sats.

4 Michael Rosen, "Children's Laureate Acceptance" (blog), June 2007, accessed February 23, 2020, http://news.bbc.co.uk/2/hi/entertainment/6740821.stm.

5 Paulo Freire, *Pedagogy of the Oppressed* (New York: Bloomsbury Academic, 2018 [1968]), 131.

6 "Tony Benn on Education," YouTube, September 16, 2009, accessed February 23, 2020, https://www.youtube.com/watch?v=5Vn83rREy5E.

British Values

1 Thomas Paine, "The Rights of Man," in *The Life and Works of Thomas Paine* (New Rochelle, NY: Thomas Paine National Historical Association, 1925), accessed January 15, 2020, http://press-pubs. uchicago.edu/founders/documents/amendI_religions57.html.

Social Mobility and Post-Society

1 David Cayley, *Ivan Illich in Conversation* (Toronto: House of Anasi Press, 1992), 8.

2   Emma Goldman, "The Child and Its Enemies," *Mother Earth* 1, no. 2 (April 1906), accessed January 15, 2020, https://theanarchistlibrary. org/library/emma-goldman-the-child-and-its-enemies.

3   Johnathan Watkins, Wahyu Wulaningsih, Charlie Da Zhou, Dominic C Marshall, Guia D C Sylianteng, Phyllis G Dela Rosa, Viveka A Miguel, Rosalind Raine, Lawrence P King, and Mahiben Maruthappu, "Effects of Health and Social Care Spending Constraints on Mortality in England: A Time Trend Analysis," *BMJ Open* 7, no. 11 (November 2017), accessed January 15, 2020, https:// bmjopen.bmj.com/content/7/11/e01772.

4   Quoted in Jesse Hagopian, "Our Destination is Not on the MAP," in Jesse Hagoian, ed., *More Than a Score: The New Uprising Against High-Stakes Testing* (Chicago: Haymarket Books, 2014), 19.

5   Alexander Inglis, "6 Basic Functions of School," Openly Voluntary, January 1, 2017, accessed January 15, 2020, https://openlyvoluntary. com/tag/6-basic-functions-of-school-by-alexander-inglis.

6   Margaret Thatcher, Speech to Conservative Party Conference ("Confrontation with Reality"), Margaret Thatcher Foundation, October 14, 1977, accessed January 15, 2020, https://www. margaretthatcher.org/document/103443.

7   See, for example, "Sir Peter Lampl Awarded Honorary Doctorate in Civil Law at Durham University" (press release), Sutton Trust, June 25, 2014, accessed January 15, 2020, https://www.suttontrust. com/news-opinion/all-news-opinion/sir-peter-lampl-awarded-honorary-doctorate-civil-law-durham-university.

8   James Kirkup, "Justine Greening's Appointment as Education Secretary Gives Real Hope for Social Mobility—and the White Working Class," *Daily Telegraph*, July 14, 2016, accessed January 15, 2020, https://www.telegraph.co.uk/news/2016/07/14/justine-greenings-appointment-as-education-secretary-gives-real.

A Conflicted Situation

1   Jeffrey Toobin, *American Heiress: The Wild Saga of the Kidnapping, Crimes and Trial of Patty Hearst* (New York: Anchor Books, 2016), 43.

2   "Training Programme," Teach First, accessed February 23, 2020, https://www.teachfirst.org.uk/training-programme.

3   "Salaried Teacher Training," Teaching, accessed February 23, 2020, https://getintoteaching.education.gov.uk/explore-my-options/ teacher-training-routes/school-led-training/school-direct-salaried.

4   Charles Dickens, *Hard Times* (London: J.M. Dent, 1920), 2, accessed December 27, 2019, https://ia800302.us.archive.org/8/items/ hardtime00dick/hardtime00dick.pdf.

Problems with Authority
1   Chris Searle, *Classrooms of Resistance* (London: Writers and Readers Ltd., 1975).

The Essential Anarchist
1   Quoted in Paulo Freire, *Pedagogy of the Oppressed* (New York: Bloomsbury Academic, 2018 [1968]), 89n4.
2   Ibid., 125.
3   Jean-Pierre Melville, *Le Samouri* (Paris: CICC, 1967).

Socialisation and the Essential Anarchist
1   "Half of Cabinet Was Privately Educated" (press release), Sutton Trust, May 11, 2015, accessed February 23, 2020, https://www.suttontrust. com/news-opinion/all-news-opinion/half-of-new-cabinet-was-privately-educated.

Wrong Questions and Wrong Answers
1   Patrick Butler, "New Study Finds 4.5 Million UK Children Living in Poverty," *Guardian*, September 16, 2018, accessed January 21, 2019, https://www.theguardian.com/society/2018/sep/16/new-study-finds-45-million-uk-children-living-in-poverty.

Playfulness
1   A.S Neill, *The Problem Child* (London: Herbert Jenkins Ltd., 1929).
2   Paulo Freire, *Pedagogy of the Oppressed* (New York: Bloomsbury Academic, 2018 [1968]), 80.
3   Pierre Clastres, *Society against the State* (New York: Urizen Press, 1977), 163.
4   A.S. Neill, *Summerhill: A Radical Approach to Child Rearing* (Oxford: Hart Publishing Company, 1960), accessed January 21, 2020, https://archive.org/stream/Summerhill-English-A.S.Neill/summerhill_djvu.txt.
5   Nancy Carlsson-Paige, "Defending Young Children," in Jesse Hagopian, ed., *More Than a Score: The New Uprising Against High-Stakes Testing* (Chicago: Haymarket Books, 2014), 87.
6   Charles Dickens, *Hard Times* (London: J.M. Dent, 1920), 262, accessed December 27, 2019, https://ia800302.us.archive.org/8/items/hardtime00dick/hardtime00dick.pdf.
7   "Playground Anarchy?" in *No! Against Adult Supremacy* (London/Bristol: Dog Section Press/Active Distribution, 2017).

The Road to Neverland

1   *No! Against Adult Supremacy* (London/Bristol: Dog Section Press/ Active Distribution, 2017).
2   Jonathan Kozol, *Savage Inequalities: Children in America's Schools* (New York: Harper Perennial, 1991).

The People's Republic of Neverland

1   A.S. Neill, *Summerhill: A Radical Approach to Child Rearing* (Oxford: Hart Publishing Company, 1960), accessed January 21, 2020, https://archive.org/stream/Summerhill-English-A.S.Neill/ summerhill_djvu.txt (italics added).
2   Zack Snyder, *300* (Burbank, CA: Warner Bros. Pictures, 2007).

The People's Republic of Neverland and the REAL WORLD

1   Albert Square is the fictional setting central to the British soap opera *EastEnders. Coronation Street* is a popular British soap opera that began broadcasting in December 1960. Its ten thousandth episode aired in February 2020.
2   "Black Papers," Wikipedia, accessed January 22, 2020, https:// en.wikipedia.org/wiki/Black_Papers.

A Long Hard Look in the Long Hard Mirror

1   Ivan Illich, *Deschooling Society* (New York: Harper and Row, 1971), accessed January 23, 2020, https://archive.org/details/ DeschoolingSociety.
2   George Orwell, *1984* (London: Secker and Warburg, 1949).
3   Phillip Larkin, "This Be the Verse," in *Collected Poems* (New York: Farrar Straus and Giroux, 2001), accessed January 23, 2020, https:// www.poetryfoundation.org/poems/48419/this-be-the-verse.
4   Emma Goldman, "The Child and Its Enemies," *Mother Earth* 1, no. 2 (April 1906), accessed December 27, 2019, https://theanarchistlibrary. org/library/emma-goldman-the-child-and-its-enemies.
5   G.P. Maximoff, ed., *The Political Philosophy of Bakunin: Scientific Anarchism* (New York: Free Press of Glencoe, 1953), 327, accessed January 23, 2020, https://libcom.org/files/Maximoff%20-%20 The%20Political%20Philosophy%20of%20Bakunin.pdf.
6   Goldman, "The Child and Its Enemies."
7   Kathleen Nicole O'Neal, "The Problem with Unschooling," in *No! Against Adult Supremacy* (London/Bristol: Dog Section Press/ Active Distribution, 2017), 231–33.

8   Ivan Illich, *Deschooling Society* (New York: Harper and Row, 1971), accessed January 23, 2020, https://archive.org/details/DeschoolingSociety.

9   László Benedek, dir., *The Wild One* (Culver City, CA: Columbia Pictures, 1953); in the now iconic exchange in the film being referred to here, Mildred, played by Peggy Maley, asks Johnny, played by Marlon Brando, "Hey, Johnny, what are you rebelling against?" and Johnny responds, "What've you got."

10   A.S. Neill, *Summerhill: A Radical Approach to Child Rearing* (Oxford: Hart Publishing Company, 1960), accessed January 21, 2020, https://archive.org/stream/Summerhill-English-A.S.Neill/summerhill_djvu.txt (italics added).

Whose Schools? Our Schools

1   A.S. Neill, "Summerhill School," in Mark Vaughan, ed., *Summerhill and A.S. Neill* (Maidenhead, NY: Open University Press, 2006), 47.

2   Ken Loach, dir., *Kes* (Beverly Hills, CA: United Artists, 1969).

3   Office of the High Commissioner for Human Rights, Convention on the Rights of the Child, November 20, 1989, accessed January 23, 2020, https://www.ohchr.org/en/professionalinterest/pages/crc.aspx.

Alchemy, Trust and Politics

1   A.S. Neill, *Summerhill: A Radical Approach to Child Rearing* (Oxford: Hart Publishing Company, 1960), accessed January 21, 2020, https://archive.org/stream/Summerhill-English-A.S.Neill/summerhill_djvu.txt.

2   Chris Searle, *This New Season* (London: Marion Boyers Publishing, 1973).

Educational Privilege and the Ruling Class: Unfit for Purpose

1   Hayley Dixon, "Academies Paying Millions to Businesses Linked to Their Directors," *Telegraph*, January 13, 2014, accessed January 23, 2020, https://www.telegraph.co.uk/education/educationnews/10567498/Academies-paying-millions-to-businesses-linked-to-their-directors.html.

2   Janet Floyd, "Private School Inspections: There Isn't the Fear You Feel with Ofsted," *Guardian*, February 18, 2016, accessed January 23, 2020, https://www.theguardian.com/teacher-network/2016/feb/18/private-school-inspections-isnt-fear-ofsted.

Never Trust a Neoliberal

1 Sally Weale, "School Heads Criticise New Reception Tests for Five-Year-Olds," *Guardian*, September 3, 2019, accessed February 28, 2020, https://www.theguardian.com/education/2019/sep/03/school-heads-criticise-new-reception-tests-for-five-year-olds; Sarah Vine, "What My Husband's Drugs Confession Has Taught Me About Trust . . . and True Friendship: Sarah Vine Opens Her Heart About Michael Gove's Cocaine Past," *Daily Mail*, June 11, 2019, accessed February 28, 2020, https://www.dailymail.co.uk/news/article-7129687/SARAH-VINE-opens-heart-Michael-Goves-cocaine-past.html.

2 British Association for Early Childhood Education, "Review of the Early Years Foundation Stage 2019–20," Early Education, accessed February 28, 2020, https://www.early-education.org.uk/getting_it_right_in_the_eyfs.

Glossary

1 George Orwell, *1984* (London: Secker and Warburg, 1949).

2 Ivan Illich, *Deschooling Society* (New York: Harper and Row, 1971), accessed January 23, 2020, https://archive.org/details/DeschoolingSociety.

3 Chris Searle, *Isaac and I: A Life in Poetry* (Nottingham: Five Leaves Publications, 2017).

4 Paulo Freire, *Pedagogy of the Oppressed* (New York: Bloomsbury Academic, 2018 [1968]).

5 Norman Wisdom was an English actor in numerous British comedies from the mid-1950s to the mid-1960s. Chaplin said he was his "favourite clown", and Wisdom was a cult figure in Albania where his comedy was recognised as dramatising the struggles of the working class.

Selected Bibliography

1 "The task of teachers, those obscure soldiers of civilization, is to give to the people the intellectual means to revolt". Louise Michel, *Mémoires* (Paris: F. Roy, Libraire Éditeur, 1886), accessed April 18, 2020, https://disciplineandanarchy.wordpress.com/2010/09/13/portrait-louise-michel-1830-1905/; English translation quoted in Portrait: Louise Michel (1830–1905), Discipline and Anarchy, April 18, 2020, https://disciplineandanarchy.wordpress.com/2010/09/13/portrait-louise-michel-1830-1905/.

About the Author

Robb Johnson was born in 1955, studied English Literature at Sussex University, trained as a teacher, and then did an MA in English literature at Manchester University. He worked as a classroom teacher by day and a songwriter by night from 1980 to 2015. He currently works part-time as a consultant for the education charity Persona Doll Training. As a songwriter, he has received widespread critical acclaim. Robb has written songbooks, edited a book of stories, *Journeys Down Denbigh Road*, for use with young children in school assemblies, edited *A Navigator's Tale*, a book collecting his father's World War II memoir and poetry, and contributed regularly to the music magazine *RNR*.

ABOUT PM PRESS

PM Press is an independent, radical publisher of books and media to educate, entertain, and inspire. Founded in 2007 by a small group of people with decades of publishing, media, and organizing experience, PM Press amplifies the voices of radical authors, artists, and activists. Our aim is to deliver bold political ideas and vital stories to all walks of life and arm the dreamers to demand the impossible. We have sold millions of copies of our books, most often one at a time, face to face. We're old enough to know what we're doing and young enough to know what's at stake. Join us to create a better world.

PM Press
PO Box 23912
Oakland, CA 94623
www.pmpress.org

PM Press in Europe
europe@pmpress.org
www.pmpress.org.uk

FRIENDS OF PM PRESS

These are indisputably momentous times—the financial system is melting down globally and the Empire is stumbling. Now more than ever there is a vital need for radical ideas.

In the years since its founding—and on a mere shoestring—PM Press has risen to the formidable challenge of publishing and distributing knowledge and entertainment for the struggles ahead. With over 450 releases to date, we have published an impressive and stimulating array of literature, art, music, politics, and culture. Using every available medium, we've succeeded in connecting those hungry for ideas and information to those putting them into practice.

Friends of PM allows you to directly help impact, amplify, and revitalize the discourse and actions of radical writers, filmmakers, and artists. It provides us with a stable foundation from which we can build upon our early successes and provides a much-needed subsidy for the materials that can't necessarily pay their own way. You can help make that happen—and receive every new title automatically delivered to your door once a month—by joining as a Friend of PM Press. And, we'll throw in a free T-shirt when you sign up.

Here are your options:

- **$30 a month** Get all books and pamphlets plus 50% discount on all webstore purchases

- **$40 a month** Get all PM Press releases (including CDs and DVDs) plus 50% discount on all webstore purchases

- **$100 a month** Superstar—Everything plus PM merchandise, free downloads, and 50% discount on all webstore purchases

For those who can't afford $30 or more a month, we have **Sustainer Rates** at $15, $10 and $5. Sustainers get a free PM Press T-shirt and a 50% discount on all purchases from our website.

Your Visa or Mastercard will be billed once a month, until you tell us to stop. Or until our efforts succeed in bringing the revolution around. Or the financial meltdown of Capital makes plastic redundant. Whichever comes first.

A Reasonable History of Impossible Demands: The Damage to Date 1986–2013

Robb Johnson

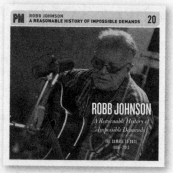

ISBN: 978-1-62963-220-9
UPC: 877746007620
$44.95   390 mins. / 64 pages

The life and times (so far!) of the UK's greatest living songwriter are captured in a deluxe box set. 92 songs, on 5 CDs with a 64-page booklet. A career retrospective traversing the acoustic and the electric, the agit-folk and the chanson, the greatest hits and a welter of unreleased material.

"So—yeah, this collection does have quite a lot of politics and protest, lots of songs doing what folk song is supposed to do—provide an alternative ordinary person's perspective to the dominant culture's hegemonic discourse, its spin and propandising on behalf of the interests of the ruling class. But there are also interpersonal songs about relationships, about being a son, being a lover, being a dad (think I may not have had room for the ones about being a Brentford supporter), above all about being a human . . . what you have here is part journal, part diary, part testament." —Robb Johnson

"An English original."
—*Guardian* (UK)

"One of Britain's most challenging songwriters."
—*Daily Telegraph*

"A creator of some of the most potent songs of the last decade."
—*fRoots*

"Britain's finest songwriter since Richard Thompson."
—*Venue*

"His songs are incisive and clever and witty and you can sing them on your way to work."
—Boff Whalley, Chumbawamba

The Liberty Tree: A Celebration of the Life and Writings of Thomas Paine

Leon Rosselson and
Robb Johnson

ISBN: 978-1-60486-339-0
UPC: 877746001628
$20.00   Double Audio CD / 20 pages

"When the rich plunder the poor of his rights, it becomes an example to the poor to plunder the rich of his property."—Thomas Paine

The Liberty Tree tells the story of Tom Paine's extraordinary life, interweaving Paine's own words, from his letters and the pamphlets which made him one of the most influential and dangerous writers of his age, with extracts from newspaper reports, diaries, letters and other documents of the times. The songs of Robb Johnson and Leon Rosselson add another dimension to the story, reflecting Paine's radical ideas and evaluating them in the context of the 21st century. This unique blend of words and music challenges received opinion in the same way Paine's writings did.

"A highly subversive pairing of two of the left's most eloquent songwriters."
—The Daily Telegraph

"Rosselson's songs are teeming with colorful characters, wonderfully descriptive passages and witty observations."
—Washington Post

"Robb Johnson is Britain's finest songwriter since Richard Thompson"
—Venue

Anarchism and Education: A Philosophical Perspective

Judith Suissa

ISBN: 978-1-60486-114-3
$19.95   184 pages

While there have been historical accounts of the anarchist school movement, there has been no systematic work on the philosophical underpinnings of anarchist educational ideas—until now.

Anarchism and Education offers a philosophical account of the neglected tradition of anarchist thought on education. Although few anarchist thinkers wrote systematically on education, this analysis is based largely on a reconstruction of the educational thought of anarchist thinkers gleaned from their various ethical, philosophical, and popular writings. Primarily drawing on the work of the nineteenth-century anarchist theorists such as Bakunin, Kropotkin, and Proudhon, the book also covers twentieth-century anarchist thinkers such as Noam Chomsky, Paul Goodman, Daniel Guérin, and Colin Ward.

This original work will interest philosophers of education and educationalist thinkers as well as those with a general interest in anarchism.

"This is an excellent book that deals with important issues through the lens of anarchist theories and practices of education . . . The book tackles a number of issues that are relevant to anybody who is trying to come to terms with the philosophy of education."
—*Higher Education Review*

Anarchist Education and the Modern School: A Francisco Ferrer Reader

Francisco Ferrer
Edited by Mark Bray and
Robert H. Haworth

ISBN: 978-1-62963-509-5
$24.95   352 pages

On October 13, 1909, Francisco Ferrer, the notorious Catalan anarchist educator and founder of the Modern School, was executed by firing squad. The Spanish government accused him of masterminding the Tragic Week rebellion, while the transnational movement that emerged in his defense argued that he was simply the founder of the groundbreaking Modern School of Barcelona. Was Ferrer a ferocious revolutionary, an ardently nonviolent pedagogue, or something else entirely?

Anarchist Education and the Modern School is the first historical reader to gather together Ferrer's writings on rationalist education, revolutionary violence, and the general strike (most translated into English for the first time) and put them into conversation with the letters, speeches, and articles of his comrades, collaborators, and critics to show that the truth about the founder of the Modern School was far more complex than most of his friends or enemies realized. Francisco Ferrer navigated a tempestuous world of anarchist assassins, radical republican conspirators, anticlerical rioters, and freethinking educators to establish the legendary Escuela Moderna and the Modern School movement that his martyrdom propelled around the globe.

"*A thorough and balanced collection of the writings of the doyen of myriad horizontal educational projects in Spain and more still across the world. Equally welcome are the well-researched introduction and the afterword that underline both the multiplicity of anarchist perspectives on education and social transformation and the complexity of Ferrer's thinking.*"
—Chris Ealham, author of *Living Anarchism: Jose Peirats and the Spanish Anarcho-Syndicalist Movement*

Teaching Resistance: Radicals, Revolutionaries, and Cultural Subversives in the Classroom

Edited by John Mink

ISBN: 978-1-62963-709-9
$24.95   416 pages

Teaching Resistance is a collection of the voices of activist educators from around the world who engage inside and outside the classroom from pre-kindergarten to university and emphasize teaching radical practice from the field. Written in accessible language, this book is for anyone who wants to explore new ways to subvert educational systems and institutions, collectively transform educational spaces, and empower students and other teachers to fight for genuine change. Topics include community self-defense, Black Lives Matter and critical race theory, intersections between punk/DIY subculture and teaching, ESL, anarchist education, Palestinian resistance, trauma, working-class education, prison teaching, the resurgence of (and resistance to) the Far Right, special education, antifascist pedagogies, and more.

Edited by social studies teacher, author, and punk musician John Mink, the book features expanded entries from the monthly column in the politically insurgent punk magazine *Maximum Rocknroll*, plus new works and extensive interviews with subversive educators. Contributing teachers include Michelle Cruz Gonzales, Dwayne Dixon, Martín Sorrondeguy, Alice Bag, Miriam Klein Stahl, Ron Scapp, Kadijah Means, Mimi Nguyen, Murad Tamini, Yvette Felarca, Jessica Mills, and others, all of whom are unified against oppression and readily use their classrooms to fight for human liberation, social justice, systemic change, and true equality.

Royalties will be donated to Teachers 4 Social Justice: t4sj.org

"**Teaching Resistance *brings us the voices of activist educators who are fighting back inside and outside of the classroom. The punk rock spirit of this collection of concise, hard-hitting essays is bound to stir up trouble.*"**
—Mark Bray, historian, author of *Antifa: The Anti-Fascist Handbook* and coeditor of *Anarchist Education and the Modern School: A Francisco Ferrer Reader*

Anarchist Pedagogies: Collective Actions, Theories, and Critical Reflections on Education

Edited by Robert H. Haworth
with an afterword by Allan Antliff

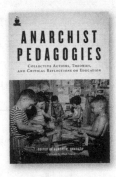

ISBN: 978-1-60486-484-7
$24.95   352 pages

Education is a challenging subject for anarchists. Many are critical about working within a state-run education system that is embedded in hierarchical, standardized, and authoritarian structures. Numerous individuals and collectives envision the creation of counterpublics or alternative educational sites as possible forms of resistance, while other anarchists see themselves as "saboteurs" within the public arena—believing that there is a need to contest dominant forms of power and educational practices from multiple fronts. Of course, if anarchists agree that there are no blueprints for education, the question remains, in what dynamic and creative ways can we construct nonhierarchical, anti-authoritarian, mutual, and voluntary educational spaces?

Contributors to this edited volume engage readers in important and challenging issues in the area of anarchism and education. From Francisco Ferrer's modern schools in Spain and the Work People's College in the United States, to contemporary actions in developing "free skools" in the U.K. and Canada, to direct-action education such as learning to work as a "street medic" in the protests against neoliberalism, the contributors illustrate the importance of developing complex connections between educational theories and collective actions. Anarchists, activists, and critical educators should take these educational experiences seriously as they offer invaluable examples for potential teaching and learning environments outside of authoritarian and capitalist structures. Major themes in the volume include: learning from historical anarchist experiments in education, ways that contemporary anarchists create dynamic and situated learning spaces, and finally, critically reflecting on theoretical frameworks and educational practices. Contributors include: David Gabbard, Jeffery Shantz, Isabelle Fremeaux & John Jordan, Abraham P. DeLeon, Elsa Noterman, Andre Pusey, Matthew Weinstein, Alex Khasnabish, and many others.

Out of the Ruins: The Emergence of Radical Informal Learning Spaces

Edited by Robert H. Haworth and John M. Elmore

ISBN: 978-1-62963-239-1
$24.95   288 pages

OUT OF THE RUINS
*The Emergence of
Radical Informal Learning Spaces*

Edited by Robert H. Haworth & John M. Elmore

Contemporary educational practices and policies across the world are heeding the calls of Wall Street for more corporate control, privatization, and standardized accountability. There are definite shifts and movements towards more capitalist interventions of efficiency and an adherence to market fundamentalist values within the sphere of public education. In many cases, educational policies are created to uphold and serve particular social, political, and economic ends. Schools, in a sense, have been tools to reproduce hierarchical, authoritarian, and hyper-individualistic models of social order. From the industrial era to our recent expansion of the knowledge economy, education has been at the forefront of manufacturing and exploiting particular populations within our society.

The important news is that emancipatory educational practices are emerging. Many are emanating outside the constraints of our dominant institutions and are influenced by more participatory and collective actions. In many cases, these alternatives have been undervalued or even excluded within the educational research. From an international perspective, some of these radical informal learning spaces are seen as a threat by many failed states and corporate entities.

Out of the Ruins sets out to explore and discuss the emergence of alternative learning spaces that directly challenge the pairing of public education with particular dominant capitalist and statist structures. The authors construct philosophical, political, economic and social arguments that focus on radical informal learning as a way to contest efforts to commodify and privatize our everyday educational experiences. The major themes include the politics of learning in our formal settings, constructing new theories on our informal practices, collective examples of how radical informal learning practices and experiences operate, and how individuals and collectives struggle to share these narratives within and outside of institutions.

Teaching Rebellion: Stories from the Grassroots Mobilization in Oaxaca

Edited by Diana Denham
and the C.A.S.A. Collective

ISBN: 978-1-60486-032-0
$21.99   384 pages

In 2006, Oaxaca, Mexico came alive with a broad and diverse movement that captivated the nation and earned the admiration of communities organizing for social justice around the world. What began as a teachers' strike demanding more resources for education quickly turned into a massive movement that demanded direct, participatory democracy. Hundreds of thousands of Oaxacans raised their voices against the abuses of the state government. They participated in marches of up to 800,000 people, occupied government buildings, took over radio stations, called for statewide labor and hunger strikes, held sit-ins, reclaimed spaces for public art and created altars for assassinated activists in public spaces. Despite the fierce repression that the movement faced—with hundreds arbitrarily detained, tortured, forced into hiding, or murdered by the state and federal forces and paramilitary death squads—people were determined to make their voices heard. Accompanied by photography and political art, *Teaching Rebellion* is a compilation of testimonies from longtime organizers, teachers, students, housewives, religious leaders, union members, schoolchildren, indigenous community activists, artists, journalists, and many others who participated in what became the Popular Assembly of the Peoples of Oaxaca. This is a chance to listen directly to those invested in and affected by what quickly became one of the most important social uprisings of the 21st century.

"*Teaching Rebellion presents an inspiring tapestry of voices from the recent popular uprisings in Oaxaca. The reader is embraced with the cries of anguish and triumph, indignation and overwhelming joy, from the heart of this living rebellion.*"
—Peter Gelderloos, author of *How Nonviolence Protects the State*

"*These remarkable people tell us of the historic teachers' struggle for justice in Oaxaca, Mexico, and of the larger, hemispheric battle of all Indigenous people to end five hundred years of racism and repression.*"
—Jennifer Harbury, author of *Truth, Torture, and the American Way*

Understanding Jim Crow: Using Racist Memorabilia to Teach Tolerance and Promote Social Justice

David Pilgrim with a foreword by Henry Louis Gates Jr.

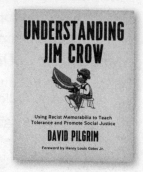

ISBN: 978-1-62963-114-1
$24.95   208 pages

For many people, especially those who came of age after landmark civil rights legislation was passed, it is difficult to understand what it was like to be an African American living under Jim Crow segregation in the United States. Most young Americans have little or no knowledge about restrictive covenants, literacy tests, poll taxes, lynchings, and other oppressive features of the Jim Crow racial hierarchy. Even those who have some familiarity with the period may initially view racist segregation and injustices as mere relics of a distant, shameful past. A a proper understanding of race relations in this country must include a solid knowledge of Jim Crow—how it emerged, what it was like, how it ended, and its impact on the culture.

Understanding Jim Crow introduces readers to the Jim Crow Museum of Racist Memorabilia, a collection of more than ten thousand contemptible collectibles that are used to engage visitors in intense and intelligent discussions about race, race relations, and racism. The items are offensive. They were meant to be offensive. The items in the Jim Crow Museum served to dehumanize blacks and legitimized patterns of prejudice, discrimination, and segregation.

Using racist objects as teaching tools seems counterintuitive—and, quite frankly, needlessly risky. Many Americans are already apprehensive discussing race relations, especially in settings where their ideas are challenged. The museum and this book exist to help overcome our collective trepidation and reluctance to talk about race.

Fully illustrated, and with context provided by the museum's founder and director David Pilgrim, *Understanding Jim Crow* is both a grisly tour through America's past and an auspicious starting point for racial understanding and healing.

Strike! 50th Anniversary Edition

Jeremy Brecher with a Preface by Sara Nelson and a Foreword by Kim Kelly

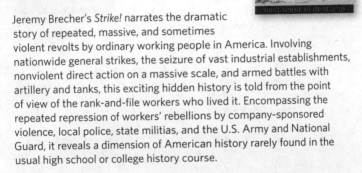

ISBN: 978-1-62963-800-3
$28.95   640 pages

Jeremy Brecher's *Strike!* narrates the dramatic story of repeated, massive, and sometimes violent revolts by ordinary working people in America. Involving nationwide general strikes, the seizure of vast industrial establishments, nonviolent direct action on a massive scale, and armed battles with artillery and tanks, this exciting hidden history is told from the point of view of the rank-and-file workers who lived it. Encompassing the repeated repression of workers' rebellions by company-sponsored violence, local police, state militias, and the U.S. Army and National Guard, it reveals a dimension of American history rarely found in the usual high school or college history course.

Since its original publication in 1972, no book has done as much as *Strike!* to bring U.S. labor history to a wide audience. Now this fiftieth anniversary edition brings the story up to date with chapters covering the "mini-revolts of the 21st century," including Occupy Wall Street and the Fight for Fifteen. The new edition contains over a hundred pages of new materials and concludes by examining a wide range of current struggles, ranging from #BlackLivesMatter, to the great wave of teachers strikes "for the soul of public education," to the global "Student Strike for Climate," that may be harbingers of mass strikes to come.

"Jeremy Brecher's Strike! *is a classic of American historical writing. This new edition, bringing his account up to the present, comes amid rampant inequality and growing popular resistance. No book could be more timely for those seeking the roots of our current condition.*"
—Eric Foner, Pulitzer Prize winner and DeWitt Clinton Professor of History at Columbia University

"*Magnificent—a vivid, muscular labor history, just updated and rereleased by PM Press, which should be at the side of anyone who wants to understand the deep structure of force and counterforce in America.*"
—JoAnn Wypijewski, author of *Killing Trayvons: An Anthology of American Violence*

No Gods No Masters: Live in Concert (DVD)

Leon Rosselson and Robb Johnson

ISBN: 978-1-60486-441-0
$19.95   2 x DVDs / 250 mins.

In this glorious 2 DVD set, Britain's finest living songwriters are captured live (on tour in Berkeley, CA), presenting two nights of their original songs, words, and inimitable performance.

Turning Silence into Song (Disc One) showcases a pair of career-spanning "greatest hits," with a suitable sprinkling of new and previously unreleased material. All introduced and contextualized with a large helping of trademark wit and dry irony.

The Liberty Tree (Disc Two) tells the story of Tom Paine's extraordinary life, interweaving Paine's own words, from his letters and the pamphlets which made him one of the most influential and dangerous writers of his age, with extracts from newspaper reports, diaries, letters, and other documents of the times. The songs of Robb Johnson and Leon Rosselson add another dimension to the story, reflecting Paine's radical ideas and evaluating them in the context of the 21st century. This unique blend of words and music challenges received opinion in the same way Paine's writings did.

Together, herein you'll find over four hours of the finest contemporary songs, stories, humor, and observation from the greatest practitioners of the craft.

". . . some of the most literate and well-made topical songs now being written"
—*The New York Times* [on Leon Rosselson]

"Britain's finest songwriter since Richard Thompson."
—*Venue* [on Robb Johnson]

"A highly subversive pairing of two of the left's most eloquent songwriters."
—*Daily Telegraph*